A Programmed Course in
Psychological Skills Exercises

Workouts to Build Psychological Strength

Joseph M. Strayhorn, Jr.

D1523174

Psychological Skills Press

Wexford, Pennsylvania

Published by Psychological Skills Press

Author's email: joestrayhorn@gmail.com

ISBN: 978-1-931773-18-8

The cover photograph of Zion Narrows is in the public domain, and was taken from Jon Sullivan's website, pdphoto.org.

Contents

Chapter 1: The Idea of Exercises for Psychological Skills.............................. 7

    The Work Ethic.. 14

Chapter 2: Alternate Reading.. 16

    The Art of Reading and Speaking Expressively 19

    Answering a More Difficult Question 23

    Mastery of Alternate Reading 24

Chapter 3: The Divergent Thinking Exercise 26

    Mastery of the Divergent Thinking Exercise...................................... 31

Chapter 4: The Celebrations Exercise... 32

    Mastery of the Celebrations Exercise 37

Chapter 5: Celebrating Others' Choices (The Search for Positive Models)............. 38

    Mastery for Celebration of Others' Choices 41

Chapter 6: The Reflections Exercise.. 42

      Prompts for Reflections 43

    Mastery of the Reflections Exercise 52

Chapter 7: Listing Values or Principles, and Reading Affirmations 53

    Mastery for the Listing Values Exercise.. 56

Chapter 8: Skills Stories... 58

    Mastery of the Skills Stories Exercise 64

Chapter 9: Brainstorming Options 65

    Mastery of the Brainstorming Options Exercise................................. 69

Chapter 10: Pros and Cons... 70

    Mastery of the Pros and Cons Exercise 73

Chapter 11: The Guess the Feelings Exercise 74

    Mastery of the Guess the Feelings Exercise 76

Chapter 12: The Twelve-Thought Exercise 78

    Mastery of the Twelve Thought Exercise 88

Chapter 13: The Four-Thought Exercise 89

    Mastery of the Four Thought Exercise 93

Chapter 14: Listening With Four Responses 95

    Mastery for the Listening with Four Responses Exercise 100

Chapter 15: The Tones of Approval Exercise 102
    Mastery for the Tones of Approval Exercise.. 106
Chapter 16: The Social Conversation Role-Play 107
    Mastery for the Social Conversation Role Play.. 111
Chapter 17: STEBC Fantasy Rehearsals 112
    Mastery of STEBC Fantasy Rehearsals.. 116
Chapter 18: UCAC Fantasy Rehearsals... 117
    Mastery of UCAC Fantasy Rehearsals 119
Chapter 19: Positive Emotional Climate Rehearsals.. 120
    Mastery for the Things to Say for A Positive Emotional Climate Exercise 123
Chapter 20: Saving a Reward for After Self-Discipline... 124
    Mastery for Saving a Reward for After Self-Discipline 133
Chapter 21: The To Do List... 134
    Mastery of the To Do List 136
Chapter 22: Listing Important Variables for a Decision 137
    Mastery for Listing Important Variables 145
Chapter 23: The Joint Decision Role Play.. 146
    Mastery for the Joint Decision Role Play 158
Chapter 24: The Decisions Exercise.. 159
    Mastery for the Decisions Exercise 163
Chapter 25: The Choice Points Exercise 165
    Mastery for the Choice Points Exercise... 168
Chapter 26: A Guessing Game 169
    Mastery for the Guessing Exercise 172
Chapter 27: Breathe and Relax 174
    Mastery for Breathe and Relax 177
Chapter 28: Mind-Watching... 178
    Mastery for Mind-Watching 179
Chapter 29: Other Ways of Relaxing or Meditating... 181
    Repeating a mantra 181
    Meditation with movement.. 182
    Visualizing relaxing scenes 183
    Imagining acts of kindness 183
        Types of Kind Acts.. 184
    The good will meditation... 185
    The pleasant dreams technique.. 185
    The psychological skills meditation 187

Simple rest 188
Mastery for Other Ways of Relaxing.. 189
Chapter 30: Task-Switching 191
Mastery for Task-Switching 195
Chapter 31: Biofeedback.. 197
Mastery for Biofeedback.. 200
Chapter 32: Concentrate, Rate, and Concentrate 202
Mastery for the Concentrate, Rate, and Concentrate Exercise 206
Chapter 33: Responding to Criticism... 208
Mastery for the Responding to Criticism Exercise 214
Chapter 34: Self-Monitoring.. 215
Mastery for Self-Monitoring 226
Chapter 35: Goal-Setting and Goal-Monitoring 227
Mastery for the Goal-Setting and Goal-Monitoring Exercise.......................... 233
Chapter 36: Examples of Brainstorming Options... 234
Chapter 37: Examples of Pros and Cons.. 240
Chapter 38: Examples of Listing Important Variables for a Decision.................. 244
Chapter 39: Examples of the Twelve Thought Exercise 247
Chapter 40: Examples of STEBC Fantasy Rehearsals 252
Chapter 41: Examples of UCAC Fantasy Rehearsals.. 260
Chapter 42: Examples of the Social Conversation Role Play 264
Conversation 1: Two hikers 264
Conversation 2: The cleaning person and the hotel guest................................ 266
Conversation 3: Two young children at a playground...................................... 268
Conversation 4: The speaker and the audience member................................... 270
Conversation 5: The spelling bee winner and the chess tournament winner,
continued 272
Conversation 6: A Chat with Superman 274
Chapter 43: Examples of the Joint Decision Role Play (Dr. L.W. Aap) 278
Appendix 1: Questions for Divergent Thinking Practice 288
Appendix 2: Choice Points 291
Appendix 3: Options for the Pros and Cons Exercise.. 297
Appendix 4: Affirmations for Psychological Skills... 300
Affirmations for Sixteen Skills and Principles 300
Affirmations for All 62 Skills 301
Appendix 5: Things To Say To Create a Positive Emotional Climate 308
Appendix 6: Self-Ratings of Psychological Skills... 310

Programmed Course in Psychological Skills Exercises

The Psychological Skills Inventory 310
One-Item Self-Rating of Psychological Skills...................................... 311
Index 312

Chapter 1: The Idea of Exercises for Psychological Skills

1. Most people know that if you want to keep your body healthy, you have to exercise often. If you want to make your heart healthier, you run or swim or ride a bicycle or do something else that makes you breathe fast. If you want to get your muscles stronger, you lift weights or do push-ups or do something else that makes your muscles work hard.

   Lots of people know which exercises strengthen certain muscles. Curls build your biceps muscles, and squats build your hip and upper leg muscles.

The main point of this section is that

A. most people know that if you want physical fitness, you have to get physical exercise regularly,
or
B. curls build up the biceps muscles, on your upper arm?

2. This book is meant to teach you how to do different sorts of exercises. These exercises are designed to increase the health of your mind. They are meant to help you strengthen good habits of thinking, feeling, and behaving. We can call this your mental health, or your psychological skills. Most people don't know about these sorts of exercises. We hope that learning about them and doing them can make your life better.

What's the main point of this section?

A. One of the most important things you can do to help your mental health is not to abuse alcohol.
or
B. This book teaches exercises meant to build up your mental health or psychological skills.

3. What do we mean by mental health? We mean the skills that will help you to be happy, to help other people to be happier, and to make the world a better place. We mean making and carrying out the decisions that will help you to live the best life you can, and to add as much good as possible to the lives of others. If you think about how important these goals are, you realize that mental health skills are the most important skills for people to learn.

What's the main point of this section?

A. Mental health is the important set of skills that help you to be happy and to make others happy.
or
B. Most people who are taught exercises for mental health don't realize the value of the "secret" that has been shared with them.

4. What sort of people can help themselves by doing psychological skills exercises? Who can gain from learning ways of being happier and making other people happier? The answer is clear: all people who can learn these skills should do so.

Some people act as if only unusual people, who have some sort of embarrassing problem, should work on psychological health. What if someone thought that only people who have had heart attacks should try to keep their hearts healthy? Or that only people who have had head injuries should wear helmets when they ride bikes? We're wise enough now to know that all people should take care of their health, not just those with visible illness or injury. It's the same with mental health as well.

The exercises of this book are not just for people with certain sorts of problems. If you are already very happy and make lots of other people happy, I hope you'll find that doing the exercises in this book will help you to have even greater success. On the other hand, if, like approximately all human beings, you can use improvement in your productivity, your emotional life, or your relations with others, then these exercises are one way to work toward those goals.

What's the main idea of this section?

A. The exercises in this book are for just about everyone, not just those with a certain type of problem.
or
B. Physical fitness is not something you achieve and then forget about; it's something you have to keep working at all your life.

5. What would you think if you went for skiing lessons in which you never practiced skiing? Or math lessons, with never any practice in doing math problems? Or dancing lessons where you sat down the whole time and talked about dancing, or singing lessons where you never sang a note? Probably all these would seem very strange, and they wouldn't work very well. Lessons in any skill should encourage you to practice the skill you want to get better at.

This book takes the same attitude toward psychological health skills. If you want to get better at decision-making, you practice listing options, thinking of advantages and disadvantages, and other parts of the decision process. If you want to get better at social relationships, you practice talking with people. If you want to resolve conflict better, you practice conflict-resolution conversations. If you want to be less angry or less fearful in certain situations, you practice doing non-angry and non-fearful things in those situations. And so forth.

What's a summary of the principle this section sets forth?

A. If you want to get good at a skill, including psychological skills, you practice doing what you want to be able to do well.
or
B. When you practice, you want to practice positive patterns rather than bad patterns that will just get you into bad habits.

6. Let's think about mental health some more. What are the skills that mentally healthy people are good at? Or in other words, what do people have to learn to do, in order to be very mentally fit?

In the next few sections, we are going to list some of the most important skills for mental health. All the exercises in this book are meant to improve our abilities in one or more of these.

The purpose of this section was to

A. make the point that getting enough sleep can improve your psychological health,
or
B. introduce the next few sections, which will talk about skills for psychological health?

7. If you want to meet your goals, you have to work at them. You have to put out effort. The habit of working hard is called productivity.

When you do good things, it's important to feel good about them. This makes it more likely that you'll do more good things in the future. Also, it's very helpful to feel good about the good things other people do for you, and about the good luck you have. Most people don't think of feeling good about good things as a skill, but it is, and it can be practiced and learned. We call this skill joyousness.

The most mentally healthy people are not selfish. They figure out ways to make other people happier. They want to find ways to relieve other people's suffering. This is the skill of kindness.

Suppose someone works very hard at a job that helps lots of people, and the person feels very good about helping people. This person is getting a chance to practice

A. productivity, joyousness, and kindness, all at once,
or
B. courage, honesty, and loyalty all at once?

8. Life goes better if you're in the habit of telling the truth and not cheating or stealing. Relationships go better if people realize that you keep the promises you make. These habits are the skill of honesty.

No matter how well we run our lives, bad things happen. We need to know how to handle it when things go badly. Sometimes we work very hard to make things better; sometimes we have no choice but to put up with what we don't like. The skill of dealing with bad things that happen is called fortitude.

Life is a series of situations or "choice points;" we choose how to handle each one of them. Choosing well is the skill of good decisions.

Some decisions involve other people. Sometimes these choice points lead to disagreements or conflicts. Decisions where two or more people choose together about how to handle something that affects all of them are called *joint decisions*. When people solve a disagreement well, they are

doing a type of joint decision that we call *conflict resolution*.

Suppose someone gets a bad illness, but doesn't let it get him too depressed. He makes the most of it. This person is giving an example of the skill of

A. honesty,
or
B. fortitude?

9. One of the biggest problems that faces the world is the fact that people so often hurt and kill one another. Avoiding hurting other people's bodies, and trying to persuade others to do the same, is the skill of nonviolence.

Unkind words can hurt people, just as hits and kicks and bullets can. Speaking respectfully to other people, unless there is a really good reason not to, is the skill of respectful talk.

How happy we are, and how happy we can make other people, are very much increased if we have good relationships with people. There are several skills involved in good relationships, including getting to know other people, arranging to be with people, having good chats with people, and helping relationships to get closer and better. These are the skills of friendship-building.

If someone is tempted to hit someone else, but decides not to, that's an example of the skill of

A. respectful talk,
or
B. nonviolence?

10. Lots of times we have a choice of two things to do. One of those things helps us reach an important goal. But the other thing feels better in the short run. For example, someone has a test coming up and wants to study so as to do well. But in the short run, it's more fun to play video games. Or someone wants to quit smoking, to be healthier, but in the short run, it feels better to smoke. Lots of times, mentally healthy people choose to do things that are not fun or pleasant, in order to achieve their goals. The ability to do this is the skill of self-discipline.

When we try to make other people happy, we can't spend time trying to help each of the billions of people in the world. Whom do we make promises to? Do we keep the commitments we make? How do we decide which people to stand by in times of trouble, and which to let fend for themselves? Good decisions in this area are the skill of loyalty.

Suppose that someone is supposed to eat a low salt diet for medical reasons. The person gets offered something that tastes really good, but the person turns it down because the food is too high in salt. The person is using the skill of

A. self-discipline,
or
B. loyalty?

11. Any person has only a limited amount of time and money. And the world as a whole has only a limited amount of natural resources such as clean water, clean air, and forests. It's an important principle not to waste any of these things. If we use our time and money well, and if we are careful not to waste the earth's resources, we are good at the skill of conservation.

The mentally healthy person takes care of his or her own health and safety. Driving carefully, eating a good diet, exercising, following doctors' advice, not smoking, not abusing alcohol or other drugs, and going to bed early enough are all ways that people use the skill of self-care.

Someone has the urge to buy a new computer. But the person learns ways of making an older computer do everything that she needs it to do. By not wasting, she is using the skill of

A. conservation,
or
B. self-care?

12. When someone obeys the law, or obeys reasonable rules, or obeys an authority like a parent or teacher or boss at work, the person is using the skill of compliance. Sometimes it's important to refuse to do what people ask you to do. People sometimes ask you to do wrong things. Part of the skill of compliance is figuring out when to obey someone and when not to.

Scientists who study the mind have found out that you can get better at things by practicing them in your fantasy. For example, you can help yourself give a speech well by rehearsing giving it to an imaginary audience. People can help themselves learn anger control by imagining themselves staying cool in the sorts of situations that often provoke anger. It's good to imagine yourself behaving in good ways. It's also good to avoid violent entertainment, so that you don't practice much violence in your imagination. Using your fantasy well to practice doing good things is called the skill of positive fantasy rehearsal.

Suppose that someone wants to get better at chatting with people. The person makes up and writes down lots of imaginary conversations where two people chat and get to know each other better. The person is using the skill of

A. positive fantasy rehearsal,
or
B. compliance?

13. The last skill on our list is courage. This means not letting fear stand in the way of doing good and wise things. For example, someone is scared of being in a dark room while waiting to fall asleep. If the person toughs it out and stays in the dark room until the fear is gone, that's an example of courage.

Courage does not mean taking unwise risks. Sometimes people do very reckless and risky things to show how brave they are.

Suppose someone wades around in a river with a swift current and slippery rocks, right above a huge waterfall, for no particular reason other than for the fun of it. This is a

A. really good example of courage,
or
B. really bad example of self-care?

14. Now we've been through the sixteen skills and principles. It is very useful to remember the skills on this list. I remember the list by using a little song. If you want to hear it, you may be able to find it on the Internet if you search for the title of the song, "What are the Qualities?" Here are the words to the jingle:

Chapter 1: The Idea of Psychological Skills Exercises

What are the qualities that make life
better?
What makes people good?
What lets people live in happiness and
peace
And brother- and sisterhood?

Productivity, joyousness, kindness
Honesty, fortitude
Good decisions made every day
Nonviolence and not being rude.

Friendship-building, self-discipline,
loyalty,
Conservation and self-care,
Compliance and positive fantasy
rehearsal
And courage, if you dare.

Which of the following is NOT one of
the sixteen psychological skills in the
list?

A. The skill of making witty
comebacks,
or
B. the skill of fortitude?

15. Would you agree that the skills
you just read about are the most
important ones that people can learn?
People have put a high value on skills
such as these since ancient times. This
book will give you ways to practice
them.
        Why can't we just practice
these skills in real life – why do we
need exercises? We need them
because the situations in real life often
come at us too fast. Or maybe we're
too emotional to think of a good way
to act. So in the heat of the moment,
we often practice bad patterns.
Psychological skills exercises give
you a chance to slow things down and
think carefully about what to do,
before you rehearse doing it.

What's one of the main points of this
section?

A. The exercises you will learn let you
have time to think carefully about
what you want to do, before you
practice handling a situation in a
certain way.
or
B. The skills of productivity,
joyousness, kindness, and so forth
have not been taught as well as they
should have been, seeing how
important these skills are.

16. If your work with this book is
successful, you will "master" a bunch
of psychological skills exercises. To
master an exercise means that if
someone asks you to do the exercise,
you can do it quickly, easily, and well.
Mastering a certain exercise means
that you are ready to use it for the rest
of your life. It does not mean that you
can check this exercise off the list and
never think about it again.

This works the same way with physical exercises. Once you can do a pull-up, you don't just check it off a list and forget about it. If you want to keep benefiting from it, you keep doing it for the rest of your life.

What's a major idea of this section?

A. Being able to keep your weight in the right range – not too much or too little, but just right – usually requires self-discipline.
or
B. Once you get good at doing an exercise, you keep doing it, to stay in good psychological shape.

17. You can read this book by yourself, and do the exercises by yourself. But the most fun way to do the psychological skills exercises, for most people, is with someone else. With most exercises you can take turns. Taking turns gets a rhythm going that makes the activity more interesting and fun. If one person is the teacher and the other is the student, both of them learn and gain from doing the exercises together. I know that this is true because I have gained very much from doing these exercises with many people.

What's the point of this section?

A. It is important to do the exercises often enough.
or
B. Taking turns and doing the exercises with someone makes them more fun.

The Work Ethic

18. Why should someone want to spend time doing psychological skills exercises rather than watching TV or a movie or playing video games? Over time, as you do these exercises, you will probably understand more and more about how very useful they are. People have made their lives lots better by doing these exercises. Improving your own psychological skills is probably the most important goal you can achieve, because it helps you to accomplish anything else you want, for the rest of your life.

But for this type of thought to make a difference to you, you have to first be interested in the question, "What's most important to accomplish?" instead of just "What's most entertaining and fun at the moment?" Being willing to work toward worthwhile goals, even when there is something else more entertaining to do, is the skill of self-discipline. It's also called the work ethic. People who learn to enjoy working have a tremendous advantage over those who don't.

What's the main idea of this section?

A. It's work to do these exercises, but if you can have the "work ethic," you will find yourself much more able to have a good life.
or
B. TV is tempting as an alternative to work, because smart people work very hard to make shows that attract your attention.

19. Sometimes the problem with doing psychological skills exercises is not that someone doesn't like working, but that there is too much other work to do.

Suppose that Jermaine is taking lots of really hard courses at school, with lots of homework. He's also on an athletic team that has long practices; he also plays an instrument in an orchestra. He's also taking dance lessons and martial arts lessons. Would it be surprising if it were hard for him to find the time to do psychological skills exercises? There is only so much time in a day. Sometimes the key to improving psychological skills is to reduce the things you have to do, to make time for what is more important. Sometimes this means saying "I quit" to one or more activities.

What's the main point of this section?

A. With enough of the work ethic, you can accomplish things that other people couldn't dream of.
or
B. No matter how much you are willing to work, there is only a limited amount of time in the day, and sometimes you have to quit doing some things so you can have time for more important ones.

Chapter 2: Alternate Reading

20. Here's what alternate reading means: Two people take turns reading aloud to each other from a book like this one – one that's divided into sections, with a question after each section. Usually the two people are called the tutor and the student. One reads odd numbered sections, and another reads even numbered sections. At the end of each section, the student answers the question. The tutor gives the student feedback on the answer to the question – for example, "I agree!" or "Yes!" or "I thought it was the other one."

The purpose of this section is to

A. tell what people do when they do "alternate reading,"
or
B. make the point that psychological skills are more important than sports skills?

21. What's the purpose of alternate reading? Of course, the main purpose is to learn what's written in the books. It's often more pleasant to read a book with someone else than by yourself. This is especially true if the two people can be nice to each other and enthusiastic about what they're doing. It takes two to do this. If you can, with someone else, create an atmosphere where alternate reading is fun, you both deserve to feel really good!

What's a main idea of this section?

A. Alternate reading, for many people, is more fun and less lonely than reading on your own.
or
B. In the age of the Internet, reading skill has become more important, not less important.

22. Reading aloud to each other has a side benefit. No matter how well you read, reading aloud usually helps you read better. When you hear yourself speak the words that you read, you get feedback on whether you have read them correctly. You tend to improve your reading habits over time. Plus, when you get used to answering many questions about what you have read, you get better and better at understanding and remembering what you read. The ability to read well is a super-important skill. This is why it's tested on almost all standardized tests!

The main point of this section is that

A. alternate reading improves your reading skill,
or
B. when we count the number of exercises you have done, we don't count alternate reading – instead we count the number of sections you've read.

23. There's another side effect of alternate reading. Reading aloud helps you to become a better speaker. This is particularly true if you try to put a lot of expression into what you read.

Reading aloud helps you become more expert at public speaking, such as giving speeches to groups. It also helps with the sort of speaking that goes on in conversations. If you have had many hours of practice of making words come out of your mouth, you will find it easier to communicate what you mean to say.

What's the main point of this section?

A. Meditation often involves experiencing something over and over.
or
B. Reading improves your speech.

24. There's one other benefit of alternate reading. It can be a relaxing and pleasant activity, in some ways like meditating. You get into the rhythm of taking turns, and it feels good. It sometimes takes weeks or months before the alternate reading starts to feel relaxing and pleasant. But if you can keep doing it long enough, you may be surprised at how pleasant it becomes.

What's the main point of this section?

A. Alternate reading from books with new words in them tends to build up your vocabulary.
or
B. After some time of doing alternate reading, lots of people begin to find the activity relaxing and pleasant, like a meditation.

25. The main requirement for mastery of alternate reading is that you figure out a way to enjoy it! There are lots of ways to do this. You can get interested in what you are reading, and become curious to find out more, and take pleasure in learning. You can take pleasure in realizing that you are becoming a better reader, or a better speaker. You can enjoy the success you get from answering the questions. You can enjoy spending time with your tutor or student. You and the tutor or student can both enjoy helping each other to be successful in your mission. You can let the rhythm of the activity feel like a meditation, and enjoy the relaxation. You can let the

images of positive behavior you find in the reading be a pleasant alternative to the scenes of violent and bratty behavior that we find on TV and, too often, in real life. You can make your life better by using the learnings you get from the reading.

Please use your own creativity and intelligence to answer these questions about alternate reading: "How can I enjoy this activity the most? How can I help the other person enjoy it the most? How can I get the most out of it?" The more you succeed at this, the more you have mastered alternate reading!

What's the main idea?

A. You master alternate reading by making the activity enjoyable for both people, and by getting a lot out of it.
or
B. As you continue alternate reading, you will probably find that you make fewer mistakes and can read faster.

26. It may take a while before you have fully found a way to take lots of pleasure in alternate reading. The activity is an "acquired taste." It tends to grow on you over time. The more you do it, the more you find ways to enjoy it, if you vigorously look for those ways.

What's the author's purpose in this section?

A. To teach the reader that something like computer programming is an acquired taste, and something like eating ice cream is less so.
or
B. To help the reader to be patient and grow the taste for alternate reading over time, rather than expecting it to be great fun from the beginning.

27. To get the most out of alternate reading, focus your attention on what you are reading. It's easy to read words while totally ignoring what they mean! One way of measuring whether you are tuned in to the meaning of the words is to see whether you can answer the questions at the ends of the sections correctly. If you are paying attention, and the words in what you are reading are not too hard, the questions should be pretty easy for you. Answering the questions makes it easier to stay "tuned in" to the reading.

Which is closer to the main idea of this section?

A. Reading comprehension skill is usually defined as the ability to correctly answer questions on what you've read.
or

B. The questions at the end of the sections help you check to see if you're "tuned in" during alternate reading.

28. Some people think that if a learner is getting all, or nearly all, the questions right in anything resembling a test, then the activity is too easy, and should be made harder. This is NOT the philosophy for alternate reading. We would ideally like to use "errorless learning," where you make no errors at all on the test questions. The theory behind errorless learning is that each time you answer a question wrong, you are practicing doing something incorrectly. We want you to practice correct performances, not incorrect ones. Therefore, the idea is to make the questions such that you have to pay attention and think to answer them, but that you make very few errors on them.

What was the idea that this section explained?

A. Everyone needs to get used to the fact that making mistakes is part of life, and you should tackle very difficult questions, even if you miss them.
or
B. Because we want you to practice doing things right, we try to make it possible to make as few errors as possible, at least in the questions for books like this.

29. What if something that you have read brings to mind some thought that you want to discuss with the person you're reading with? Then it's often great to speak up and comment and tell your idea. You can have some good discussions about what you are reading.

On the other hand, if you want to go straight through the reading without feeling the need to discuss, that's OK too. We want the activity to be relaxing and pleasant, not stressful and pressured.

What's an idea present in this section?

A. If you want to have a fun discussion about some idea that you read, you have the opportunity to do it in the middle of alternate reading.
or
B. There are important goals that can be accomplished by reading aloud, that can't be accomplished as well by reading silently.

The Art of Reading and Speaking Expressively

30. Have you ever listened to a recording of a book or story, read by a trained actor? Or have you heard an expert storyteller put on a

performance? Or even, have you noticed the way people speak on almost any movie or TV show? The people in these performances speak *expressively*. Can you imagine what it would sound like if they read their lines in a tired monotone voice? It is hugely more fun to listen to people and watch them when they speak expressively. And in real life, it's usually lots more fun to talk with someone who puts lots of expression into the voice. People tend to have more confidence and interest in people who speak expressively than in those who don't.

Which idea does this section communicate?

A. It's good to be able to predict the consequences of options, so that you'll be able to decide which option you want to carry out.
or
B. Speaking with expression in your voice tends to let you have a bigger effect on other people than speaking with a monotone.

31. Reading and speaking expressively are fine arts. Most of us can never get to be as good at it as great actors are. But when alternate reading gets easy for you, and you want an extra challenge, you can work on being an expert expressive reader. Learning to

use expressive speech helps you to communicate with people more effectively, every time you open your mouth to speak! Reading aloud in alternate reading gives you practice in speaking expressively, with every word you read!

Which idea does this section communicate?

A. Doing alternate reading with these manuals can give you great practice at speaking expressively.
or
B. There is a connection between the brain and various nerves and the muscles of speech; with more practice, these connections probably work better.

32. One way to read (and speak) expressively is to think about which words in each sentence you want to accent or emphasize with your voice. When we speak words, we accent or emphasize certain syllables. For example, when you say the word *possibly*, you accent the first syllable, the *poss* part. When you say the word *completely*, you accent the second syllable, the *plete* part. And when you say the word *understand*, you accent the third syllable, the *stand* part. Just as you accent syllables in words, you also emphasize words in sentences. How you choose to emphasize the

words has a lot to do with what the sentence means!

What's the main point of this section?

A. In Spanish it is much easier to predict which syllable of a word will be accented than in English.
or
B. Your reading (and talking) are much more effective if you choose well which words to emphasize.

33. Let's look at an example. Suppose the sentence you are reading is "How did he do that?" If you emphasize the words *how* and *do*, saying, "*How* did he *do* that?" then it sounds as if you're surprised that what he did was possible. If you say, "How did *he* do that?" then it sounds as if it's more surprising that he did it, than that someone else did. And if you say, "How did he do *that*?" then it sounds as if the important thing is that he did the particular thing he did, and not something else. On the other hand, there's another way of reading it that carries the message "I don't really care what this says – I'm just trying to get the words out and get this over with. Try reading the same sentence that way: "How … did … he … do... that...."

What's the purpose of this section?

A. To give an example of how emphasis can change the meaning of a sentence.
or
B. To make the point that different words are accented on different syllables.

34. Here's an example where it makes a big difference what words you emphasize. Suppose someone hears that a friend has gotten an A+ on a test, and says to the friend, triumphantly, "You got an *A*+!!" emphasizing the last words. The friend would probably feel good that you were celebrating with her. But if you say, "*You*, got an A+??" then it sounds as if it's hard for you to believe that your friend, of all people, should be the one to get a good grade. Your friend might feel insulted. The same words could have a very different effect, depending only on the tones with which you say them.

What's the main purpose of this section?

A. To make the point that you should avoid insulting people without a very good reason.
or
B. To give an example of how emphasis and tones of voice can change the effect your words have on other people.

35. Another part of reading aloud well is pausing at the right places. Punctuation marks give us important clues about when to pause. Without any punctuation or pauses, it's hard to figure out what this sentence means:
It was and I said not but.
But now try reading it with the pauses and emphasis that the punctuation signals to you:
It was "and" I said – not "but."
Here's another example. See what the following means to you:
How I wonder does the sun make light.
It sounds as if you are saying how much you wonder whether the sun makes light or not. On the other hand, if you read it like this:
How, I wonder, does the sun make light?
This way, it sounds as if you are wondering how the sun gives off light – for example is it by burning or by nuclear fusion?

What's the main idea of this section?

A. If you use the pauses signaled by punctuation, you communicate the meaning more effectively.
or
B. The sun creates light energy by nuclear fusion.

36. Here's another important idea about expressive reading. The more the pitch of your voice changes, the more emotion you communicate. Think about the sentence, "I would love to do that." Can you read it a few times, and make the pitch of the word *love* get higher and higher?

I would love to do that.
I would *love* to do that.
I would LOVE to do that.
I would LOVE!!! to do that!

So which way seems to communicate the most eagerness to do whatever it is? It's the one where the word *love* goes up the most in pitch, don't you think?

What's the main point of this section?

A. If you would like to do something with someone else, you should communicate that.
or
B. One of the main ways people communicate emotion is by making the pitch of their voices go up and down.

37. Here's one more thing to work on while you are reading: try to read very clearly, so that someone who can't hear well can still understand you. How do you do this? You have to speak loudly enough, but loudness is

not the main secret to being understood. The main secret is putting force into the consonant sounds in words. For example, if you're reading the word pl*ates*, you make the t say "tuh!" forcefully – so that your listener is sure you're saying *plates* instead of *plays*. And for the s sound at the end, you hiss forcefully, so that your listener knows for sure that there is more than one plate. If you bang out your consonant sounds, you can speak clearly without getting loud!

What's the "secret" of speaking clearly that this section presents?

A. Just speak up loudly enough.
or
B. Say the consonant sounds of the words forcefully.

38. The expert reader constantly tries to get the full meaning of the words. At the same time, the expert reader figures out how to use the voice to communicate that meaning. This is a very complicated activity for our brains to carry out! But when our brains work hard on this, we understand what we're reading more, and the activity is more fun! For this reason, you often get a lot more out of reading aloud and hearing someone read aloud, than you get out of reading silently.

This section provides

A. A reason for reading aloud rather than silently.
or
B. A reason to practice the exercises every day.

Answering a More Difficult Question

39. Sometimes people can answer each of the questions at the end of sections in manuals like this one. But then, when they are done, and someone asks them, "What did you learn from this?" they shrug their shoulders and can't name one thing. This isn't surprising. It's much more difficult to summarize what you have read than to pick the correct summary when someone else supplies it. If you really want to test how well you understand anything you read, and spur yourself to understand it better, try to retell the main points of what you have read.

One idea in this section is that

A. To better understand what you're reading, practice retelling.
or
B. People in conversations very much appreciate it when a person listens very carefully and checks his or her understanding.

40. Sometimes you can't answer the question, "What did you learn from this?" Perhaps you very much disagreed with what you read. Or maybe you already knew whatever the author was telling you, and you got reminded of something rather than learning it for the first time. In that case, we can phrase the question: "What did this chapter say?" Or, "What was the writer telling you in this part?" Or, "Please summarize this part." Or, "What can you remember from what you read in this whole book?" If you get into the habit of trying to answer this sort of question often, you'll be a better reader.

This section told you

A. The brain pathways that explain why summarizing what you have read helps you to understand writing better.
or
B. There are several different good ways of putting to yourself the question, "What do I remember from this?"

41. For each exercise in this book, we will list the ways to know if you have "mastered" that exercise. Mastery does not mean that you check the exercise off a list, consider it finished, and never return to it again. If you have mastered an exercise, you can do it well, as it is meant to be done, and as you should continue doing it.

What's the main idea?

A. Alternate reading is measured mainly by how many sections you have read.
or
B. Mastery of an exercise means that you are doing it with good form, not that you should forget about it and consider it finished.

Mastery of Alternate Reading

1. At the first level, you are simply able to do alternate reading and answer the questions.

2. At the second level, you read with some expressiveness, not in a monotone, reading the punctuation as well as the words. You pay attention to the reading well enough to answer almost all the questions correctly. You are able to take pleasure in the rhythm of alternate reading.

3. At the third level, you read very expressively. You can not only answer the questions at the end of the sections, but also give good answers if someone asks, "What do you remember from this?" or "What was

this trying to tell you or remind you of?" You are able to take much pleasure in the rhythm of alternate reading.

Chapter 3: The Divergent Thinking Exercise

42. Divergent thinking is the skill of generating a bunch of different ideas about things. Usually there's some sort of question that the ideas are meant to answer.

Much of education in schools trains you in remembering the one right answer to something, or finding the one right answer to a problem; this is called convergent thinking.

Here's an illustration of the difference, using math questions:
Convergent thinking:
What is 6 + 8?
Divergent thinking:
There is a math problem with 14 as the answer. What could the problem have been?

Which of the following questions most encourages or requires divergent thinking?

A. How many miles is it from the earth to the sun?
or
B. Someone needs to fix something that is broken. What are a bunch of possibilities for what the broken thing could be?

43. Divergent thinking really comes in handy when you need to come up with a creative solution to a problem or come up with ideas. It's very useful when you want to write. It also comes in handy when you are having some social conversation – it helps you think of more interesting and fun things to talk about.

The point of this section is that

A. convergent thinking tends to get you high grades on tests,
or
B. divergent thinking helps very much in solving practical problems?

44. Sometimes the question at hand is, "What possible ways can I survive in this situation?" or "How can I let other people survive?" In such cases, divergent thinking can save lives.

Let's imagine a situation where something poison gets into the water supply. Some people just give up when their supplies of water are out, and die of thirst. But some figure out how to grind up wild plants that are a high fraction water, and drink the plant juice. Others figure out how to make their freezing compartments of their refrigerators frost up quickly, and then drink the water they get by defrosting. Others figure out how to boil water and let it condense again in a way that distills out the poison. Others get water that is condensed from a room dehumidifier or an air conditioner. Others rig up ways of collecting the water that falls on their roofs when it rains. All of these methods could possibly give water that is dirty or unhealthy, but they could let people survive. Divergent thinking skills are meant to help us survive!

A major purpose of this section was to

A. give an example where divergent skills help with survival,
or
b. make the point that doing psychological skills exercises is lots of work, but it can be fun?

45. In addition to helping us survive, divergent thinking is also meant to help us have fun and enjoy life. Suppose there are two people with some time to spend waiting somewhere. They are away from electronic entertainment, with "nothing to do." One just sits feeling bored.

    The other thinks up all sorts of possibilities: getting some exercise by running or doing pushups, getting into a conversation with any of the other people nearby, writing a letter to someone, writing an essay for a newspaper, playing "twenty questions" with someone, reviewing in the mind what has been learned so far in a course in school, thinking of math problems and solving them, thinking up a fun plot for a movie and imagining the movie being played; thinking about how to solve some of the world's problems, playing a version of volleyball with someone, using a wadded up piece of paper, taking a nap, and so forth.

The example in this section was meant to illustrate that

A. divergent thinking can help people figure out how to have more fun,
or
B. if people can stay cool when they have disagreements, they are much more likely to solve their problem well?

46. Divergent thinking also helps us enjoy talking with other people. Every time you are in a conversation, and it's your turn to talk, you can say any one of lots of different things. Divergent thinking lets you have something to say or ask. For example: there is a lull in a conversation. Someone thinks of saying, "Guess what happened to me today!..." and "I read something interesting this morning..." and "I'm curious about something you said: could you tell me more about ____?"

and "Please tell me about how you like to spend your time," and "I've been working on an idea; do you want to hear about it?"

The person described in this section was using

A. convergent thinking,
or
B. divergent thinking?

47. There are various other psychological skills exercises described in this book that will draw upon your divergent thinking skill. For example, one asks you to think up examples of psychological skills. Another asks you to think up options for what you could do in a certain situation. A third asks you to think of possible advantages or disadvantages of an option. Another asks you to talk about anything you want, while someone else listens. If you practice the exercise of this chapter, you'll be more ready for the exercises that future chapters will describe.

What's the point of this section?

A. Divergent thinking will help you with other psychological skills exercises.
or

B. Answering the questions that follow each of the sections of this book requires convergent thinking.

48. Here's the way the exercise of this chapter works. There is a question, that could have a very large number of answers. You simply think up lots of answers – probably not as many as you can, because that would take too long. Just think of a good number, a number that feels as if you've exercised your divergent thinking skills. If you're doing this with a trainer or tutor, it's much more fun to do this exercise taking turns. You take turns telling the other person a possible answer, and listening to the other person's answer.

The purpose of this section was to

A. tell some advantages of being skilled at divergent thinking,
or
B. describe how the divergent thinking exercise is done?

49. Here's how the divergent thinking exercise might sound. The question is: "Someone gives someone else a gift. What is the gift?"
Tutor: A sweater.
Student: A phone.
Tutor: A free computer repair.
Student: A new exit sign, given to a school that has a broken one.

Tutor: I like that one. OK, my turn. A bunch of zucchini squash that someone grew in their garden.
Student: Someone gives a gift to people who use the Internet, by making a book available for free.
Tutor: A rich person gives a gift to a town by buying land and giving it to use as a community garden.
Student: A rich man tries to impress his girlfriend by giving her a diamond studded wastebasket.
Tutor: A mother bird gives her baby a worm for breakfast.
Student: A public health clinic gives some kids some free vaccinations.
Tutor: A pirate gives a boy a map showing where treasure is buried.
Student: Someone gives some food and water to someone who is starving.

The purpose of this section was to

A. give information about the brain structures that are used for divergent thinking,
or
B. give an example of what the divergent thinking exercise might sound like?

50. As you can see, in the example of the last section, the tutor and student were trying to stretch their divergent thinking skills. In answering the question of possible gifts, they could have created more conventional ideas:

a watch, a tie, a belt, a videogame, a gift card – and this would have been perfectly fine too! If it's fun for you to try to think of more unusual or creative answers to the question, go to it, and if what pops into your head are more conventional answers, that's great too.

The attitude expressed in this section is that

A. unusual and conventional answers to the question are both OK for the divergent thinking exercise,
or
B. the more unusual and creative the answers, the better?

51. Here's another example. To speed things up, we'll leave out the two people's commenting on, or complimenting, each other's ideas in this section. The question is: Someone is feeling stressed. What's the person feeling stressed about?

Person 1: She's getting ready to go to school, and can't find the calculator she needs for her chemistry test.
Person 2: He dropped a glass and broke it, and there are little bits of glass all over everywhere.
Person 1: He really needs to use his computer, but when he tries to turn it on, he sees a blank screen.

Person 2: She hears noises in her house at night that she thinks could be an intruder.
Person 1: Her parents are having a bad argument.
Person 2: He was taking a walk in the woods, and he realizes he doesn't remember how to get back.

In this part of the example, did the two people comment on or give feedback on each other's ideas?

A. Yes,
or
B. No?

52. The divergent thinking example continues with the question, "Why was the person feeling stressed?"

Person 1: The person had a certain deer that he liked to see in the woods, and hunting season was beginning.
Person 2: That's an interesting one. The person had an envelope that wouldn't stick, and when the person looked for some tape to seal it, she couldn't find the tape.
Person 1: I still remember what envelopes are – people used to use them a lot before email was invented! OK, my turn: the person has an important test the next day and is trying to sleep, but people are making noise outside and he can't sleep.

Person 2: That's a good one. The person is taking a test, but she realizes she has gotten off on the numbering system and has most of the marks in the wrong bubbles.
Person 1: OK! The person has a huge amount of homework to do, and also has a play practice to do on the same night.
Person 2: I've been in that situation! The person goes to school and some bullies are really mean to him.
Person 1: That's really a frequent cause of stress.

In this section, did the people comment on and compliment the other person's ideas?

A. Yes,
or
B. No

53. Where do you find questions to use in the divergent thinking exercise? There's a list of them in an appendix near the end of this book. I encourage you to work through these. If you use them all up and still want to do the exercise further, you can do a divergent thinking exercise in which the question is,
"What are possible questions that are good to use for the divergent thinking exercise?"

The purpose of this section was to

A. tell where to get questions to use in the divergent thinking exercise,
or
B. tell why the divergent thinking exercise is useful?

Mastery of the Divergent Thinking Exercise

1. At the first level, you can think of at least 4 nonviolent answers to the question.

2. At the second level, you can think of lots of answers – ten or more. Hopefully at this level the exercise is fun for you.

3. At the third level, you can think of lots of answers – ten or more – and also do it quite quickly, without much hesitation. At this level the exercise should be fun for you. You should also contribute some questions for yourself and others to use in the exercise.

At all levels, you think of ideas that are as conventional or unconventional as you want, according to what makes the exercise most enjoyable for you.

Chapter 4: The Celebrations Exercise

54. Here's how you do the celebrations exercise. First, you do some good examples of psychological skills. If a tutor and a student are working together, you both make good decisions and do good things. You are almost certainly already doing this, whether you're aware of it or not! Then you take turns telling each other about the things you're glad you've done. After each brief story that you tell, you figure out together at least one of the psychological skills that your action was an example of.

What's a summary of this?

A. Most people do more good things than they are aware of.
or
B. To do the celebrations exercise, you take turns telling about good things you've done, and figure out which skill your acts are examples of.

55. To get the most out of the celebrations exercise, you don't just recall and tell about the good things you've done. You also *feel good* about those things. The celebrations exercise is meant to give you the opportunity to practice a very important part of the skill of joyousness: taking pleasure in realizing you've done something good.

A main idea of this section is that

A. it's good to be able to remember lots of good things you've done,
or
B. it's good to build the skill of feeling happy about the good things you've done.

56. If you start watching for your own good and wise deeds, you should always be able to think of something you are glad to have done. Sometimes those things seem very minor or unimportant. But you shouldn't feel satisfied with saying, "There's nothing I've done that I'm glad I've done." Are you glad you've eaten rather than starved yourself? That's self-care. Did you cross the street without walking in front of a car? You probably made a good decision about when to walk. Did you feel good about anything, even some relief at getting to stop doing something you didn't like? That's joyousness. If you didn't feel good about anything, then did you put up with anything you didn't like? That's fortitude. At this moment, you are probably choosing to keep

breathing rather than trying to hold your breath till you pass out. If you can't think of anything else, you can celebrate that excellent decision you are making and that example of self-care! You are making another good decision by working on this book now: that's productivity. It's also joyousness if you're enjoying it, and maybe fortitude if you aren't!

Does the author feel that it's reasonable to say, "I haven't done anything lately that I'm glad I've done?"

A. Yes.
or
B. No.

57. Here's what it might sound like when a tutor and a student do the celebrations exercise together.

Tutor: Let's do the celebrations exercise! I'll go first. Today I was in my apartment, and my roommate had been on a trip. When my roommate came in, I said, "Hi, welcome back! I'm glad you had a safe trip!"

Student: That sounds like an example of joyousness and friendship-building.

Tutor: Yeah, I think those are good labels for it! OK, your turn!

Student: Let's see... This morning when the alarm went off I was having a great dream, which I've forgotten, and I really didn't feel like getting out of bed. But I did anyway, and just went off to school.

Tutor: Hey, an example of self-discipline! Congratulations.

In the example above, the person who labeled the example as a certain psychological skill was

A. the person who told about the positive example,
or
B. the person who was listening?

58. Here's a continuation of how it might sound as the tutor and the student do the celebrations exercise.

Tutor: My turn again. Today I was set to take a test. Just fifteen minutes before the test, I decided to review things really quickly. I turned the pages of my textbook and my notes and brought things back to my mind quickly. Then when I took the test, I think I could remember things better for that reason.

Student: Sounds to me like an example of good decisions and productivity! Congratulations to you!

Tutor: Thank you! Your turn again.

Student: Today at school, somebody called me a name as I walked down the hall, and I just gave the person a glance and went on walking, and didn't even get too upset, because this person does this sort of thing for no reason.

Tutor: Wow, that's a great example of fortitude, anger control, and nonviolence. Congratulations to you!

Student: Thanks!

In these examples, there were two "rounds" of the celebrations exercise. Who went first in each round:

A. the tutor,
or
B. the student?

59. The examples you've read so far are the type that come when the student is really familiar with the sixteen skills and principles. While the student is getting familiar with them, or at any other time, it's just fine for the tutor to do the work of figuring out which skill label goes with each example. At the beginning, the student may be doing enough work just to remember some positive examples.

What's the main point of this section?

A. The examples people think of don't have to be big and important – life consists of lots of small situations.
or
B. It's fine to let the tutor figure out which skills the stories are examples of, especially at the beginning.

60. Here are some more examples of what it might sound like when people do the celebrations exercise. In these examples, the student leaves it to the tutor to figure out how to label the story as an example of a certain skill.

Tutor: Here's a celebration. When I did this today, I thought, I look forward to celebrating this with my student! I was walking, and there was a really icy and slick paved path, that was very steep. So I decided I would get off the pavement and walk down in the snow beside the path rather than on the slick walkway. And I think that was an example of … self-care! Your turn.

Student: OK. There were just a few strawberries left after supper. My sister asked if she could have them, and I said she could, even though I might have liked them too. It made her happy.

Tutor: Congratulations, sounds like a really good kindness celebration!

34

In the examples above, the person labeling the celebration story as an example of a certain psychological skill was

A. the person listening to the story, or
B. the tutor?

61. Why is the celebrations exercise such a good thing to do? Why is it good to remember the good things you do, and to feel good about them? First, the more you feel good about doing good things, the more likely you are to do similar good things in the future. Second, the more you feel good about the good things you've done, the happier you feel and the less likely you are to become depressed.

What's the main point of this section?

A. The celebrations exercise is meant to help you do more good things and to feel happier about the good things you do.
or
B. It's fine to celebrate in your own mind, but it can be even more special to do it with someone else that you like.

62. Our brains are built so that we do more of the behaviors that get rewarded, that result in our feeling good. Suppose there were someone to follow each of us around and give us a reward (otherwise known as *positive reinforcement*) every time we did something productive, joyous, or kind. We would probably have a world full of hard-working, happy, and kind people! There will never be such a huge army of people rewarding others for their good acts.

But what if we could train ourselves to reward ourselves for these good acts? What if we each learned to feel good about our acts of productivity, joyousness, kindness, and so forth, even when there is not someone else there to reward us? We can call this the skill of *self-reinforcement*. People who learn to feel good about the right sorts of things have an enormous advantage in life. You can practice that skill when you do the celebrations exercise, if you approach it with the right attitude.

Which is a better example of the skill of self-reinforcement, the skill of feeling good about your good acts, that is spoken of in this section?

A. Members of a football team get themselves psyched up before a game.
or
B. Someone feels really good about making a younger kid feel happy by playing with the kid in the park, even

though no one else congratulated the person for this.

63. What if you can't think of any good things that you've done lately? The celebrations exercise is something you get better at over time. If you pay attention to the situations you're in and the things you do, you'll start to see more and more celebrations. Did you do any schoolwork or work around the house? That's productivity. Were you nice to anyone? That's kindness and/or friendship-building. Did you eat a healthy meal? That's self-care. Did you really enjoy something you ate? That's joyousness. Did you make a choice that turned out well? Good decisions. Did you make a choice that turned out badly, but learn from your mistake? That's a branch of fortitude.

The author is making the point here, without saying it directly, that

A. it's a kind act to be reinforcing when someone else celebrates with you,
or
B. almost every situation you're in gives an opportunity for a celebration-worthy action?

64. If you still have trouble thinking of things to celebrate, go out and do more celebration-worthy things on purpose! Do some good work. Act cheerful with someone. Do something nice for someone. Realize when you are making choices, and decide carefully. Get into a good conversation with someone.

In other words: 1) plan to do good things, 2) do them, and 3) tell about them!

The advice given in this section is

A. if you have trouble remembering your celebrations, write them down, or
B. go out and do celebration-worthy things on purpose?

65. When you've done the celebrations exercise enough, you start to realize something about life that is very important. Almost every situation in your life provides you an opportunity to do something worthy of celebration. If you can make the most of these opportunities, and feel good about doing so, your life is going to be much better. When you see life as an endless series of opportunities to do good things that you deserve to feel good about, you have a life view that will help you and the people you are close to, throughout your life.

What's the point of this section?

A. It's nice to have a view of life as one situation after another where you can do things worth feeling good about.
or
B. The celebrations exercise gives you practice at telling brief stories, which is also a very important skill.

66. One way to make the celebrations exercise even more useful is to write down at least some of your celebrations, so that you won't forget them. If two people are doing this together, perhaps one of them can be the secretary and jot down some of the highlights of the celebrations. You can review this celebrations diary often; each time you do, you send positive examples through your mind and rehearse them. As you review the celebrations diary, you can see whether you are coming up with examples for all the groups of psychological skills, or just some of them.

Which is a summary of this section?

A. To make the celebrations exercise even better, keep a written record of celebrations and review it often.
or
B. Courage and fortitude often go together, just as kindness and respectful talk do.

Mastery of the Celebrations Exercise

1. At the first level, you are able, perhaps with some help, to come up with at least one celebration-worthy thing you've done, ever in your life, on any given occasion. You also can figure out at least one skill it is an example of.

2. At the second level, you're able to think, without prompting, of five or six celebration-worthy things you've done in the last day or so, and link them to the skills they are examples of. At this level hopefully you feel pleasure at recalling these good things you've done. You also hopefully report some more pleasure at the time you do the things, at the thought, "Here is a celebration for me."

3. The third level is like the second, only you have kept a diary of your celebrations containing at least 40 examples. At this level you should really feel that every moment gives you a chance to do something celebration-worthy, and should feel lots of pleasure in making and carrying out celebration-worthy choices.

Chapter 5: Celebrating Others' Choices (The Search for Positive Models)

67. The exercise for this chapter is very much like the celebrations exercise; the only difference is that you look for and tell about celebration-worthy things that other people have done. "Other people" can include people of history, people in the news, family members, friends or acquaintances, and other real people. "Other people" can also include imaginary characters – people in novels, stories, movies, plays, television shows, poems, song lyrics, or any other artistic production. If you are on the lookout for positive models, you can find lots of them.

What's a summary of this section?

A. Some behaviors are good examples of one skill but bad examples of another.
or
B. In celebrating others' choices, you find and report the positive models carried out by any other person, living, dead, or imaginary.

68. What do we accomplish by doing this exercise? The more positive examples of thought, feeling, and behavior we store in our memory, the better decisions we can make. Part of

the way our brains make decisions is by searching through our memories of how people have acted in similar situations. The more we can put into our memories really useful and good examples, the more easily we can find good options to use in our own life's situations.

What's a summary of this?

A. The more positive examples we have stored in memory, the more resources we have for making good decisions.
or
B. Some people make decisions impulsively, doing the first thing that comes to mind; others agonize too much over decisions.

69. Here's what the exercise on celebrating others' choices might sound like.

Person 1: Let's do the celebrating others' choices exercise. I have one. I was reading about the march on Washington, where Martin Luther King gave his "I have a dream" speech. The celebration is for the thousands of people there who protested bad conditions, but did so without hurting anyone or breaking things. So that's a nonviolence example.

Person 2: OK. I was reading a book called The Voyages of Doctor Dolittle. Doctor Dolittle went to a place where there was a custom of bullfighting. In this story he could talk to animals, and he made a plan with the bulls that resulted in no more bullfighting in that place ever again. This is an example of kindness and nonviolence.

Person 1: Great. Here's another one. I saw a movie called The Scarlet Pimpernel where a man rescued innocent people who otherwise would have been executed during the French Revolution. He used all sorts of clever disguises, and many times he risked getting killed, but he managed to save himself and others. There were examples of good decisions and courage.

Person 2: There's someone on our street who has done really well in school, and has won scholarships to college. Her mom mentioned that she studied and worked on her schoolwork about 50 hours a week.

What person 2 just told about is an example of

A. productivity and self-discipline, or
B. friendship-building and joyousness?

70. Here's more of what the exercise can sound like.

Person 1: My mom had a lot of paperwork to do, that she had let herself get behind on. She sat down at the dining room table and worked on it all day for about two days without stopping, and finally got it all done. That was self-discipline and productivity.

Person 2: Good example. I read about the legend, which may or may not be true, in which George Washington chopped down a cherry tree when he was a boy. His parents were upset to see it chopped down, and asked if he knew anything about it. He told them he did it. This is an example of honesty.

Person 1: Thanks for that example! There was a kid at school who was being bullied by a bunch of other kids. These kids said to others that they would beat up anybody who told on them. But one boy went to the guidance counselor and told, and after that, other kids were able to tell about it too.

Person 2: Is that something you read about, or saw in real life?

Person 1: It happened in real life, when I was in school, in another class.

Was the true story that Person 1 just told an example of

A. conservation, productivity, and joyousness,
or
B. courage, kindness, and good decisions?

71. Here's more of what the exercise can sound like.

Person 2: My mom sent a pretty nice graduation present to each of her nieces, and neither of them wrote her a thank you note. But she didn't hold it against them or let herself get resentful. She said, "There have been lots of times where I haven't written a thank you note when I should have in my life, so I don't want to feel entitled to get one from them." That was a good example of fortitude and anger control.

Person 1: Wow, I like that example. A friend of our family has back pain that never goes away. But this person decided to just act as if the pain weren't there. She works really hard to support her family, and says that work

is actually good for her because it distracts her from her pain.

The last is an example of

A. friendship-building and respectful talk,
or
B. fortitude and productivity?

72. Here's more of what the exercise can sound like.

Person 2: That's a great example. OK, my turn. My dad gets this newsletter on how to keep yourself healthy. I think it's called the University of California at Berkeley Wellness Letter, or something like that. He reads it every time it comes, and he fairly often eats more or less of something, or does more of a certain type of exercise, or something like that, because of things it suggests.

Person 1: That's a good example of self-care; congratulations to him. OK, I read a little biography of Elizabeth Fry, a woman who lived in England in the early 1800's. She visited a prison and started working very hard to reduce the cruelty in prisons. She started a school for the children of female prisoners. She also set up one of the first homeless shelters.

Person 2: Sounds like some good models of kindness and productivity. Today when I was walking down the hall at school, someone I haven't even met smiled at me, in a way that was not laughing at me, but just nice.

Person 1: A good example of kindness and friendship-building. I have an aunt who lost a lot of money. She and her husband tried a business, but it failed. But after that, she worked really hard, and spent almost no money, and saved almost everything she made. Finally they had enough money saved up that they didn't have to worry.

The last thing Person 1 talked about was an example of

A. conservation,
or
B. friendship-building?

73. If you want to make the celebration of others' choices exercise even more useful, write down the positive models you observe. You can review this written record often. The more frequently you run positive models of psychological skills through your mind, the more likely you are to do similar positive examples yourself.

     If you write down positive models well enough, you may accumulate a book that will be very helpful for other people to read.

What's a summary of this section?

A. Please make sure that the positive models you pick really increase the happiness of someone rather than just attracting attention.
or
B. If you keep a written record of positive models, it may help both you and others.

Mastery for Celebration of Others' Choices

1. At the first level, you are able to think of something that someone else has done that is a positive example, each time this exercise is done, on a few occasions.

2. At the second level, you are able to think of 5 or 6 examples of positive things that other people have done, on several occasions. At this point you should feel yourself becoming more aware of the positive models going on around you, and should take some pleasure in finding them.

3. At the third level, you can think of 5 or 6 celebrations of others' choices at any time. You take pleasure in searching for and finding positive models. You have kept a diary of positive models containing at least 40 examples.

Chapter 6: The Reflections Exercise

74. Suppose someone says something to you. You say back what you heard, in your own words, to check out that you understood right. For example:

First person: I've been thinking about whether I want to keep on doing gymnastics. Lots of people expect me to do it, but it's getting more dangerous and I'm enjoying it less.

Second person: So if I understand you right, other people want you to keep on doing gymnastics, but you're having second thoughts, huh?

What the second person did is called a reflection.

The purpose of this section was to

A. say why reflections are good,
or
B. to explain what reflections are, and give an example of one?

75. In the reflections exercise, one person talks, and the other does reflections. What is the point of this? There are two main benefits. The first is that it helps with concentration and attention skills. To do an accurate reflection, you have to really focus on what you are hearing. The second benefit is that reflections are a big help in social conversation. When people talk, they want to be understood; when you do an accurate reflection, both you and the other person know that you have understood.

What are the two benefits of reflections that this section mentioned?

A. good decisions and loyalty,
or
B. concentration skill and understanding between people?

76. Doing reflections is not as easy as it may seem. Most of us have much more practice in asking a question or making a comment on what the other person has said, rather than reflecting to make sure we understood it.

　　　　Particularly at the beginning, it's lots easier to be sure you're doing a reflection if you start off in one of the following seven ways, and fill in the blank with what you heard the other person saying. The first few times you do the reflections exercise, it's good to start your reflections with these prompts. You start with the first one and go straight down the list. You do one reflection with each of them, and you start back at the top of the list when you've used all seven of them.

Prompts for Reflections

So you're saying _____?
What I hear you saying is _____.
In other words, _____?
So if I understand you right, _____?
It sounds like _____.
Are you saying that _____?
You're saying that _____?

The author in this section recommends

A. Calling up a relative whom you think would like to hear from you, and doing a reflection every now and then as you listen.
or
B. The first few times you do the reflections exercise, start your reflections with the seven prompts. Start at the top of the list and go straight down the list.

77. A person says, "It bothers me that we have to memorize so much in school, but yet we don't have time to study the really important stuff, like how people can get along with each other and be happy and be organized."

Which of the following is a reflection?

A. That's because people are too worried about falling behind other countries.
or
B. In other words, you feel that people are putting out lots of effort in school, but it would be more useful if they spent more time on psychological skills, huh?

78. In the reflections exercise, one person is the talker. This person just tells about his or her own thoughts or feelings or experience or anything else. The talker should stop talking often, to give the listener a turn. Each time the talker stops, the listener does a reflection. They keep doing this for as long as they want, usually between five and twenty turns for each. Then, if they want, they can switch roles. The person who was listener becomes talker. That person tells about something while the other person reflects.

What's a summary of how to do the reflections exercise?

A. The two people take turns making up a story, with one person writing it down.
or
B. One person talks, and the other does a reflection, or summary of what the first person said, each time the first person stops talking.

79. Here's an example of the reflections exercise.

Talker: When I was 8 years old, my father brought home a cute little beagle dog from an animal shelter to stay with us for a while.

Listener: So you're saying that when you were 8, your dad brought home a beagle dog.

Talker: Yes. I wanted to go and pet the little dog right away. But then I learned that I couldn't do that just yet.

Listener: What I hear you saying is that you wanted to pet the dog, but you found out that you couldn't?

Talker: That's right.

So far, is the listener beginning at the top of the list of 7 prompts for reflections, and going in order?

A. Yes,
or
B. No?

80. The conversation continues.

Talker: The dog had been mistreated by someone. He was scared of people. He was so scared that he wouldn't let anyone within about 10 meters of him.

Listener: In other words, the dog had been treated so badly that he was scared of people.

Talker: Right. So I took on the job of helping the dog get over being scared of people. Right away I read directions on how to do this, and people talked with me about how to do it, too.

Listener: So if I understand you right, you quickly studied how to help the dog get over being scared.

Talker: That's right. So first we let the dog get hungry. Then I would put little pieces of food down in the yard. I would walk away a certain distance, and sit down on the ground. The dog had to come within a certain distance of me to get the food.

Listener: It sounds like you used the food to give the dog a motive to come closer to you.

Talker: You're right.

About how long would you say the talker in this example speaks before stopping and giving the listener a chance to reflect?

A. About 3 to 5 minutes,
or
B. About 10 to 40 seconds?

81. The conversation continues.

Talker: I had to pick the distance carefully. If the food was too close to me, he wouldn't come. If it was too far away, he wouldn't make progress. I had to pick just the right distance. Gradually I put the food closer and closer to me as he learned he wouldn't be hurt.

Listener: Are you saying that as you kept doing this, the dog gradually was able to come closer and closer?

Talker: Exactly right. It took several days, and a lot of patience. Finally he was able to come next to me, and stay there. And then I started in the same way teaching him to let me touch him. Finally he learned to let me pet him, and to even enjoy it. And then he learned the same thing with other people.

Listener: You're saying that you gradually taught him to enjoy being with people!

In this example so far, are the listener's reflections usually

A. shorter than what the talker said,
or
B. longer than what the talker said?

82. The example of the reflections exercise continues.

Talker: That's right! After all this, the dog could be adopted by a family that came to the animal shelter. But the people lived near us, and I got to go over and see him often, for years after that. And I got to be friends with the people in the family, too.

Listener: So you're saying the dog found a home with another family, and you got to keep being friends with him and his new family for a long time afterwards.

Talker: Yes!

In this conversation, did the listener use, in order, each of the listed ways start a reflection, and go back to the start of the list after coming to the end?

A. Yes,
or
B. No?

83. Here's another example of the reflections exercise. The talker is telling about an activity done in a school class.

Talker: Today in one of my classes I had a good time. We got to practice something called biofeedback.

Listener: So you're saying that you enjoyed doing biofeedback?

Talker: That's right! Biofeedback means that you use a gadget to measure something about what your body is doing, and then you play around with seeing whether you can control it. So for example you might be measuring how fast your heart beats, or how hot or cold your hands are.

Listener: What I hear you saying is, with biofeedback you measure something about your body, and see if you can change it around?

Talker: Yes, that's it! Today we were measuring how tense and tight our muscles were. We taped little things onto our skin, and then attached wires to them, and the wires went into a little machine that showed a number. The more tense our muscles were, the higher that number was.

Listener: In other words, you worked with a machine that told you how tense your muscles were?

Talker: Exactly right!

So far, has the listener done a reflection each time the talker stopped talking?

A. yes,
or
B. no?

84. The conversation continues.

Talker: So I got hooked up so that the machine could measure the tension in the muscles around my forehead. If I would raise my eyebrows or frown or grit my teeth, the number would go way up. If I relaxed the muscles in my face and head and neck, the number would go down.

Listener: So if I understand you right, the biofeedback machine measured how tense your face muscles were.

Talker: That's a good reflection, yes! Since I did this, I've been more aware of how tense my muscles are. Sometimes I find that I've tensed them up without realizing it.

Listener: It sounds like doing this has helped you realize it when you're tensing your muscles.

Talker: That's right! And part of the whole idea of doing this is that keeping your muscles too tense for too long can make your head hurt. People with headaches can sometimes help themselves by learning to relax their muscles more.

Listener: Are you saying that one of the main points of doing this stuff is to get fewer headaches?

Talker: Yes, I am! But it also helps people in all sorts of other ways, to learn to relax more – such as getting less fearful, or getting to sleep more easily.

Listener: You're saying that there are more goals of biofeedback than just fewer headaches, and these include less fear and better sleep?

Talker: I am saying that. Great listening! Now it's your turn to be the talker.

In this example, which did the talker do after the listener did a reflection?

A. Confirm that the listener's reflection was correct, and then go on talking about the same subject.
or
B. Say something else about a different subject, without telling whether the listener had heard right or not?

85. Sometimes the listener doesn't understand accurately what the talker was saying. In this case, the talker lets the listener know that the message

didn't get across, and they both try again. Here's an example.

Talker: I don't like how in most schools, the grade you get depends on how everyone else does. The people who do better than most classmates get good grades. The people who do worse than most classmates get bad grades. People are made to compete with each other.

Listener: So you're saying you don't like competition?

Talker: Well, no, I'm not really saying that. I like competition sometimes. For example, I like to play chess, and I enjoy some sports. I like competition as long as people get to choose whether they want to compete against each other. I don't like it when people have to compete in school, whether they want to or not.

Listener: What I hear you saying is that you're not against competition, as long as people get to choose, but you think that in schools, people have to compete with each other whether they want to or not.

Talker: That's exactly right!

In this example, the listener

A. Understood correctly on the second reflection, but not on the first,

or

B. Understood correctly on the first reflection, but not on the second?

86. The conversation continues.

Talker: For example, my cousin recently finished his first year of high school. At the end of the year, the school sent everyone their class rank. Someone was in first place, and someone was in last place. You knew you were doing well by how many people you beat.

Listener: In other words, it sounds like your cousin didn't like finding out he was in a game against everyone else.

Talker: No, that's not really correct – my cousin really enjoyed finding out that he was close to the top of the class. But I just happened to think about those people who were close to the bottom. I'm sure they feel like they've failed.

Listener: So if I understand you right, you think that the people close to the bottom of the class ranking for grades are failures?

Talker: No, I don't think that at all. I'm saying that it bothers me that other people, or they themselves, think

they've failed, only because someone else scored higher.

In the last two reflections, what did the listener do?

A. Understand correctly both times,

or

B. Misunderstand both times?

87. The conversation continues.

Listener: OK, now I think I understand. Are you saying that you don't like it when school people call it "success" when someone does better than others, even when that person hasn't learned much, or call it "failure" when the person does worse than others, even though that person may have learned a lot?

Talker: That's right. That's exactly what I'm getting at. Why can't teachers just make a list of what they want people to learn. If everyone in the class learns everything on the list, they all get the top grade.

Listener: You're saying that rather than students' being in a game against each other, the class can have goals, and if everyone meets the goals, they can all get high grades?

Talker: That's exactly right!

In the last two reflections, the listener has

A. understood correctly both times,
or
B. misunderstood both times?

88. The conversation continues.

Talker: If students aren't playing a game against each other for grades, they will want to help each other more. As it is, the winners need for other students to do badly. But if students aren't playing against each other, the students who catch on quicker can help the others, to try to help them succeed.

Listener: Are you saying that everyone should be guaranteed to succeed all the time, no matter how smart they are or how much work they do?

Talker: No, I'm not saying that. There may be people who can't learn the things that are on the list of goals. But it should at least be possible for everyone to succeed. And schools should try to make that happen. Students shouldn't have to have a bunch of people who do worse than they do to be called a success.

Listener: So if I understand you right, you think that school shouldn't be a competition that students play against each other. You think the grading system should encourage people to cooperate and help as many people as possible to achieve a set of goals.

Talker: That's exactly right, yes. Thank you.

Which of the following do you think is the better reflection of what the talker has been saying in this conversation?

A. So you're saying that school should be a lot easier, so that no one feels any stress or has any risk of failing?
or
B. So you're saying that teachers should measure students' success by whether they learned certain things, and not by how many other students they beat?

89. In real life conversations, when people hear a high-quality, very accurate reflection summarizing just what they were trying to say, they often feel good. But to hear a low-quality reflection sometimes feels irritating or frustrating to people.

Suppose the first person says: "Wow, what a day it is outside! The sky is the most beautiful shade of blue. It's nice and cool. There's a fresh feeling in the air. It makes me want to just run and skip!"

Here are two possible reflections.

The first: "So if I understand you, the sky is blue today."

The second: "Hey, the beautiful day has gotten you full of energy, huh!"

The person doing the first reflection just picks a random bit of information and repeats it back. The person doing the second is trying harder to really understand the most important idea and feelings the speaker is trying to get across.

The author is trying to illustrate that

A. both of these are good reflections, or
B. the first would be irritating while the second would probably feel good to hear?

90. Here's another example. The speaker says, "I keep trying to teach these students to play the piano. And I think I'm teaching well. But how can they learn when they don't practice? And then people blame me when they don't get better!"

Here's the first reflection: "How frustrating it must be when you're doing your work, but your students aren't doing theirs, and you get blamed!"

Here's the second reflection: "If I understand you correctly, piano students aren't learning well."

What do you think the author is trying to illustrate?

A. The second reflection is better because it starts with one of the seven prompts for reflections listed near the beginning of this chapter.
or
B. The first reflection is better because it shows understanding of the main point the speaker is making, whereas the second reflection misses the point and would be irritating to the speaker.

91. Here's another example of high and low quality reflections.

The speaker says, "The people who run my school seem to feel so good about all this anti-bullying stuff they're doing. But I think kids are just as mean to each other as ever, and if you ever want to talk to anyone about it, no one has any time."

Here's the first reflection: "In other words, you think kids are mean to each other in your school?"

Here's the second: "In other words, despite all the talk about stopping bullying, people aren't really taking the time to do what would help the problem the most?"

Which reflection is of higher quality?

A. The first,
or
B. The second?

92. Here's another example of high and low quality reflections.

The speaker says, "I heard the greatest speech! It was about choosing a mission or purpose in life, something that lets you leave the world better because you've lived. And I really want to do it!"

Here's the first reflection: "It sounds like you've gotten really inspired to make the world a better place!"

Here's the second: "If I understand you right, you went and heard someone give a speech, and the speech was good."

Which reflection is of higher quality?

A. The first,
or
B. The second?

93. Here's one more example of reflections of high and low quality.

The speaker says, "People invite me to sleepovers. And I really want to go and have fun with them. But they always stay up almost all night. It messes up my sleep rhythm, and I get headaches when that happens."

Here's the first reflection: "It sounds like you have a real dilemma: you want to have fun with your friends at sleepovers, but you've found that messing up your sleep rhythm gives you headaches."

Here's the second reflection: "What I hear you saying is that you've been getting headaches lately, and also that you like having fun with friends at sleepovers."

The higher quality reflection is

A. The first,
or
B. The second?

94. Here's still another example of high and low quality reflections.

The speaker says, "You're nice to me when we're alone together. But I don't like how when we're with other people, you make fun of me and leave me out in ways that you wouldn't do if it were just you and me."

Here's the first reflection: "So you're saying you like being one-on-one better than being with other people, and that you like not having those other people to have to share attention with?"

Here's the second: "What I'm hearing is that when we're with other people, you see me trying too hard to impress those others, and I say hurtful things or leave you out and am not loyal enough to you. Is that right?"

Which reflection is the better one?

A. The first,
or
B. The second?

Mastery of the Reflections Exercise

1. At the first level, you can consistently do a reflection each time the other person stops speaking.

2. At the second level, you can do the exercise both as the speaker and the listener. Plus, your reflections are not only technically reflections, but they are getting to be "high quality" reflections at least some of the time. At this level hopefully it is pleasant both to listen and to talk in the exercise.

3. At the third level, you can do this exercise easily as both listener and speaker, and your reflections are of high quality almost all the time. When you are the speaker, you can talk about your own life fluently. At this level hopefully it is quite pleasant to talk and to listen.

Chapter 7: Listing Values or Principles, and Reading Affirmations

95. It's important to have "a good sense of values." What are your values?

It's important to know the difference between right and wrong, to follow good ethical principles. *Ethics* is the branch of philosophy that thinks about right and wrong behavior. What ethical principles do you think people should live by?

What advice would you give someone if the person asked you, "How should I live? What guidelines should I follow?"

What are the characteristics you would like to see in a friend, a spouse, an employee, a boss? What are the traits of people that make them good to be in relationships with?

All of these are different ways of wording one very important question.

What's a summary of this section?

A. There are lots of different ways of asking the very important question, "What principles should we live by?" or

B. When you choose a job, it's good to think about the personality of your boss.

96. Many people can't answer the question, "What are the important principles that you want to live by?" Many people simply say, "I don't know." But life goes better if you know important principles that wise people have used to guide themselves.

An exercise for this chapter is simply to think of principles to live by, and say them. It's often more fun if two people do it together, taking turns. Or, one person can simply list those principles by himself or herself. We can call this the listing values or principles exercise.

The more proficient you get at this exercise, the more you are able to give a very complete and fluently expressed answer to the question.

What's the exercise that this section talks about?

A. Using principles to decide what to do in choice points.
or

B. Listing the principles that we use in making good decisions about what to do and how to be.

97. Sometimes people give a blank stare when asked for important guidelines for living, even when they have read a lot about the 16 skills and principles. (To review: these are productivity, joyousness, kindness, honesty, fortitude, good decisions, nonviolence, respectful talk; friendship-building, self-discipline, loyalty, conservation, self-care, compliance, positive fantasy rehearsal, and courage.) Sometimes people don't make the connection in their minds: that these principles are the product of hundreds of hours of study on the question of what good behavior is, as well as what psychologically skillful behavior is. This list is also very similar to many other lists of character strengths or ethical principles that other people have come up with. These principles have been inspired by writings in philosophy, ethics, and various religions, as well as from psychology. If you are asked what values are important or what ethical behavior is, the 16 skills and principles are meant to be an answer. If there are other principles you want to add or substitute, you are of course free to do so!

What's the main point of this section?

A. The psychological skills (productivity, etc.) are also meant to be answers to the question about values or ethics.
or
B. It is ethical and good to take care of yourself as well as to do things to make others happy.

98. The sixteen skills and principles are actually a condensation of a longer list. Under many of the sixteen skill groups are several different skills. For example, under joyousness, we can think about enjoying several different types of events: your accomplishments, your acts of kindness, kind things other people do for you, silliness or glee, and humor. Under productivity, it's good to have a sense of purpose that leads you to worthy pursuits; it's good to be able to persist long enough to get a job done; it's good to organize your effort.

A master list of 62 skills is good to get familiar with.

What's the main idea of this section?

A. The skill of decision-making includes both individual decisions and decisions that people make together.
or
B. There is a longer list, of 62 skills and principles, that is good to study.

99. Let's now describe another exercise that's closely related to listing values: the affirmations exercise. It's meant to get you familiar with the various skills and principles. An affirmation, in this case, is a statement declaring, or affirming, to yourself that you want to act according to a certain principle. For example, "I want to be able to work hard to get worthy goals accomplished," is an affirmation having to do with productivity. "I want to treat other people in ways that make them happy," is an affirmation of the value of kindness.

In an Appendix near the end of this book is one set of affirmations having to do with the 16 skills and principles, and another set having to do with all 62 skills and principles. To do the affirmations exercise, you simply take turns reading these affirmations to each other.

What's a summary of this section?

A. In the affirmations exercise, you take turns reading aloud a set of sentences about values.
or
B. Some people make up affirmations that are worded as if you are already doing a great job with the skill in question; the author does not prefer this type.

100. One of the purposes of the affirmations exercise is to let you read a list, a menu, from which you may wish to choose some of your important values. You may wish to get some of them from other sources, or think them up from your experience. The choices of your most important values are, of course, up to you.

What's an idea that this section communicates?

A. The affirmations listed in the Appendix can be thought of as possibilities for what you might choose for your own values, along with other possibilities.
or
B. The long list of 62 principles is illustrated in the last chapter of the book called *Programmed Readings for Psychological Skills.*

101. What is the purpose of values and ethical principles? You use them to decide what to do. If people don't have useful ethical principles and values in mind, they often default to seeking entertainment, and to complaining of being bored when there is nothing to entertain them. They sometimes default to seeking power by defeating or dominating or bullying those who are around them. They also default to seeking physical

pleasure, often in the form of using drugs.

What's the main point of this section?

A. When people don't cultivate useful values, they tend to default to entertainment, power, and pleasure as values.
or
B. Violence, and cultivating skill in violence, very often are aimed at having power over other people.

102. The pursuits of entertainment, power, and pleasure are not bad in and of themselves. People's wishes to be entertained can inspire great works of art. The motive for power can lead people to do very useful work in order to get money, or to get the power that comes from being an expert in something. It can inspire people to learn to speak eloquently and persuasively. (There is a longer discussion of nonviolent means of gaining power and influence in my book on conflict-resolution and anger control.) And we could not enjoy the skills of joyousness without the motive for pleasure.

A big job for all people is to harness our drives for entertainment, power, and pleasure in good ways. First, we need to use these motives in ways that take care of ourselves over the long term, not just feel good right

now. Second, we need to use these drives to help other people as well as ourselves. The people who pick their values most successfully are most able to achieve long term happiness for themselves and to deliver long term happiness to others.

What's a summary of this section?

A. The drives for entertainment, power, and pleasure are not bad – they need to be used in a way that take into account the future and not just the present, and other people and not just ourselves.
or
B. When someone repeatedly gives in to something that feels good now but is bad for him or her in the long run, that may be called an addiction.

Mastery for the Listing Values Exercise

1. At level 1, you are able to answer the question about values or ethical principles in a way that makes sense.

2. At the second level, you're able to list several different values or ethical principles and say why they are desirable.

3. At the third level, you remember all of the sixteen skills and principles that this curriculum emphasizes, and

you're able to add any others that are
in your personal value system. You're
able to explain, for each principle,
why human society works better when
people follow it than when they don't.

Chapter 8: Skills Stories

103. The skills stories exercise is a good one for people to do together. You go through the psychological skills and principles in order, making up an example of each one of them. Each example is a very brief story. So for example, a tutor makes up an example of productivity. Then the student makes up an example of joyousness. Now it's the tutor's turn for kindness, and so forth. To make this exercise a little shorter, you can do the first half of the sixteen skills and principles one time and the second half next time.

What's a summary of this section?

A. The skills stories exercise consists of going through the skills and principles in order, making up an example of each.
or
B. It's good to "take turns" in psychological skills exercises, because turn-taking is fundamentally satisfying to the human brain.

104. What's the point of thinking up positive examples of the skills and principles? Why is this "good exercise" for our mental fitness? One of the keys to a happy and successful life is simply doing lots of good examples of these skills. The more of those positive examples we have in mind, the easier it will be to actually perform them. Each time we imagine a positive example of a skill, we are practicing using that skill. This is the principle of positive fantasy rehearsal – the more we visualize positive examples, the easier it will be to carry them out.

What's a summary of this section?

A. You can do the Skills Stories exercise while performing a physical movement, and thus work on physical and mental fitness at the same time.
or
B. With every performance of this exercise, you do positive fantasy rehearsals of important skills.

105. When you think up examples of the skills, you can think of ordinary, everyday examples, or more imaginative and whimsical examples. Both are good. The first type lets you rehearse the behaviors that you'll get the opportunity to carry out often. The second type lets you practice your creativity and keeps the exercise from getting boring.

What's the main idea of this section?

A. Both long and detailed stories and short plot outlines are useful.
or
B. Both ordinary, everyday actions and more exotic and improbable fantasies are useful.

106. Here's an example of a tutor and a student doing the skills stories exercise, using fairly everyday examples.

Tutor: Let's do the skills stories exercise.

Student: OK!

Tutor: How about I go first with productivity. A person studies really hard for a test at school. Your turn for joyousness.

Student: Someone invites two friends over and they have fun joking around and talking.

Tutor: Good example. My turn for kindness. Someone sees someone at school who looks lonely, and the person smiles and says hi to the lonely person.

Student: That's a good example too! My turn for honesty. Someone has so much homework that she just didn't have time to finish it all. A teacher

asks why she doesn't have it, and she is tempted to make up an excuse but just says, "I just couldn't work fast enough to finish all my work last night."

Tutor: Nice example. My turn for fortitude. Someone invites someone to come over and hang out, but the person doesn't want to. The person feels bad, but he gets over it and asks someone else. Your turn now for individual decisions.

Student: Someone gets the urge to make a bet that might win some money, but after he studies the chances of winning and losing, he figures out that it would be an unwise bet, and hangs onto his money.

Tutor: Good one! My turn for good joint decisions, or conflict-resolution. Two people want to eat supper together, but one is hungry now and the other isn't yet. They talk about options, and decide that the hungry one will get a little snack so he or she can wait comfortably.

Student: My turn for nonviolence. Somebody has the urge to hit his or her brother when the brother acts bratty, but walks away instead.

Tutor: That's a useful example. My turn for respectful talk. Some people are talking about politics, and one has the urge to say, "You don't know what you're talking about." But he resists the urge and says, "Here's some evidence for a different way of looking at that."

In this exercise so far, who more often complimented the other on the quality of the examples?

A. the tutor,
or
B. the student?

107. The tutor and student continue the skills stories exercise with fairly ordinary examples.

Student: So it's my turn for friendship-building. Someone is at a party, and he sees someone he doesn't know, and he goes up and introduces himself and they talk some.

Tutor: My turn for self-discipline. Someone is trying to eat healthy food and not gain weight. He passes up some cheesecake.

Student: Loyalty: Someone goes on a hike with his friend, but the friend can't keep up with the rest of the group. The guy stays back and walks with his friend so the friend won't be left behind alone.

Tutor: Conservation: Instead of buying a bunch of new clothes, a person just keeps wearing the ones she's already got.

Student: Self-care: Someone puts on sunscreen when she goes out in the sun to keep from getting skin cancer some day.

Tutor: Compliance: Someone pays all the taxes that the law says he has to pay.

Student: Positive fantasy rehearsal: Someone gets over a fear of heights by imagining being in high places.

Tutor: Good example! And my turn for courage. Someone is afraid of public speaking, but the person gets up and gives speeches anyway, and gradually gets used to it. And we are now done with all of the skills and principles, congratulations to us!

The point of this section and the last was to
A. give an example of what the skills stories exercise sounds like,
or
B. persuade you that you should do the skills stories exercise at least once a day?

108. Now let's have the tutor and the student go through the skills stories

exercise all over again. But this time they get a little more imaginative and whimsical in their examples.

Student: I'll go first for productivity. Someone builds an amazing castle out of Popsicle sticks, and sells it for thousands of dollars at an art show, to help out his family.

Tutor: My turn for joyousness. Two people are in a dungeon right next door to each other. They have fun at night teaching each other songs and singing them together.

Student: My turn for kindness. A lion decides he is going to be kind to the antelopes that live nearby, so he stops eating them and eats antelope-flavored soybeans instead.

In the example for joyousness, if you think about their finding fun despite being in a dungeon, this could also have been an example of

A. honesty,
or
B. fortitude?

109. The tutor and the student continue.

Tutor: My turn for honesty. Somebody is in a math contest, where you're not allowed to change answers

in a previous section once you're working on the next section. A kid works every question right, except she realizes that she got one wrong in a previous section. Instead of going back and changing it, she writes a note to the graders telling them she realizes she got one wrong and what the answer should be. So the person sponsoring the contest gives the winner a million dollars, but gives this girl a million also for coming in second place and being honest.

Student: I like it! My turn for fortitude. Somebody gets an illness that leaves him unable to move except for blinks of his eyes. He figures out how to communicate with people in code with eye blinks. He works with people on finding a cure for his illness, and he makes some progress, even though he never finds it, but he feels good about what he's doing anyway.

Tutor: Good! My turn for good individual decisions. Someone is captured by a bad person who says she has to choose which of her two children will live. She says that what she chooses is to try to persuade the bad person to become a good person. She eventually does this, and both of her children lived happily ever after.

In the examples so far, the example for fortitude, where the person worked toward a cure of his own disease, could also have been an example of

A. productivity,
or
B. compliance?

110. The tutor and the student continue.

Student: Good joint decisions: There are two countries that are heavily armed with nuclear weapons, who are about to get into a war that will destroy the whole world, because country A thinks that the huge compost pile that country B has is too stinky and the smelliness blows into their country. So they work out a plan that country A will rake up its tree leaves and put it on country B's compost pile so it won't smell bad. So nuclear war doesn't take place and the world is saved.

Tutor: All right! My turn for nonviolence. Somebody makes a time machine, and goes back to the time when the Greeks and the Trojans were fighting each other. The person pulls out a karaoke machine, with a bunch of contemporary Greek and Trojan songs on it. It turns out that Achilles and Odysseus and Hector and all the

ones fighting the war get so into singing karaoke that the war is ended.

Student: My turn for respectful talk. Once there was a talking wasp who got trapped in someone's car. A person in the car saw the wasp and cussed at it and tried to smush it. The wasp had the urge to cuss back, but instead, he used respectful talk and said, "I can see how you'd be afraid of me. But I can assure you I'm not interested in stinging you. If you'll kindly open the window, I'll fly away and we'll both be happy." The person opened the window and the wasp flew back to his nest where his fellow wasps greeted him warmly.

The last example given could also have been an example of

A. conflict-resolution or joint decision making,
or
B. productivity?

111. The tutor and the student continue.

Tutor: My turn for friendship-building. Someone is held captive. But he's so good at finding out about his captors and listening when they talk with him, that they start to like him, and they decide to let him go.

Student: Self-discipline. Someone has to earn money for his family. The only job he can find is cleaning up very disgusting stuff that's too disgusting for me to even go into. He doesn't like it, but he keeps doing it to make money for his family.

Tutor: Good one. My turn for loyalty. Two kids went to camp together, and were best friends. Then they came home and went to two different schools, where they each played on a football team. They found themselves lined up across from one another. Instead of hitting one another, they just shook hands. They asked the coaches to have them not have to play opposite each other. The coaches were so mad that they didn't let them play that game, so they sat on the bench together and chatted.

In the last example, the kids chose that they had more

A. loyalty to their best friend,
or
B. loyalty to their sports team?

112. The tutor and the student continue.

Student: My turn for self-care. Someone discovers that the receipts she's been giving out at her restaurant have a special paper with a chemical that does bad things for people's health. So she makes the receipts on regular paper, and finds most people don't want a receipt anyway.

Tutor: My turn for compliance. A person's psychological skills trainer asks him to do 500 fantasy rehearsals of something. He does it, and he finds his life greatly improved!

Student: My turn for positive fantasy rehearsal. A person is held captive by someone who says he can get loose only if he can jump into the air and turn a flip, without practicing. The person does lots and lots of practicing in his fantasy, and the story ends with his doing it successfully.

Tutor: And courage. An amoeba is very scared of splitting into two parts. He's scared the two parts he splits into won't like each other. Finally he has the courage to go ahead and split in two, and the two amoebas he splits into become best friends.

The last story in this set could have also been about

A. friendship-building,
or
B. honesty?

113. Skills stories may be a difficult exercise for some people to do well.

Some people find it much easier to let stories come into their minds than others do. But it's a skill that can improve with practice. It also is a skill that improves when you've read lots and lots of models. I would recommend that before taking on this exercise, you read all the skills and principles stories at the beginning of *Programmed Readings for Psychological Skills*.

A point made in this section is that

A. this exercise is fun to do with pictures,
or
B. this exercise is easier to do if you have read lots and lots of models of the psychological skills.

114. If a tutor and student get into doing this exercise, you might want to write down the story ideas you come up with. There is always a need for more positive models of psychological skills, and you could make a contribution by thinking of examples that will be useful to other people!

In this section the author invites you to

A. write down the stories you make up, so they can help other people,
or

B. record the stories you make up, and listen to them as you fall asleep at night?

Mastery of the Skills Stories Exercise

1. At the first level, you can think up or remember a story that's an example of each of the skills, with some help remembering the skills if you need it.

2. At the second level, you can think up a story that's an example of each of the skills, being prompted only by being given the next skill on the list. The stories have some originality or creativity.

3. At the third level, you are able to remember all the skills yourself, in order. You can think up a story that's an example of each, with no prompting. The stories have more originality and creativity. Furthermore, you have created a written diary of skills stories with at least 40 brief stories.

Chapter 9: Brainstorming Options

115. If you're awake, then your job, at any moment, is to decide what to do and do it. The quality of your life depends upon the quality of the decisions you make. If you make really good decisions, one after another, you're very likely to have a great life!

Many people go through their lives not thinking much about what to do – they just do the first thing that pops into their heads. As soon as they get an urge to do something, they do it. This isn't the best way to make important decisions. Thinking before acting, especially on important choices, is a very important habit!

A summary of the second part of this section is that

A. An important thing to think about when making decisions is the probability that a certain consequence will occur.
or
B. Many people do the first thing that occurs to them, but happier and more successful people think more before acting.

116. One of the most important words in decision-making is *options*. An option is something you could possibly do, but haven't done yet. For example, if someone earns a lot of money, one option is to pay for repairs to his car, another is to give money to a charity, another is to put money in the bank, and another is to buy investments that he hopes will earn more money. When you have an important choice point, it's good to think of several options, the best ones you can, and then try hard to figure out which ones will work the best.

What's a summary of this section?

A. A key to good decision-making is thinking of several options, and then trying to pick the best ones.
or
B. It's good to keep observing what the consequences of people's actions are, because your decisions are only as good as your predictions of consequences.

117. In the brainstorming options exercise, you consider a situation: a choice point, or a problem, or a goal, and you list options on what a person could do in that situation. As with most of the exercises, it's usually more fun if you take turns. The tutor thinks of an option, and then it's the student's turn, and then it's the tutor's

turn again. Your goal is to see how many good options the two of you can come up with, and to think of the best options you can. You are not in competition with each other to see who can think of more options.

Sometimes you will have a situation for which other people have already generated options. In this case, you can have the additional goal of seeing how many of their options you can think of.

What's a summary of this section?

A. In the brainstorming options exercise, you think of as many good options as you can for what to do in a certain situation.
or
B. In the pros and cons exercise, you take a certain options and think of the advantages and the disadvantages of it.

118. The word *brainstorming* also refers to an important process. When you are brainstorming, you try to think of as many ideas as you can, without being critical of your ideas. Your first priority is to get lots of ideas on the table; you can always discard the ones you don't like, later. You don't get bogged down in debating with yourself about which option is the best until you're through listing. You devote all your energy to coming up

with ideas, putting off till a little later the job of figuring out which idea is best.

What's a summary of this section?

A. The word *brainstorming* means that you put all your energy into coming up with ideas, and leave till later the decision on what is best.
or
B. The expected payoff for a certain option is how good the consequences would be, on the average, if you chose that option many times.

119. Even though the idea of brainstorming means generating lots of ideas without being too critical of the ideas, it's still good to leave out options that are obviously stupid or bad. For example, let's say the problem is that I am eating at a restaurant, and I think the people there have made a mistake in adding up my bill. If I think of options like pouring water on my head, kidnapping the waitress, lying on the floor while kicking and screaming, or getting up on a table and dancing, I'm wasting time and energy that I could use in really seriously trying to figure out what to do.

What's a summary of this section?

A. When you think of options for a real life problem, it's a good idea to write them down so you can remember them.
or
B. When you do the brainstorming options exercise, it's usually best to leave out options that are obviously not good ones.

120. Here's an example of what the brainstorming options exercise may sound like.

Tutor: Let's do the brainstorming options exercise. I have a situation in mind.

Student: OK! What's the situation?

Tutor: Bill has a friend named Dave, whom he likes to get together with. But Dave is friends with Scott, and wants to include Scott lots of times when they do things together. But Bill really dislikes Scott very much. That's the situation; let's think of some options!

Student: OK, I'll go first. Bill could just tell Dave how he feels, and ask Dave to get together with Bill only when Scott is not along.

Tutor: OK! My turn. Bill could not tell Dave that he doesn't like Scott, but just find out each time if Scott is going to be with Dave, and turn down any invitations where Scott will be present.

Student: If Bill dislikes Scott for a reason that is not very important, Bill could try to learn to get along with Scott better.

Tutor: Good! Bill could invite Dave to do things more often, that are of the sort that Dave wouldn't be so likely to invite Scott along to. For example, Dave might be more likely to invite Scott if they are playing sports, and less likely if Bill's invitation is for Dave to come over and have supper.

So far, what have the tutor and student done?

A. They have listed five options, and have talked in detail about the reasons why one option is better than the others.
or
B. They have listed five options, without discussing which one would work best?

121. The tutor and student continue listing options.

Student: If Bill does that option you just said and Dave still invites Scott to come along, Bill could nicely ask him not to do that.

Tutor: If Scott is doing a certain thing that Bill doesn't like, Bill could ask him to please stop doing it.

Student: Bill could work on making some new friends, just in case things don't work out with Dave because of Scott.

Tutor: That makes me think of, Bill could work on enjoying doing some more things by himself, just in case things don't work out with Dave because of Scott.

Student: Bill could work on just ignoring whatever unpleasant things Scott does, and not let them bother him.

Tutor: Bill could get together when he's within walking distance of home or when he has transportation, and just say goodbye and go home when he is with the other two and doesn't have a good time. That way he won't be stuck in a situation he doesn't like.

Student: If Scott does or says particular mean things to Bill, Bill could tell Dave about these sometime when they're alone, so Dave would understand why Bill doesn't want to have Scott with them.

Tutor: Wow, we've come up with 11 options, and every one of them seems pretty reasonable to me! Congratulations!

Student: Congratulations to you, too!

What was the purpose of this section?

A. To continue to give examples of what it's like to brainstorm options with a problem.
or
B. To make the point that if you have a friend, you should be able to ignore unpleasant things that friend's friends do.

122. What if the student runs out of options very early in the exercise? Then one possibility is that the tutor can say, "OK, listen to some more, please, and sometime we'll do this same situation again, but you'll have the benefit of having heard a bunch of options." Then the tutor reads, or makes up, a bunch of good options. In a while, or even immediately if they want to, they start over and do the same situation again.

What possible solution to a problem did this section suggest?

A. Working on divergent thinking exercises as described in this book, to

improve divergent thinking before doing much brainstorming options.
or
B. The tutor's listing or reading some options, and then coming back to the same choice point and listing options on it again later.

123. What if the student often runs out of options early enough that this activity isn't fun? Then there's an activity that will be less frustrating, but which will move the student toward greater skill in option-generating: alternate reading on choice points and options. The student and the tutor just read choice point situations, and they read options that people have thought of for those situations. That way the student gets the benefit of lots of models of option-generating before being asked to practice this skill.

Reading options that have been written down for choice points is a very good exercise even for tutors and students who are already very skilled at generating options. It's a part of the option-generating enterprise that is recommended for everyone. A few examples of brainstorming options are provided in an appendix to this book.

The exercise recommended in this section is

A. listing advantages and disadvantages of a certain option,
or
B. reading options that other people have made up as possibilities for choice points?

Mastery of the Brainstorming Options Exercise

1. At the first level, take turns thinking of options with your trainer for at least three situations, and think of at least two or three reasonable options for each.

2. At the second level, given five test situations, be able to think of a large fraction of the good options that have been listed by others for those situations.

3. At the third level, given ten more test situations, think of most of the options that have been listed by others; also think of very high quality options and express them articulately.

Chapter 10: Pros and Cons

124. With the brainstorming options exercise, you take a situation and think of options. With the pros and cons exercise, you take an option and think of advantages (pros) and disadvantages (cons) of it.

This exercise really asks you to guess the consequences, or results, of an option. If you think a certain good consequence will happen, that's an advantage of the option. If you think the option may lead to a bad consequence, that's a disadvantage of the option.

What's a summary of this section?

A. With the brainstorming options exercise, it's good not to waste your time on obviously bad options.
or
B. The pros and cons exercise lets you practice thinking of good and bad consequences of an option that might occur; these are called pros and cons or advantages and disadvantages.

125. The pros and cons exercise gives practice in a very important part of decision-making. Once you've noticed what's going on and have listed options for what to do, you have to figure out which options are best. You do that by trying to predict what will happen. The more the advantages of the options outweigh the disadvantages, the smarter it is to choose that option. The skill of choosing good options, and avoiding bad ones, is key to happiness and success!

What's the point of this section?

A. The pros and cons exercise gives practice in figuring out which options are best, and this is a really central skill for having a good life.
or
B. When deciding, you want to take into account how likely it is that each good or bad consequence will occur.

126. When you do the pros and cons exercise, you don't actually decide whether the option should be done or not. To make the decision, you would have to compare the pros and cons of one option to those of the other options. The pros and cons exercise gives you concentrated practice in doing one part of the decision process, without doing the whole thing. In this way it's like the brainstorming options exercise.

What's the point of this section?

A. The pros and cons exercise does not ask you to make the decision, but to practice one part of the decision-making process.
or
B. One of the goals of the pros and cons exercise is not to leave out any very important advantages or disadvantages of an option.

127. Here's an example of what the pros and cons exercise might sound like.

Tutor: Let's do the pros and cons exercise. Some people in a family are considering the option of adopting a pet dog. I'll go first. A disadvantage is that the people might fight with each other over who has to feed the dog and take him out and so forth.

Student: An advantage is that they could have a lot of fun playing with the dog and petting him.

Tutor: An advantage is that they could get some good exercise by taking him out for walks.

Student: A disadvantage is that the dog could bring in ticks that could get on the people and give them Lyme Disease.

Tutor: An advantage is that by being friendly and nice to the dog, the

people might get into the habit of being more friendly and nice to each other.

Which of the following have they NOT thought of so far?

A. The advantage of getting exercise taking the dog for walks,
or
B. The disadvantage of having hair on things, if the dog sheds?

128. The pros and cons exercise continues, with the same option, adopting a dog.

Student: A disadvantage is that the people could get so busy that no one would have time to spend on the dog, and the dog is not taken care of well.

Tutor: A disadvantage is that dog could whine and bark and keep people awake when they are trying to sleep.

Student: An advantage is that the people will feel loved by the dog and will be happier because of that.

Tutor: A disadvantage is that they would have to spend money on dog food and vet bills and other things.

Student: A disadvantage is that every time they take a trip, they would have to find someone to take care of the dog.

Tutor: Congrats! We've thought of 10 of them, and really good ones, too!

Which of the following occurred in this example?

A. Both the tutor and the student thought of both advantages and disadvantages.
or
B. The tutor thought only of disadvantages, while the student thought only of advantages?

129. Here's another example of the pros and cons exercise.

Tutor: Let's do the pros and cons exercise. Here's an option: someone is considering trying out for a football team.

Student: A pro is that he could turn out to be good at it and get lots of respect from his fellow students.

Tutor: A pro is that he could get lots of exercise that makes him stronger and more fit.

Student: A con is that he could get several concussions and get brain damage that would make him stupider for the rest of his life and get a dementia early.

Tutor: Another similar con is that he could get an injury some place other than his head, that would bother him for the rest of his life, like a knee or ankle injury.

Student: A pro is that he could end up having a lot of fun playing the game.

Which of the following have they NOT thought of so far?

A. The con of getting many concussions and brain damage,
or
B. The pro of making a lot of friends by getting to know his teammates?

130. The pros and cons exercise continues, with the same option.

Tutor: A con is that he would have less time to do his schoolwork because of all the practices.

Student: A con is that even if he doesn't get hurt, he could hurt someone else.

Tutor: A pro is that he could have the experience of working hard at something and having his efforts pay off.

Student: A con is that he could participate in a pretty violent sport that tends to model violence for lots of people.

Which of the following pros or cons have they NOT thought of?

A. The pro that if he is good enough at football, he could win a college scholarship.
or
B. The con that by modeling violence, he has a part in making other people a little more violent.

Mastery of the Pros and Cons Exercise

1. At the first level, when you are given an option, you can take turns with the trainer and come up with at least one or two reasonable advantages or disadvantages.
2. At the second level, when you are given an option, you can think of several important advantages and disadvantages on your own.
3. At the third level, when you are given several options, you can generate all or almost all the most important advantages and disadvantages of each of them, on your own.

Chapter 11: The Guess the Feelings Exercise

131. Suppose that someone wakes up and sees that it has snowed last night. Does the person feel angry, or happy? It's hard to answer that, isn't it, without any other clues. Now suppose you find out that the person saw the snow and thought, "Darn it! Now I have to do lots of shoveling to get out of my driveway, even with my back already sore! Drat!" This clue would give away the answer, wouldn't it? On the other hand, suppose instead that you found out that the person thought, "Oh boy! I love the snow. I'll get to go cross-country skiing, and it will be so beautiful!" Now it would still be easy to guess, but the answer would be the opposite one, wouldn't it?

What does this section illustrate?

A. That we feel emotion partly based on what sort of bodily reaction we feel ourselves making to a situation.
or
B. That the emotions we feel about a situation depend upon what we think about that situation.

132. Here's another example. A person gets back a test, and finds that the grade is 92 out of 100. Does the person feel proud, or angry? Again,

it's hard to say. Suppose you found out that the person thought, "Yay! I got an A on this! This is by far the highest grade I've gotten so far! My new method of studying is working!" The person would feel proud. On the other hand, suppose the person thought, "They took off points for no good reason! I should have had a perfect score! Why can't I get what I deserve!" In this case, the person would feel angry.

This section, like the previous one, is illustrating the effect of

A. thought upon emotion,
or
B. emotion upon thought?

133. The fact that our thoughts greatly influence how we feel is a very important idea. People have used this idea to make themselves less depressed, less anxious, and less angry. By changing our thoughts, we can sometimes very effectively change how we feel about things.

   The guess the feelings exercise gives lots of practice in grasping this very important idea. To do it, you make up a situation and give two choices for how the person felt. Then, you give the important hint: you tell what the person thought – in other words, what the person said to himself or herself. Now the other person should be able to guess correctly how the person felt. Then, the other person tells what the person might have thought that would have given the other answer.

The purpose of this section is to

A. Tell what the point of the guess the feelings exercise is, and tell how to do it,
or
B. To give evidence that when you are feeling a certain way, your thought patterns are affected by your feelings.

134. Here's an example of what it might sound like when two people do the guess the feelings fxercise.

First person: Let's do the guess the feelings exercise. I have one for you.

Second person: OK!

First person: Someone is deer hunting. The person sees a deer, but the deer sees the person and runs away. Does the person feel relieved, or disappointed?

Second person: Hmm. What's my hint about what the person thought?

First person: The person thought, "Whew. Thank goodness the deer got away. I just came along on this hunt to be with my friends. It would have felt so bad to shoot such a cute deer!"

Second person: Great hint! So now I know he felt relieved, huh?

First person: Yep.

Second person: So he would have felt disappointed if he had thought, "Aw, too bad. I wanted to be able to feed my family some deer meat. I missed my chance."

First person: Sounds good! Your turn for one!

In this exercise, do you think the first person was trying to

A. keep the second person from getting the right answer,
or
B. help the second person to get the right answer?

135. Here's another example of how the guess the feelings exercise might sound.

Second Person: A person has a test at school today. Does the person feel confident, or scared?

First person: And can you give me a hint by telling what the person thought?

Second person: The person thought, "Oh, no. What if I don't know the answers to any of them. I'll be so embarrassed to get a bad grade – that will be terrible!"

First person: Scared! And if the person had felt confident, the person would have been thinking, "I've studied a lot, and practiced answering lots of questions just like those on the test. I'm well prepared."

Second person: All right!

How difficult did the second person try to make it, to guess the right answer?

A. Very easy,
or
B. Very difficult?

136. Here, for your convenience, is a list of the steps you do in the guess the feelings exercise.

1. The first person tells a situation, and gives two choices for how the person felt in the situation.

2. The second person asks for the hint, of what the person thought about the situation.
3. The first person tells the thoughts.
4. The second person guesses correctly.
5. The first person confirms the guess.
6. The second person says what the thought would have been to make the other guess correct.

As you can see, the hardest part in this exercise is not guessing the feeling, but coming up with a situation and coming up with thoughts that would explain both of the feelings.

What's a point made in this section?

A. Each time you do the guess the feelings exercise, you remind yourself of the Big Idea of cognitive therapy: how you feel is greatly influenced by what you think.
or
B. The main challenge in the guess the feelings exercise is coming up with situations and thoughts, and not just making the correct guess.

Mastery of the Guess the Feelings Exercise

1. At the first level, when the trainer presents you with situations, choices for feelings, and thoughts, you can

guess the feeling correctly. You can say what feeling the person would have had when the trainer gives you the alternative thoughts. In other words, you can guess the feelings correctly for several situations.

2. At the second level, you can go through the six-step process listed above. in the role of the "second person." That is, you listen to the situation and choices, ask for the hint of thoughts, guess correctly, and make up the thoughts that would make the other feeling correct.

3. At the third level, you can go through the six-step process listed above in the role of the first person: that is, you make up a situation, tell the two choices, give the hint of the thoughts, and confirm the correct choice. You are able to do this for several situations.

Chapter 12: The Twelve-Thought Exercise

137. The twelve-thought exercise is one of the most useful psychological skill-building activities that we have discovered. In it, you practice thinking about a certain situation in twelve different ways. The goal is to help you think about any situation in the way that is most helpful, the way that brings about the best results. Most of us get into certain habits of thinking in certain ways, and stick with those habits whether they are working well or not. To be able to choose the thoughts that work the best is a life-changing liberation. The twelve-thought exercise has helped a number of people greatly improve their lives.

Which of the following is one of the points made in this section?

A. A goal of the twelve-thought exercise is taking more control over your own thoughts.
or
B. It is useful to do fantasy rehearsals out loud, so that you can hear yourself creating a practice in imagination.

138. Here are the twelve types of thoughts:

1. Awfulizing
2. Getting down on yourself
3. Blaming someone else
4. Not awfulizing
5. Not getting down on yourself
6. Not blaming someone else
7. Goal-setting
8. Listing options and choosing
9. Learning from the experience
10. Celebrating luck
11. Celebrating someone else's choice
12. Celebrating your own choice

Of course, not every thought falls into one of these categories. But these categories cover fairly well the important things we say to ourselves. Most people can benefit greatly from learning to choose well among just these twelve.

The author feels that

A. there are so many types of thoughts that it's impossible to classify them usefully,
or
B. the twelve categories we list here are enough to cover pretty well the important ways of thinking that we use?

139. Before doing the twelve thought exercise, it's good to practice with an easier exercise that we can call twelve thought recognition. In twelve thought

recognition, rather than having to come up with examples, you read or hear examples that someone else has come up with. You then practice deciding which of the twelve thoughts each is an example of. The *Journey* story in *Programmed Readings for Psychological Skills*, and the chapter on the twelve thought exercise in that same book, give lots of practice on twelve thought recognition. Let's do some quick twelve thought recognition practice right now. Even if you haven't read the other books that define the twelve types of thoughts, I'll bet you can figure them out just from their names.

What's the main point of this section?

A. Before generating your own examples of the twelve thoughts, it's good to practice classifying the examples someone else has written.
or
B. When you list options, you should not just list a bunch of bad options and one good one; you should shoot for listing several good options.

140. The situation is that someone is playing an electronic game. A family member has said, "We're going to have to leave, so you will have to finish up in the next 15 minutes." Then, 15 minutes later, the family member says, "You need to finish up now."

Suppose the person thinks, "Oh no! I'm still not at a stopping point! This is terrible!" Is that

A. awfulizing,
or
B. celebrating luck?

141. In the same situation, suppose the person were to think, "It's so stupid for me to get upset over a game, when other people are doing really important things." Would that be

A. listing options and choosing,
or
B. getting down on himself?

142. If the person thought, "How can she be so mean! Doesn't she know I'm in the middle of this? She shouldn't be interrupting me!" This is

A. learning from the experience,
or
B. blaming someone else?

143. Suppose instead the thought were this: "OK, I can handle this. It's not such a big deal. It's only a game."

A. not awfulizing,
or
B. getting down on himself?

144. If the person thought, "I don't like it that I'm feeling so upset about this, but it won't help to get down on myself about that now, so I won't," this is

A. not getting down on himself,
or
B. celebrating someone else's choice?

145. "My family member even went out of her way to warn me ahead of time. She doesn't deserve any blame at all." Is this

A. getting down on himself,
or
B. not blaming someone else?

146. "I want to handle this in a rational way. I want to produce a pleasant outcome for me and for my family member. I want to show maturity." Is this

A. goal-setting,
or
B. celebrating luck?

147. "I could take just a few seconds to wrap things up. Or I could just stop immediately, to give myself more practice in self-discipline. I could say nothing, or I could say, 'Thanks for reminding me.' I'm choosing to stop immediately and say 'Thanks for reminding me!'" Is this

A. listing options and choosing,
or
B. not getting down on himself?

148. "Next time, when I become aware that I only have a few minutes left, I'll stop as soon as I've reached a good stopping point. I'm learning that I can't do both of two things: I can't use every second that's available to me, and at the same time stop when things feel finished. I've learned that I have to choose one or the other, and I'm choosing to finish early." Is this

A. blaming someone else,
or
B. learning from the experience?

149. "I'm so lucky that the frustrations I'm dealing with are things like stopping playing games, whereas lots of other people are having to deal with things like war and famine." Is this

A. celebrating luck,
or
B. goal-setting?

150. "I'm really glad that my family members planned for us to go where we're going now. It's a better use of time than sitting around playing games."

A. listing options and choosing,
or
B. celebrating someone else's choice?

151. "I feel really good about staying cool and stopping playing the game right away. This is a self-discipline triumph for me."

A. celebrating his own choice,
or
B. not blaming someone else?

152. When two people do the twelve thought exercise together, they first select or think up a situation to use. They will use this same situation for all twelve thoughts. Then they take turns. The first makes up a way of awfulizing about that situation. The second makes up a way of getting down on himself or herself when in that situation. Then it's the first person's turn for blaming someone else. They keep going until they've done all twelve. Each of the twelve thoughts is a possible reaction to the same situation.

When a tutor and a student do the twelve thought exercise together,

A. the tutor listens while the student makes up all twelve thoughts,
or

B. the tutor and the student take turns as they make up examples of each of the twelve thoughts, about the situation they've picked?

153. Here's a model of the twelve thought exercise.

Tutor: Let's do the twelve thought exercise. I have a situation. Someone gets back a graded test from school. Points are taken off for answers that the student thinks are actually correct, and are mistakes by the grader.

Student: OK, do you want to start?

Tutor: Yes, I'll start with awfulizing. This is terrible, and so unfair. I do things right and get them counted as wrong! Your turn for getting down on yourself.

Student: It must be that I did something wrong, and I'm not able to even figure out what it is.

Tutor: All right! My turn for blaming someone else. The person that graded this is a bad grader. He doesn't know what he's doing. Your turn for not awfulizing.

Student: It's not such a big deal. It's just a few points. It probably won't make any difference to my grade in the long run, even if it's not corrected.

Tutor: Good example! My turn for not getting down on myself. It's true that I don't understand what I did wrong, but I don't want to punish myself for that. It could be that I did nothing wrong, and it could be that I made a mistake I can learn from. Your turn for not blaming someone else.

Student: The person who graded this is capable of making mistakes, just as I am. I don't want to waste my energy getting super angry over this.

So far, how many of the twelve thoughts have the two of them gone through?

A. four,
or
B. six?

154. They continue with the twelve thought exercise.

Tutor: My turn for goal-setting. My goals are to understand the answer to the question, and perhaps to get the points back if I deserve them, and in any case to stay cool. Your turn for listing options and choosing.

Student: I could study the book or look up other explanations to understand the answer better. If I still think I was right, I can just forget about it, or I can talk with the teacher about it before class starts. Or I can send the teacher an email or write a note. I think I'll study first, and then if I still think I'm right, get to class early and ask the teacher about it.

Tutor: Good job. My turn for learning from the experience. I learned from this that it's good to check over things that are graded, because mistakes happen. Your turn for celebrating luck.

Student: I'm lucky that I'm thinking about getting back a few points on a test rather than having to deal right now with someone's dying, or a war's starting, or my not having enough to eat.

Tutor: Good. My turn for celebrating someone else's choice. I'm glad that my friend has been supportive in times like this, and that even if the points were unfairly taken away and I can't get them back, at least I can talk with my friend about it. Your turn for celebrating your own choice.

Student: I'm glad I've stayed cool and made a good plan. And I'm glad I did well on the test in any case.

The good plan that the student made when listing options was

A. to talk with his parents,
or
B. to study the subject matter the question dealt with, and ask the teacher about it if it still appeared he got the question right?

155. Here are some tips for doing the twelve thought exercise well.

How do you do "not awfulizing" when the situation really is awful? You can choose to think about something other than how awful it is. For the worst case scenario, if the situation is that a nuclear bomb is headed toward your house, not awfulizing might be, "I want to spend the next few moments doing something other than going over how terrible this is."

Likewise, you can "not get down on yourself" when you really have done something bad. If you have robbed a bank, a reasonable way to not get down on yourself might be to think, "I did make a mistake, but I'm choosing at this time to do something more useful than to keep thinking what a bad thing I did."

What's the principle that these examples illustrate?

A. You can "not awfulize" or "not get down on yourself," without thinking something that isn't true, even when the situation is bad or you've made a mistake.
or
B. That all the thoughts are useful at some points – there is not one of them that you should never do.

156. The same point goes for "not blaming someone else." You can be aware that someone else did a bad act, and still choose to use your mind in ways other than repeating to yourself how bad that person is. You don't need to deny that someone has done something bad.

What would be an example of not blaming someone else in a way that follows this principle, if you know for sure that someone purposely burned down your house?

A. It's not their fault. It must have been an accident.
or
B. Even though the person did a bad thing, I have better things to do with my mind right now than to keep going over what a bad thing he did.

157. It is possible to awfulize, get down on yourself, or blame someone else in useful ways. Useful thoughts stick close to the evidence at hand about this situation, without generalizing to all sorts of other situations or exaggerating how bad

things are. For example, suppose someone discovers that the factory he works for is releasing very harmful poisons into the environment, and he thinks, "This is a really bad situation!" This is a useful thought. It will tend to make the person do something useful about the problem. On the other hand, thoughts like "I can't stand this! I just can't handle it!" tend to make the person feel helpless.

In this section the author gives an example of how someone can

A. celebrate even when bad things happen,
or
B. awfulize in more constructive or less constructive ways?

158. Using the same example, if the person who works for the factory were to think to himself, "It's a mistake that I didn't notice this earlier," that's getting down on himself without overgeneralizing. On the other hand, if he thinks, "I'm a terrible person for not finding this earlier; I don't deserve to ever be liked by anybody ever again," then he's overgeneralizing and exaggerating.

If he thinks, "Other people at this factory also should have been on top of this earlier," then he's blaming other people in a limited and probably useful way. If he thinks, "This factory is full of horrible people," he is probably overgeneralizing.

In giving these contrasting examples, the author has the goal of

A. teaching how to use awfulizing, getting down on yourself, and blaming someone else in more constructive ways,
or
B. encouraging you to do the twelve thought exercise many times, not just a few?

159. In doing the twelve thought exercise, often it's useful to think of not very constructive examples of awfulizing, getting down on yourself, or blaming someone else, so that you will recognize thoughts of this type when you find yourself doing them. It's also useful to practice the more constructive versions of these three thoughts, so that you get practice at them. When you do the twelve thought exercise, it's up to you to choose which way will be more useful to you!

The author advises

A. avoiding the nonconstructive types of awfulizing, getting down on yourself, and blaming someone else thoughts when doing the twelve thought exercise,
or

B. thinking of either constructive or nonconstructive examples of the first three types of thoughts, whichever you feel will be more useful to you?

160. What's the difference between goal-setting and listing options and choosing? In goal-setting, you decide on the result you'd like to bring about. In listing options and choosing, you try to figure out what to do to bring about that result. For example, suppose the situation is that someone stands on your foot. The goal is the situation you want to bring about: the person is off your foot, and a fight has not started. The options are different things you might say and do to bring about this desired result.

Choosing your goal influences what options you consider. In the situation of the person standing on your foot, if you were to choose the goal of punishing and dominating the other person, you would think of different options than if the goal were simply to get the person off you.

What's a summary?

A. Goal setting is figuring out what outcome you want, and listing options and choosing is deciding how you want to bring about that outcome.
or

B. People who are depressed tend not to do much celebrating about anything.

161. When listing options, many people list several bad options, followed by one good option, and to choose the good option. For example, "I could hit the person, or I could scream at him, or I could just politely but firmly inform him that he's on my foot. I'll choose the last one." You will improve your decision-making skills more if you think of several good options, for example: "I could say, 'You're standing on my foot,' or I could say, 'Please get off my foot,' or I could say, 'Move off my foot please," or I could just jerk my foot out from under his. I'm going to choose to say the first one while jerking my foot out from under his."

In this section the author advocates

A. practicing the twelve thought exercise with positive situations as well as problem situations,
or
B. thinking of several good options when listing options and choosing – not several bad options and only one good one.

162. How do you celebrate luck, when the situation is that something bad has happened? You can celebrate that

something even worse didn't happen. Or you can search to find one positive aspect of the situation and celebrate that. For example, if the situation is that a piano has fallen out of a building and landed on my leg, I can celebrate that it hasn't landed on my head. Or I can celebrate that this happened fairly close to a good hospital.

A summary is that

A. you can celebrate luck when bad things happen by celebrating that even worse things didn't happen, or by finding some positive part of the situation.
or
B. celebrating luck tends to make you feel good about the world you're living in, whereas celebrating your own choice tends to make you feel good about yourself?

163. How do you celebrate someone else's choice when the situation is that someone has done something bad to you? You can think of someone else who has been nice to you, and celebrate what that person did. For example, if I'm doing the twelve thought exercise with the situation where someone burned down my house on purpose, I can celebrate someone else's choice by thinking, "I'm glad my family members have

chosen to be tough in situations like this and not to just moan and wail."

The point is that

A. When you're celebrating someone else's choice, you can think about someone the situation didn't even mention.
or
B. Your thought should have something to do with the situation you are working on, rather than just being a random thought.

164. When you celebrate your own choice, you can make up a good way of handling the situation, and then imagine and celebrate that you have handled the situation in that way. For example, in the situation where someone burned down my house, I can imagine that my choice was to call up the insurance company that insures our house, and report this to them and talk with them about making a claim. Thus I can celebrate a choice that the situation description didn't mention.

A summary is:

A. It's good to relax your muscles while doing the twelve thought exercise with unpleasant situations.
or
B. When celebrating your own choice, you get to imagine yourself making

and enacting a good choice, and then celebrating having done that.

165. Now let's look at another example of the twelve thought exercise.

The situation is that someone goes for lunch at school, but the only things at the cafeteria are things the person doesn't like.

1. Awfulizing: This is a really undesirable situation. I was looking forward to eating something good, and now it looks like I can't.

2. Getting down on myself: I should have known this would happen and should have prepared for it. I don't think ahead enough.

3. Blaming someone else: Why can't those people come up with something good? This is a bad food service they're running.

4. Not awfulizing: This isn't so bad. At least I'm not starving.

5. Not getting down on myself: I could have foreseen this and prepared for it, but I don't want to punish myself about that.

6. Not blaming someone else: They're just trying to make the food more healthy. I don't want to waste energy blaming them.

When the person "awfulized," he could have said, "I can't stand this! This shows that nothing ever comes out right!" Compared to this, do you think the way the person really awfulized in the example above, by thinking "this is an undesirable situation," was

A. more useful to do in real life, because it didn't overgeneralize so much,
or
B. less useful to do in real life, because overgeneralization is good?

166. The twelve thought exercise continues.

7. Goal-setting: My goal is to pick something to do now that will make things come out OK, and to plan what to do about this in the future.

8. Listing options and choosing: For now, I could skip lunch and eat when I get home. I could eat the stuff that is best for me, even if I don't like it. I could just get something to drink that will tide me over. I think I'll get tough and eat the healthiest stuff even though I don't like it. For the future, I think I'll bring my lunch more often.

9. Learning from the experience: I learned from this that if I want to eat only what I like, I should bring it from home rather than buying it here.

10. Celebrating luck: I'm glad that I have enough to eat, unlike a lot of people.

11. Celebrating someone else's choice: I'm glad that at home, my parent gets lots of foods that I like.

12. Celebrating my own choice: I'm glad I chose to eat healthy stuff I don't like, and thus have a self-discipline triumph!

When you realize that you have made a triumph in a certain type of psychological skill, you are almost always

A. celebrating your own choice,
or
B. not awfulizing?

Mastery of the Twelve Thought Exercise

0. At a preliminary level, the student is able to recognize any of the twelve thoughts when they are presented – as for example in the Journey story or the examples given in this chapter.

1. At the first level, when the trainer presents a situation, the student is able to take turns with the trainer, and make up the appropriate thoughts when prompted by the trainer. The student should do this for at least two situations, doing the odd numbered thoughts for one and the even numbered thoughts for the other.

2. At the second level, you should be able to compose examples of the thoughts that are of higher quality than those at level 1 – you use the tips mentioned in this chapter. You list some very good options, and no options that are obviously bad. You can come up with the thoughts fairly quickly.

3. At the third level, you can make up a situation yourself, give examples of all twelve thoughts, and have the thoughts be really good examples, for several situations. You generate several really good options. You can come up with these thoughts fluently. You remember the 12 thoughts in order without prompting.

Chapter 13: The Four-Thought Exercise

167. In real life, when you are busy responding to situations, you will seldom take the time to go through all twelve thoughts and then choose which ones are most useful. Life goes by too quickly.

But when unwanted things happen, you can go through a certain four thoughts fairly quickly. These four thoughts serve as a nice all-purpose reflex for dealing with unwanted situations. It's useful to take lots and lots of unwanted situations and practice until these four thoughts become a strong habit. This habit can improve your skills of fortitude, nonviolence, self-discipline, courage, conflict-resolution, and others.

What's the main point of this section?

A. Most people can improve several psychological skills by practicing responding with four certain thoughts when unwanted things happen.
or
B. When you have practiced the twelve-thought exercise many times, it's good to practice the "negative" thoughts without overgeneralizing.

168. What are the four thoughts that are useful to practice as a reflex for dealing with unwanted situations? They are as follows:

not awfulizing
goal-setting
listing options and choosing
celebrating your own choice.

If you wanted to make a phrase that would help you remember these four, by making the first letter of each word in the phrase give you the first letter of each of the four thoughts, which phrase would work?

A. freedom always is good,
or
B. not gonna lose cash?

169. What do we mean by "unwanted situations"? Sometimes the situations are the type that tend to make people mad. We can call these provocations. Someone criticizes you. Someone wakes you up by playing loud music. Someone commands you to do something you don't feel like doing.

Other types of unwanted situations are those that trigger fear or disgust or pain. Someone has to get blood drawn. Someone who is afraid of snakes sees a snake in the path in front of him. Someone who is afraid of public performances has to give a speech. Someone who is afraid of bees sees a wasp flying around. Someone who has a strong aversion to the image of vomiting sees someone else get sick and throw up.

How did this section try to communicate what was meant by the phrase, "unwanted situations"?

A. By defining both the word *unwanted* and the word *situations*, or
B. by giving several examples of unwanted situations?

170. Sometimes situations that have unpleasant or unwanted parts are also very much wanted. For example, someone has won an important part in a play. The night of the play comes up. The person very much wants to do the play, but the situation still brings out a lot of fear. Or a person gets a job which is very much wanted, but the thought of getting out of bed and driving in to work is unpleasant.

The point of this section is that

A. you can use the four thought exercise with situations that mix wanted and unwanted parts, or
B. it's good to learn to relax the muscles as well as to think the four

thoughts as you handle lots of difficult situations?

171. Let's look at some examples of the four thought exercise.

The situation is that I find out that a good friend of mine is moving to a different city.

Not awfulizing: I don't like that my friend is moving, but I am strong enough to handle it.

Goal-setting: I want to keep up the relationship with my friend who's moving, and also have enough other friends that I feel supported.

Listing options and choosing: I can keep in touch with my friend by phone calls, emails, Facebook, letters, and in-person visits. I can invite other people to go for walks with me or to have work parties with me or just to come over and hang out. I can join some clubs, or get more active in some groups I already belong to. I think the main plan I want to explore is having phone conversations with my friend while going for walks. We can do that wherever we both are.

Celebrating my own choice: I think I did some good thinking about this.

Which of the following goals did the person NOT set?

A. to feel supported,
or
B. to keep the friend from moving?

172. Here's another example. A person who is afraid of going to sleep in the dark turns out the lights when he goes to bed.

Not awfulizing: I feel scared, but that doesn't mean I'm in danger.

Goal-setting: I want to keep exposing myself to this situation until I get much less scared than I am now.

Listing options and choosing: While I'm lying here, I could do the "pleasant dreams" exercise by making up nice fantasies, relax my muscles, feel good about my courage in doing this, or make plans for the future. I think I'll mainly make up pleasant fantasies, relax my muscles, and congratulate myself.

Celebrating your own choice: I made a good choice about what to do, I think, and I also made a great choice by having the courage to do this exposure.

The major goal of the person in this situation was

A. to get lots of work accomplished while doing the exposure,
or
B. to get less afraid of lying in bed in the dark?

173. Here's another example of the four-thought exercise. Here the situation is that a boy is having fun, but his parent calls him to get ready for bed.

Not awfulizing: I wish I didn't have to stop, but it's not the end of the world. I've had a good bit of fun time already.

Goal-setting: My goal is to make it as painless as possible to quit playing and start getting ready for bed. My goal also is to have a self-discipline and compliance triumph.

Listing options and choosing: I could put it off for just a second, or I could start this very second, so as not to prolong the misery of facing quitting. I can yell "Bye, thanks for playing with me," to the people I'm with as I go back. I can walk, or I can run. I'm choosing to start running back, this very second, and yell "Bye, thank you," over my shoulder.

Celebrating my own choice: I'm glad I decided to start running right away, because that made it less painful. I'm glad I was polite to my friend. Hooray, that was a self-discipline and compliance triumph!

Why do you think the person decided not to put off starting to run back for even a few seconds?

A. Because the person thought that would make it less painful for himself, or
B. because the person wanted to sleep as long as possible?

174. You can take turns with someone else in doing the four thought exercise. I recommend that one person do the complete four-thought exercise (all four thoughts) for one situation, and the other do the complete exercise for another situation.

The author advises that

A. one person do one thought, and the other person do the next thought, or
B. one person does all four thoughts for one situation, and the other person does all four for another situation?

175. One of the biggest challenges in doing the four-thought exercise well lies in thinking of good options and choosing options wisely – the skill of good decision making. After each

person has done the four thought exercise, if the other person has some ideas about other options that might have been considered or chosen, it's often good to spend a short time discussing these.

It's important, when doing the four-thought exercise, to put some imagination into celebration of your own choice. You don't want to do just a little bored-sounding "Yay for me" just to get the celebration over with. You want to sincerely congratulate yourself.

What if you're not sure that you made the best choice? Then you can even say, "I'm not sure I made the best choice, but given that I can't know what will work out best, I celebrate that I chose as well as I knew how!"

Which parts of the four-thought exercise does this section give tips on?

A. not awfulizing and goal-setting, or
B. listing options and choosing and celebrating your own choice?

176. Where do you find situations for the four-thought exercise? There is a long list of provocations and another list of conflict situations near the end of my book on anger control. Also, in an appendix near the end of my book on anxiety-reduction, there is a survey

of situations that are sometimes scary for people. There's a list of choice points in an appendix to this book. I recommend that at the beginning of your work, you use these situations.

Why is it useful to use "standard" situations rather than situations drawn from your own life? First, most people will find that the situations on standard lists have lots in common with the situations that cause trouble in your own life. Second, the custom of using standard situations reinforces the idea that tutoring is to build skills useful for all situations, rather than to come up with particular solutions to problems in your life.

What's the point of this section?

A. It's good to use standard lists as sources of situations for the four-thought exercise.
or
B. You must do many repetitions of the four-thought exercise to build up the habit of calm, rational responses to unwanted situations.

177. After you have done the four-thought exercise many times, you may become ready to add to these lists yourself, using your knowledge of situations in your own life. You can write down situations that provoked more anger or fear than you wanted

them to. You can then practice with the situations you've made up.

Even then, remember that when you do the four-thought exercise, you are not making a firm decision as to what to do about a situation. You are practicing a type of thinking that will probably be very useful in deciding how to act. But you can always list options and choose again, and perhaps come to a different choice.

One of the points the author makes is that

A. When you practice the four-thought exercise, the choice you make is for practice and not a commitment: you can always decide later what you want to do in real life.
or
B. You should always pick goals that are in keeping with high values – peace and harmony, for example, rather than dominance and revenge.

Mastery of the Four Thought Exercise

1. At the first level, you can come up with examples of each of the four thoughts for a certain situation, when the tutor presents the situation and prompts you for each of the four types of thoughts.

2. At the second level, you can remember the four types of thoughts easily, and when given a situation, you can come up with good and appropriate examples of each of the four thoughts. You list several good options, and no bad ones.

3. At the third level, you can do all the things listed at the second level, but the thoughts are of even higher quality, with more good options, and you can do the exercise very fluently, with several situations. You can also think of your own situations to do the exercise with.

Chapter 14: Listening With Four Responses

178. When you do the reflections exercise, one person talks and the other listens. Every time the first person stops, the second person does a reflection.

The reflections exercise provides great practice of important skills. Doing reflections helps you get good at listening very carefully to another person. But in an ordinary real-life conversation, using a reflection many times in a row would sound unnatural. It might distract the person who's speaking to you.

The exercise called listening with four responses helps you to be a great listener while at the same time sounding natural.

What's a main point of this section?

A. In doing a reflection, you say something like "What I hear you saying is ____," and you fill in the blank.
or
B. While the reflections exercise gives great practice in listening, doing nothing but reflections usually sounds unnatural; listening with four responses, however, sounds like very natural good listening.

179. What are the "four responses?" They are: 1) reflections, 2) facilitations, 3) follow-up questions, and 4) positive feedback. These are explained in a chapter of *Programmed Readings for Psychological Skills* called "Ways of Listening to Another Person." We'll go over them again now. We already talked about reflections in another chapter.

Someone gave the word *facilitation* to responses like this:

Uh huh.
Yes.
OK.
I see.
Humh.
Is that right.
Oh.
Wow.

These can be said with any degree of approval and enthusiasm. They mean something like, "I'm receiving your message. Keep going!"

When someone says, "I've been thinking about moving to Canada," and the second person replies, "Oh?" the second person is using a

A. reflection,
or

B. facilitation?

180. A follow-up question is asking for more information on the topic the other person already was talking about. Suppose the first person says, "I've discovered something important." If the second person were to say, "What have you discovered?" that would be a follow-up question. We also count replies like, "Please tell me more, " as a follow-up question, even though it doesn't end with a question mark.

When a first person says, over the phone, "It's hot here," and the second says, "How hot is it?" the second person is using a

A. follow-up question,
or
B. facilitation?

181. Positive feedback means letting the other person know you liked something he or she said or did. It's usually positive feedback when someone says any of the following:

"That's a good point."
"How interesting."
"I'm glad you told me that."
"Thanks for telling me about that."
"Good idea!"
"I think you made a good decision!"
"Well said!"

Suppose the first person says, "I did some research on the Internet about which jobs our planet most needs people to do." Suppose the second person says, "That sounds like a smart thing to do. What did you find out?"

The second person did

A. positive feedback, then a follow-up question,
or
B. a facilitation, and then a reflection?

182. When you do the listening with four responses exercise, one person speaks, and stops speaking often. Each time the speaker stops, the listener responds with one (or more) of the four responses.

In one way of doing this exercise, the speaker names, or thanks the listener for, the particular response that the listener made, before going on talking – for example, "Thanks for the reflection," or "That was a facilitation." In the other way, the speaker simply goes on talking.

After a while, the speaker and the listener switch roles.

What was the purpose of this section?

A. To explain how to do the listening with four responses exercise.
or

B. To explain the advantages and disadvantages of the speaker's naming or thanking the listener for the particular type of response that the listener gave.

183. Here's an example in which the speaker does name the type of response the listener gave.

Speaker: I've been reading about how people improve their sports performances by practicing not just in real life, but in imagination.

Listener: Oh? Please tell me more.

Speaker: Thanks for the facilitation and follow-up question. About forty years ago someone did an experiment finding that ski racers could improve their times by vividly imagining themselves going through the ski course just the way they wanted to go in real life. We can call what they did, "fantasy rehearsal."

Listener: So if I understand you right, someone did a scientific experiment about fantasy rehearsal with ski racers several decades ago.

Speaker: Thanks for the reflection, and it's very accurate. Around the same time, a very famous golfing champion revealed that before every shot he took, he vividly imagined how he wanted to move and how he wanted the ball to move. He did "fantasy rehearsals" throughout the whole match.

Listener: That's very interesting! Please tell me more.

Speaker: Thanks for the positive feedback and follow-up question.

The topic the speaker is talking about so far is

A. how sports are useful for getting physically fit,
or
B. how fantasy rehearsal has been used to improve performance in sports?

184. The speaker continues.

Speaker: I read that almost every Olympic athlete these days uses fantasy rehearsal in some form or another to improve his or her performance.

Listener: So you're saying that fantasy rehearsal is so useful for athletes that almost all Olympic competitors use it, huh?

Speaker: Yes, that's a correct reflection. It turns out that people have used fantasy rehearsal for all sorts of other things: public speaking, musical performances, you name it. Someone did an experiment where people who were scared of snakes got over their fear by imagining themselves handling snakes fearlessly.

Listener: Humh!

Speaker: Thanks for the facilitation. Now lots of people have gotten over fears by what is called virtual exposure, where they watch videos of being in the situation they are scared of – being in an airplane, going over bridges, giving a speech, whatever.

Listener: In other words, people watched videos to get used to things they had been scared of, and this was another form of fantasy rehearsal.

Speaker: Thanks for the reflection.

In this section, the speaker turns from how fantasy rehearsal is used in sports, to

A. how fantasy rehearsal helps people get over fears,
or
B. how sports can produce lots of injuries?

185. The speaker continues.

Speaker: So what are we to think about the fact that millions of guys are spending billions of hours doing video games in which they are fantasy rehearsing shooting people, one after another, rapidly? If we believe that fantasy rehearsal helps people get over fears and aversions, it can also make them more comfortable with hurting or killing someone else.

Listener: That's a good point. You're saying that in video games, there's a massive program for fantasy rehearsal of shooting people.

Speaker: Thanks for the positive feedback and reflection. Could this have anything to do with the fact that senseless shooting rampages have gotten more and more frequent in recent years?

Listener: I see. You believe that shooting rampages may have something to do with the huge amount of violent games that provide fantasy rehearsal of violence.

Speaker: Thanks for the facilitation and reflection, and thanks for listening to me talk about this!

In this section, the speaker has taken up what topic?

A. How fantasy rehearsal through video games may contribute to shooting rampages.
or
B. How fantasy rehearsal can be used to overcome unwanted fears.

186. Now here's another example in which the speaker is a student. The speaker does not identify or thank the listener after each response. Both variations of this exercise have their advantages, and it's good to do both of them.

Speaker: I'm thinking of starting an anti-bullying club at my school.

Listener: What a worthy goal! What sorts of things would the club members do?

Speaker: There are all sorts of possibilities. We could put on presentations for other students about the bullying issue. We could organize a questionnaire to see how much bullying goes on. We could talk with teachers and other staff about how bullying is handled. We can get discussion groups going among students.

Listener: You've been doing some good thinking! Please tell me more, what else have you thought of?

In this section, each of the listener's responses consisted of

A. first a facilitation, and then a reflection,
or
B. first positive feedback, and then a follow-up question.

187. The listening with four responses exercise continues:

Speaker: We're also thinking of naming some students that other students could go to and talk with, when they're being bullied. Those students could then watch carefully, and if the bullying is repeated, they could be witnesses about exactly what happened. That way the bullied student, or the one who is supposedly bullying, for that matter, wouldn't find himself in a "my word against his" situation.

Listener: I see. So one of the roles you think students can play is to watch carefully and report very accurately exactly what does go on.

In this section, the listener responded with

A. A follow-up question, followed by a positive feedback,
or

B. A facilitation, followed by a reflection?

188. The exercise continues.

Speaker: Another thing this club might do is to find good things people have written on the subject, for students to read in class. We're also thinking of sponsoring an essay contest where students write their ideas on how to create a "culture of kindness" at the school, where people are nice to each other.

Listener: Sounds like you're figuring out ways to mix reading and writing practice with your goal. That's pretty smart, because that way you're less likely to run into the objection that "We don't have time for that, because we have to teach reading and writing."

In this section, the listener responded

A. first with a reflection, and then with positive feedback,
or
B. first with a facilitation, and then with a follow-up question?

189. The listening with four responses exercise continues.

Speaker: Thank you. One of the interesting things I find when reading about this is that when lots of nice words and approval go on between people, either in schools or in families, this tends to make people happier and protect them from mental health problems. On the other hand, when they are very critical and mean to each other, they are more miserable and they have more mental health problems.

Listener: Those sound like some very important findings. I'm glad you're studying this kind of stuff.

In this section the listener responded with

A. A facilitation,
or
B. positive feedback?

Mastery for the Listening with Four Responses Exercise

1. At the first level, you can recognize each of the four responses (facilitations, reflections, positive feedback, follow up questions) when you hear them. Also, in response to a sample piece of talk by someone else, you can make up an example of each of them.

2. At the second level, when someone talks and stops talking often, you can

answer with one of the four responses each time. You can also do the exercise from the role of the talker, responding with acknowledgement or reinforcement of the other's responses.

3. At the third level, you can do the second level tasks with very skillful choices of which response to make, and such high-quality responses, that you sound like a very skilled listener or interviewer.

Chapter 15: The Tones of Approval Exercise

190. When we speak, our voices don't just say words. We use different pitches and rhythms to show how we feel about what we are saying. Imagine that you tell someone else a good idea that you've had. You say, "I think this could really work!"

Imagine that the other person says, in a very sarcastic voice, "Yeah, right."

Now imagine instead that the person says, with great enthusiasm and joy, "Yeah! You're right!"

There's a tremendous difference in how you would feel about the other person's response, isn't there?

What's the point of this section?

A. Not just the words we say, but the tones of voice in which we say them, determine what it feels like to get the message.
or
B. Higher pitches usually correspond to higher excitement or greater emphasis.

191. Tones of voice can communicate lots of different things. But perhaps the most important message in tones of voice is that of approval versus disapproval. If I say in a very approving tone the word "Oh!" I'm telling the other person, "I like what you just said," or "Hooray for that," or "That makes me feel friendly to you," or "I want you to feel good about that!" On the other hand, if I say in a disapproving and disappointed tone the word "Oh..." I'm signaling the other person, "I don't like that," or "I'm suspicious of that," or "I want to discourage that." Knowing whether our words and actions get approval or disapproval from others is very important.

What's the main idea of this section?

A. In addition to approval or disapproval, our tones of voices signal how energetic we are feeling.
or
B. A very important message that our tones of voice communicate is how much we approve or disapprove of the other person's behavior.

192. Let's think of five degrees of approval and disapproval in people's tones of voice.

Large disapproval

Small to moderate disapproval
Neutral
Small to moderate approval
Large approval

You may want to take a phrase like, "Look what you did," and try saying it in each of these five ways. Or listen to someone else say the same thing in each of these ways. See if it's easy or hard for you to tell the difference between the various degrees of approval.

This section suggests

A. shifting the amount of approval in your own tone of voice more toward the approving end of the spectrum, or
B. practicing saying a phrase in each of the 5 ways, just to experience the difference between them.

193. If you get into the habit of listening for the amount of approval or disapproval in people's voices, you may notice several things. You may notice that the people you like the most, and enjoy being with the most, are the ones who give more approval and less disapproval. You may notice that families or classrooms or other groups of people who exchange more approval and less disapproval contain people who are happier and even physically healthier. You may notice

that people learn better and faster when they get more approval and less disapproval for their efforts.

The examples given in this section seem to make the point that

A. Relationships where more approval is exchanged seem to be better for people.
or
B. Sometimes words that don't mean much by themselves, such as "huh," or "ummh," communicate lots of meaning when you hear the tone of voice they are spoken in.

194. Observing that people seem happier when lots of approval goes on doesn't mean that we should say everything with large approval! We like some things more than others, and it's good to let our tones of voice vary so that people can tell what we really like.

You'll hardly ever find anyone who says everything with large approval. However, there are lots of people who seem to say most things with a neutral, monotone, expressionless tone of voice. These people would communicate better if they would let their tones of voice vary more. Maybe sometimes people speak without expression because they want to keep secret from the other person how much they approve or disapprove.

This section has to do with

A. How much to let your tone of voice vary, from one thing you say to another.
or
B. How the difference between small to moderate and large approval has more to do with high and low pitch than with how loudly you speak.

195. When we do the tones of approval exercise, we usually think about these three tones:

neutral
small to moderate approval
large approval

One person says something in one of the three tones, and the second guesses which tone the first one was trying to use. When both people can vary their tones of voice in each of these three ways, and each can recognize accurately the other's tones, you achieve the purpose of the exercise.

What's a summary of this section?

A. When people don't give much approval, others may adjust their expectations, and think things like, "For *him*, that's large approval."

or
B. To do the tones of approval exercise, one person says something and the other guesses which tone the person was trying to use.

196. Here's what the tones of approval exercise sounds like. If you are reading this section aloud, I recommend that you read it silently first, so that you can get into mind the tones of voice that should be used. We're pretending that the first person is very experienced in the tones of approval exercise, and the second person is less so.

First person: Let's do the tones of approval exercise!

Second person: OK!

First person: How about we start with me being the one who says the different things, and you guess how much approval I'm aiming for.

Second person: Sounds good.

First person: Here I go. Wow! You *got it*!!

Second person: Large approval?

First person: Yes! How about this one: I see.

Second person: Neutral.

First person: That's right! Here's the next one. I like that!

Second person: Large approval?

First person: I was trying for small to moderate approval. If I were doing large, I might have said, "I *like* that!!"

Second person: OK.

First person: Here's the next. How are you today?

Second person: Small to moderate?

First person: That's what I was aiming for! Want to switch roles now?

Second person: Sure. How about this one: Great job!

First person: Small to moderate?

Second person: I was trying for large. Let me try again. Great *job*!!

First person: That sounded large!

What was the purpose of this section?

A. To suggest what sorts of scientific studies should be done on approval, or

B. To give an example of how the tones of approval exercise is done?

197. Here are some phrases you can use when you do the tones of approval exercise.

Look at that.
Good job.
Again, please.
Thanks for doing that.
I see.
You got it.
I see what you mean.
How did you do that?
You finished it.
I agree.
I would love to do that.
Tell me more, please.
I understand.

But you can use just about any phase or sentence you can think of. You could use words like, "Ducks and geese," or "That's five dollars," or "Under and over," or "Whatever you want!"

What do you think the author's purpose is in this section?

A. To give a list of phrases for you to use in the tones of approval exercise, so you can concentrate on the tones and not worry about coming up with something to say.
or

B. To present the major reasons why the tones of approval exercise should be done?

Mastery for the Tones of Approval Exercise

1. At the first level, you can identify with good accuracy whether the trainer is using tones that are neutral, of small to moderate approval, or of large approval.

2. At the second level, you can do the following test exercise with good accuracy: when the trainer says a phrase with a certain level of approval, you can identify the level of approval and repeat it with the same level of approval.

3. At the third level, you can do the exercise for the second level with total proficiency. You can do an exercise where you are given a list of phrases to say with specified degrees of approval, and you can use the specified degree of approval accurately. Finally, in real life interactions, you use the full range of tones of approval appropriately and enthusiastically.

Chapter 16: The Social Conversation Role-Play

198. The social conversation role play is not an easy exercise, but it's a great one. Social conversation means just chatting with someone else, for the fun of it. It can be one of the great pleasures of life, if you cultivate it well enough. In the social conversation role play, you practice doing social conversation, and hopefully have fun doing it. You pretend to be some character, and let someone else pretend to be the other character, and you have a chat. Or, you play both parts.

This section

A. Tells what the social conversation role play is.
or
B. Tells why schools should not be focused so much on test scores, but also help people learn to have fun chatting with one another.

199. While doing the social conversation role play, you use what you've practiced in the reflections exercise, the listening with four responses exercise, and the tones of approval exercise. You use what you may have learned about greeting and parting rituals (just saying hi or hello or "how are you" at the beginning, or good-bye or "nice talking with you" or something like that at the end). You may want to help yourself come up with things to talk about by referring to a list of topics people often talk about (places, activities, people, events, reactions and ideas: remembered by the word PAPER). You probably will want to have the people introduce themselves if in the role play we pretend that they don't already know each other's names. You have each person talk for a length of time that is not too long or too short before letting the other person have a turn. You have each person make a good blend of telling about him-or-herself and finding out about the other person.

Your goal is to create a conversation that would be fun and interesting to both people. You want each person to feel that the other is friendly and interested in getting to know him or her better.

What's the purpose of this section?

A. To present data showing that people who are able to enjoy social conversation are mentally healthier throughout their lives.
or

B. To list some of the skills that go into doing social conversation well.

200. Here's an example of the social conversation role play. The first person is a spelling bee contest winner, and the second is a chess tournament winner. They happen to sit down next to each other at a lunch where several types of contest winners are being recognized. They don't know each other.

First person: Hi, how are you today?

Second person: Good, thanks, and you?

First person: Doing fine. I'm grateful that they are having this for us today.

Second person: Me too. Looks like it's a nice lunch. Did you win something, or do something else that got you invited?

When the first person said, "Hi, how are you today?" was that a

A. reflection,
or
B. greeting ritual?

201. The social conversation role play continues.

First person: I got invited because I won a spelling bee.

Second person: Congratulations. That must have taken lots of work, learning how so many words are spelled.

First person: Thanks. It did take work, but sometimes I think that I could have spent my time better doing something that actually benefited somebody.

Second person: Isn't that something, I've had thoughts like that myself. I'm here because of winning a chess tournament, and I've spent tons of hours studying chess, but I sometimes think, what if I could spend as many hours actually doing something that made people happier.

First person: So you've felt the same way, huh! I didn't know other people felt like this – I thought that most people are just focused on winning and proving they are better than other people.

When the first person says, "So you've felt the same way, huh!" that's an example of a

A. follow-up question
or
B. reflection?

202. The social conversation role-play continues.

Second person: I've always thought it would be better if I could heal sick people or stop violence or build homes for people that don't have them, but it's hard to figure out how to do those kinds of things. Plus I may not be good at them. It was actually easier for me to learn to win chess games.

First person: I really admire your attitude. I know exactly what you mean. My school and my town have all sorts of opportunities for kids to compete with each other, but not many chances for them to actually help make people happier.

When the first person says, "I really admire your attitude," is that a

A. reflection,
or
B. positive feedback?

203. The role-play continues.

Second person: You're exactly right, competition is all around. In playing chess, a lot of the people I've played against have been fairly rude to me. So I've taken a lot of pleasure at beating them. But I sometimes wonder if they would be so rude if we were

working together on something rather than pitted against each other.

First person: Good point! What I think I hear you saying is that some of the rude talk that goes on is maybe because of the competitive situation people are in, and not just their personalities.

Second person: That's right.

When the first person said, "Good point! What I think I hear you saying is ..." and what followed, that first person was doing

A. positive feedback followed by a reflection,
or
B. a follow-up question followed by a facilitation?

204. The social conversation role-play continues.

First person: So how did you get into thinking about this competition versus cooperation stuff?

Second person: Hmm. It's hard to remember. Maybe I read an article about it somewhere. I think that was it. It was talking about how the life of kids is a lot like that it is in the book, *The Hunger Games*, not with killing each other, but with competing in all sorts of other ways.

First person: Very interesting. I've read some stuff about this too. I ran across a book on cooperative games. People made up all sorts of games where people would be not working against each other, but trying to break their own record, or something like that.

Second person: Sounds interesting. Why don't we be in touch some more, and see what ideas we can come up with on this stuff? My name is Lee Scott, by the way.

First person: Glad to meet you, Lee; my name is Pat Robbins.

When the first person asked how the second got into thinking about the idea of cooperation versus competition, the first person was using a

A. follow-up question,
or
B. parting ritual?

205. As the role play continues, the two people pretend to exchange phone numbers or email addresses. Then the role-play concludes like this.

First person: Looks like somebody's going to give a little talk. Well it's been nice talking with you, Lee.

Second person: You too, Pat; I look forward to talking with you more.

This part of the conversation is called a

A. facilitation,
or
B. parting ritual?

206. Here's a checklist for the social conversation role-play.

How much success was there, in each of the following?

0=None
2=Very little
4=Some but not much
6=Moderate amount, pretty much
8=High amount
10=Very high amount

1. Enough to say. Were you able to chat without being overly shy or inhibited and to think of things to tell about yourself and ask the other? (Mnemonic PAPER)

2. Stopping talking. Did you stop talking often enough that the other person had plenty of chances to

influence the direction of the conversation?

3. Good Topics. Did you tune in to, and respond to, the signals from the other person about whether the topic was interesting? Did you try to find a topic of mutual interest? Were the topics not so personal so as to be threatening to the other person, but personal enough to be interesting?

4. Listening. When the other person talked, did you respond in a way that showed you had listened: follow-up questions, facilitations, reflections, and positive feedback? Were these responses of high quality?

5. Tones. Did your voice tones often communicate approval and enthusiasm? Did you reinforce the other person for talking to you? Was a good portion of what you said of a positive, upbeat nature?

Mastery for the Social Conversation Role Play

1. At the first level, you're able to take part in a role-played social conversation between two imaginary characters, having enough to say and stopping talking often enough. Someone else plays the part of the other person.

2. At the second level, you're able to do the role-play several times, consistently meeting all 5 requirements well: enough to say, stopping talking, good topics, listening, and tones of approval and enthusiasm.

3. At the third level, you're able to do the role-play several times, meeting all 5 criteria well, playing *both* parts yourself. At this level you are also able to have good real-life social conversations with someone else, meeting all 5 criteria well.

Chapter 17: STEBC Fantasy Rehearsals

207. One of the big ideas behind the whole program of training in psychological skills is positive fantasy rehearsal. When you imagine yourself doing something smart or good, you practice doing that thing. Thus it's good to imagine yourself very often handling situations in just the way you want to handle them. It's especially good to do this in words, either by speaking the rehearsal out loud, by writing it, or by reading aloud a fantasy rehearsal you've written.

What's a summary of this section?

A. It's good to fantasy rehearse the types of good things you'd like to do more often, in words.
or
B. Nearly every type of Olympic athlete uses some form of fantasy rehearsal to help to get peak performance.

208. How you do a fantasy rehearsal? It's good to describe thoroughly and imagine vividly the *situation* you are in. You say aloud the *thoughts* you would like to think in the situation. You imagine feeling the *emotions* that you would most prefer to feel, and you name those. You imagine doing the *behaviors* that are best to do in this situation, and you tell about this as if you are doing them in the present. Finally, you imagine yourself *celebrating* the fact that you handled the situation so well, by thinking something like, "Hooray, I handled that in just the way I wanted to!"

The words situation, thoughts, emotions, behaviors, and celebration make the letters STEBC. These are the "steps" of fantasy rehearsal.

What's a summary of this section?

A. Fantasy rehearsals can be used to practice any of the psychological skills.
or
B. To do a STEBC fantasy rehearsal, you describe the situation, followed by the desirable thoughts, emotions, and behaviors you'd like to use, followed by a celebration of handling the situation well.

209. What if you don't know how you'd like to handle a situation? Then you probably aren't yet ready to fantasy rehearse that situation! With that situation, maybe the best plan is to list options, think of pros and cons, or get more information, so that you

can make a decision. Fantasy rehearsals are for situations for which you have already come up with good response, and you want to practice that response.

What's the point of this section?

A. You use fantasy rehearsals when you've already decided on good thoughts, feelings, and behaviors to use in the situation.
or
B. One of the important parts of the decision-making process is to choose what your goals or objectives are.

210. It's very important to realize that in fantasy rehearsals, you practice the best way of handling the situation that you can possibly come up with. You don't rehearse what you usually would do in the situation – you practice what you would like to do when the situation comes up in the future.

Some people decide on the best way to handle a situation, but then object to handling the situation that way, saying, "But that's not *me*! That's not the way I act!" These people may not realize that if you practice enough times doing something that feels foreign to you, it will gradually feel part of you.

In any case, the overall guiding rule is not "Be yourself." The guiding rule is, "Do the thing that brings about the best long-term results, the thing that is kindest to yourself and others, whether it feels like 'yourself' or not."

Which of the following is the attitude expressed in this section?

A. You want to practice the best response to the situation, even if it isn't your usual habit.
or
B. The more vividly you imagine the situation in fantasy rehearsal, the more benefit you will get from it.

211. You can use a STEBC fantasy rehearsal to practice any of the psychological skills. Here's an example where someone is practicing at least a couple of them.

Situation: I have some free time. I could turn on the television. But I have on my to do list an article that I want and need to write.

Thoughts: I think that if I did get some good work done on my article, I would feel good about myself. I'm deciding to work for an hour and then do something relaxing and fun.

Emotions: I feel determined to get lots of work done and to make it come out good eventually.

Behaviors: I go to my desk and get things organized and start writing. I don't worry when things don't come out perfect. I keep going as productively as I can.... By the end of an hour I've made lots of progress!

Celebration: Hooray, I was really productive!

Which psychological skills is the person practicing?

A. nonviolence and loyalty,
or
B. productivity and self-discipline?

212. Here's another example of a STEBC fantasy rehearsal.

Situation: I have to give a speech in front of some people today. This has always been a scary situation for me.

Thoughts: Even the worst thing that can happen with this is not a tragedy – it would just be embarrassing, but no one would be hurt or killed.
It will be a really nice accomplishment when I do this. My speech is all written out, and all I have to do is to read it. I've practiced lots of times, and I know I can do it well.

Emotions: I feel relaxed and confident. I look forward to having fun doing this.

Behaviors: I get up and give my speech, enthusiastically, and I emphasize the right words, and I make gestures that help me make my points.

Celebration: Hooray, I did a great job with this!

This was a fantasy rehearsal of which skill?

A. courage,
or
B. kindness?

213. In fantasy rehearsing the speech, the person imagined himself handling the situation without fear, but feeling very confident. It was as if a miracle had occurred, to take away all his fear. We refer to this sort of rehearsal as a *mastery* fantasy rehearsal. The person imagined that he had already mastered the situation. You may want to remember what mastery fantasy rehearsals are by the fact that the words *mastery* and *miracle* both begin with the letter m.

What's a summary of this section?

A. The type of rehearsal other than a mastery rehearsal is called a coping rehearsal.
or

B. In a mastery rehearsal, you imagine yourself handling a difficult situation with all the confidence and calm that you would like to, as if a miracle had taken away all negative emotion.

214. But mastery fantasy rehearsals are not enough. Lots of times you will need to act wisely in situations where you feel really scared or angry or disgusted – you'll need to cope with your bad feelings while doing the best thing to do. For that reason, it's good to fantasy rehearse feeling unpleasant feelings but doing the best thing anyway. This sort of fantasy rehearsal is called a *coping* rehearsal.

What's the main idea of this section?

A. In addition to mastery rehearsals, it's good to do coping rehearsals, which are imagining yourself doing the best thing despite having feelings that might get in the way.
or
B. You will not appreciate the power of fantasy rehearsals unless you do lots and lots of them.

215. Someone has a fear of vomiting and seeing other people vomit. Here's an example of a fantasy rehearsal that the person uses.

Situation: I'm getting ready to go to a class at school. The thought occurs to me that I could get sick and throw up. I feel nervous.

Thoughts: The chance that this will happen is low, since I've experienced many days, and I've only thrown up on a very small fraction of them. And even if it should happen, it would be unpleasant but not horrible. I'm not in danger. I want very much to do what I need to do, no matter how I feel.

Emotions: Even though I realize that I'm not in danger, I still feel scared, about 7 on a scale of 10.

Behaviors: I relax my muscles, and this helps a little bit. I put one foot in front of the other and walk into class. I focus my attention on what is going on, despite the fact that the possibility of vomiting runs in the background. I gradually relax some. Time goes by. Now class is over.

Celebration: Hooray, I felt the fear but did what I wanted to do anyway!

Which of the following is true about this section?

A. This section illustrated a fantasy rehearsal of friendship-building skills.
or
B. This section illustrated a coping rehearsal, because the person did the

desired behavior while coping with unwanted feelings or urges.

Mastery of STEBC Fantasy Rehearsals

1. At the first level, when you are given a situation by the trainer where there is a pretty clear desirable response, and you are prompted for thoughts, emotions, behaviors, and celebrations, you can go through the STEBC of fantasy rehearsal.

2. At the second level, you can do both mastery and coping fantasy rehearsals without prompting, when given situations to practice with.

3. At the third level, you can do STEBC fantasy rehearsals, both mastery and coping, with no prompt other than the request to do a useful fantasy rehearsal. You can do fantasy rehearsals of a wide variety of psychological skills. Furthermore, the choices of thoughts, emotions, and behaviors are of high quality.

Chapter 18: UCAC Fantasy Rehearsals

216. UCAC fantasy rehearsals are particularly useful in practicing thinking before acting – in practicing resisting impulses. You imagine getting an impulse, or an urge to do something that is not the best idea. Then you imagine yourself celebrating that you caught the behavior at the urge stage rather than acting on it right away. Then, you imagine choosing an alternative that's better, and carrying it out. Then you imagine celebrating handling the situation so well. So UCAC stands for Urge, Celebration, Alternative, Celebration.

What's a summary of this section?

A. In UCAC fantasy rehearsals, you imagine getting an urge but not acting on it, and choosing and enacting a better alternative; you celebrate resisting the urge and also doing the better alternative.
or
B. The words *urge* and *impulse* mean about the same thing; both of them refer to an option's coming into mind for something to do.

217. Here's what a UCAC fantasy rehearsal sounds like. The person is a student.

Urge: I'm in class, and there's a discussion going on. The rule is that you have to raise your hand and get recognized before you talk. People are discussing something I know a lot about, and I really want to just go ahead and say it.

Celebration: I'm glad I caught myself while this was just an urge!

Alternative: I'll hold up my hand and see if I get called on.

Celebration: Hooray, I handled this in exactly the way I wanted to handle it!

The rehearsal that the person did was meant to help the person with

A. compliance with a rule,
or
B. nonviolence?

218. Here's another UCAC fantasy rehearsal. The speaker is a female who has had the habit of pulling some of her hair out; she wants to break this habit.

Urge: I'm by myself at home, feeling restless, and I get the urge to pull some of my hair out.

Celebration: Great, I recognized this urge before I actually did it.

Alternative: I'm going to try exercising a little bit, quickly, and then relaxing. I'm doing that instead.

Celebration: Hooray, I stopped myself before hair-pulling and did a much better alternative!

The rehearsal that the person did was meant to help with

A. honesty,
or
B. self-care?

219. Here's another example of a UCAC fantasy rehearsal. The speaker is a middle school male.

Urge: When a classmate says to me, "You're in love with Pat," in a very taunting tone of voice, I have the urge to hit him right in the face.

Celebration: I'm glad I caught myself while this was still an urge and not an action!

Alternative: I think I want to give him a little silent eye contact, with just a little roll of the eyes after that.

Celebration: Hooray, the choice I did was much better than the urge I had.

The UCAC rehearsal this person did was to help the person with

A. nonviolence,
or
B. productivity?

220. Here's another example of a UCAC fantasy rehearsal.

Urge: My sister tells about a big success that she had in a play. I get the urge to say, "You think you're really great, don't you?"

Celebration: I'm glad I caught myself before saying that!

Alternative: I decide to be a bigger person and not to act jealous. I say, "Congrats, that's a cool accomplishment!"

Celebration: I'm really glad I thought before acting and chose the alternative I did choose.

This UCAC fantasy rehearsal was meant to help the person with

A. conservation,
or
B. respectful talk?

221. Here's another example.

Urge: I see a pretty shirt in a store, and I have the urge to buy it right away, even though it's really expensive.

Celebration: I'm glad I caught myself so that I can think about this.

Alternative: I think about how much money I have, and how much this would cost, and whether I really need this. I finally decide that I already have enough clothes for now, and I'll save my money.

Celebration: I just saved a bunch of money; hooray!

This UCAC fantasy rehearsal helped the person to practice

A. kindness,
or
B. conservation?

Mastery of UCAC Fantasy Rehearsals

1. At the first level, when you are given a situation by the trainer that tempts you to an urge that you clearly want to resist, and you are prompted for urge, celebration, alternative, and celebration, you can go through the UCAC fantasy rehearsal.

2. At the second level, you can do UCAC fantasy rehearsals fluently, without prompting, when given situations to practice with. Your rehearsals are of high quality.

3. At the third level, you can do UCAC fantasy rehearsals with no prompt other than the request to do some useful UCAC fantasy rehearsals. You can make up situations for impulse control that help in a wide variety of psychological skills. Furthermore, the choices of alternative responses are of high quality.

Chapter 19: Positive Emotional Climate Rehearsals

222. What is a positive emotional climate? It is present when people in a relationship, or in a group of people, feel good about being with each other. It's the sort of relationship where people make each other happy, approve of one another, trust each other, and are kind to each other. It's the opposite of the sort of climate where people scream at each other, refuse to speak to each other, and frequently criticize each other. In a positive emotional climate, people often help and have fun with each other.

Positive emotional climates tend to produce psychological health. People are less likely to be depressed or angry when they spend lots of time in relationships or groups with positive emotional climates. People are happier in positive emotional climates.

What's a summary of this section?

A. Commanding, criticizing, contradicting, and threatening are the main things that make negative emotional climates.
or
B. Positive emotional climates are relationships where people are kind to each other. People are happier and have fewer psychological symptoms in such climates.

223. The big idea of this chapter is that you can make your relationships have a more positive emotional climate. A big way to do this is just by saying certain things more often, and by saying them with tones of approval and enthusiasm. A list of these things is present in an Appendix of this book, entitled "Things to Say to Create a Positive Emotional Climate." Some of these things are simple greeting and parting rituals, like "Good afternoon!" and "I'll look forward to seeing you later!" Some are congratulating or complimenting or thanking the other person, such as "Good job," or "Interesting point!" or "Thanks for doing that!" Some are offers to help: "May I help you with that?" (This one is usually followed by actually helping!) Some are inviting the other person to talk with you more: "Please tell me more about that." Some are inviting the other person to do something else with you: "Would you like to (take a walk, play a game, have a work party, eat lunch, hang out, etc.) with me?"

What's a summary of this section?

A. Emotional climates are better when people are not lazy and are willing to do what feels like more than their share of cleaning up and housework.
or
B. You can improve emotional climates simply by saying certain things more often.

224. The exercise for this chapter is another way of doing fantasy rehearsals. In it, you look at the list of things to say to create a positive emotional climate. You pick one of them. You imagine yourself in a situation where it is appropriate to say that, describe that situation out loud, and then say the statement. Here's a really simple example, for the first statement on the list, which is "Good morning."

I come downstairs to get some breakfast, and I see my father there. I say, "Good morning, dad!"

In doing this exercise, do you

A. pick a situation from a list, and then make up what to say in it,
or
B. pick something to say, from a list, and then make up a situation where you could say that thing?

225. Here's what it might sound like if a trainer and a student do this exercise together.

Trainer: Are you ready to do the positive emotional climate rehearsal exercise? Are you at the list near the end of the book?

Student: Yep!

Trainer: OK, I'll go first.
I'm in my room, in the evening, and my roommate walks in, and after I say hi, I say, "How was your day today?"

Student: I see that my mom has cooked supper for the family. I say, "You cooked a nice supper; thanks for doing that!"

Trainer: My roommate celebrates with me that she got a good score on a test. I say, "Good job! Congratulations to you!"

Student: I see a rainbow, and I call my family members to see it. I say, "Look how beautiful that is!"

What category did the last example in this section fall into?

A. Positive feelings about the world and the things and events in it.
or

B. Wishing well for the other person's future.

226. The sample exercise continues.

Trainer: I call my mom in the morning, before she goes to work. Before we hang up, I say, "I wish you the best for your day of work today!"

Student: My father is moving a bookshelf. He sees me and says, "Could you please help me with this bookshelf?" I say, "I'd love to help you in that way!"

Trainer: One of my friends asks me to go outside and throw a Frisbee back and forth. I say, "Yes, I'd love to do that with you."

Student: I sat down at lunch with someone who was alone, and got to know that person better. Then later in the evening, I say to my dad, "I feel good about something I did. Want to hear about it?"

Trainer: In a visit home, my mom spills some water on me, and apologizes. I say, "That's OK; don't worry about it. It's no problem."

Into what category did the last example in this section fall?

A. Positive feelings about oneself,

or
B. Forgiving and tolerating frustration.

227. The point of this exercise, of course, is to prepare you to actually say more things that improve emotional climates in real life. Give it a try and see what happens!

When you start saying more of the things on the list, you should not be discouraged if people don't immediately respond by being nicer and more pleasant to you. It takes a while for the effects of these utterances to take place.

With some people, you can say these utterances all you want and they will never respond in a positive way! Regardless of the other person's response, you are getting into good habits that will serve you well in relationships throughout your life.

What's a summary of this section?

A. Be patient; it may take a while (or even forever) before you see evidence of a better emotional climate in real life when you say these things. But in any case you're practicing good habits.
or
B. A positive emotional climate depends on other things as well as the utterances in the list, such as whether people take time to spend with one another, whether they keep their

promises, whether they do their share of the work, and others.

Mastery for the Things to Say for A Positive Emotional Climate Exercise

1. At the first level, taking turns with your trainer, you are able to look at the list of Things to Say for a Positive Emotional Climate and come up with situations that make the things appropriate to say. You do this for at least 10 of the things to say.

2. At the second level, you do this for 10 more of the things to say, including some of those that feel harder for you. You make up good situations for them. You model saying them in the tones of voice that would promote a positive climate. You also report saying some of these things to friends and family members and report the result.

3. At the third level, you make up situations and practice saying the positive things with approving tones of voice, for 12 more things to say, without looking at the list, but using your memory of the things on the list. At this level you should report saying these things to people in real life a lot more often than before, with some confirmation from someone in your life.

Chapter 20: Saving a Reward for After Self-Discipline

228. One of the keys to happiness and mental health is what I call the *effort-payoff connection*. The effort-payoff connection means that you do some work or make an effort on something, and your effort results in your getting something you want – a payoff.

For example, someone works in a job, and as a result, she gets a paycheck that lets her buy what she needs. Or a student studies for a test, and as a result, the student gets a good grade. Someone starts a conversation with someone, and as a result has a good time talking and makes a friend.

When you have an effort-payoff connection, you see your effort as worthwhile. Your work is not just a waste of time. The way you're spending your time gets you somewhere.

In order to have an effort-payoff connection,

A. People have to believe that their efforts cause the payoffs to occur.
or
B. The payoffs have to be objects that you can see and touch.

229. Our prehistoric ancestors probably spent most of their lives searching for food. The payoff was that they got to eat, and to survive. Their lives were very likely quite dangerous and unpleasant in many ways, but at least those that did survive had an effort-payoff connection. Even young children probably began to work for food as soon as they were physically able to. Through centuries of evolution, the human brain developed in conditions where the connection between effort and payoff was crucial to survival. Perhaps for that reason, we tend to feel happy when we believe that our effort will pay off, and unhappy when we believe that our efforts make no difference.

What's the main point the author is making?

A. Our brains are probably designed by natural selection so that we are happiest when there is a strong effort-payoff connection.
or
B. Even though today's kids may not have as strong an effort-payoff connection as prehistoric ones, they should still feel glad to be alive today.

230. A lot of research done recently tells us that people are happiest when

there is a strong effort-payoff connection in their life situations.

What is the opposite of the effort-payoff connection? One is the situation where "I can't get what I want, no matter what I do." For example, a student is in a class that is totally over his head. No matter how hard he works, he still flunks every test. You could call this type of situation one where "rewards are impossible" or even where "punishment is certain." This situation is depressing.

Another opposite of the effort-payoff connection is the situation is one we can call "unearned rewards": the payoffs come no matter what you do, regardless of your effort. For example, some children get nearly everything they could wish for, without having to work for anything. Work or not, the payoffs keep coming. This is the sort of situation more people would like to be in, but it also tends to make people unhappy.

What's a summary of this section?

A. Animals in zoos who have to work for their food have been shown to be happier than those who are given their food for free.
or
B. Uncontrollable punishment, impossible rewards, and unearned rewards tend to lead to unhappiness.

231. Here's another example I've used to help people understand that the effort-payoff connection leads to enjoyment. Let's imagine three video games. In each of them, there is a main character who is trying to get to a certain place in order to be able to save some other people.

In the first game, no matter what you do, your character very quickly falls into a deep hole from which there is no exit. This game is called "Impossible Rewards or Uncontrollable Punishment."

In the second game, the character accomplishes the goal with ease, no matter what you do. However you push the controls, or even if you don't touch them, the character goes swiftly along and quickly you find that you've won the game. This game is called "Unearned Rewards."

In the third game, if you work the controls in the right way, you win, and if you don't, you lose. There's a way of figuring out how to win, and it isn't hopelessly hard, but it isn't so easy as to be boring. This game is called "The Effort-Payoff Connection."

The first two games would be no fun at all. The third one would probably be fun.

The point the author is making by this example is that

A. Things are much more fun when there is an effort-payoff connection than when there are either impossible rewards or free rewards.
or
B. People in today's world are wasting too much time on video games when there are much more important things to be done.

232. Suppose that you are a young adult and a very good tennis player. You have your choice between two opponents. The first is another young adult who is about as good at tennis as you are. The second possible opponent is a 90 year old man who has pretty bad arthritis, has never played tennis, and is likely to forfeit as soon as he's allowed to. Which opponent would you choose? You want to win, don't you, and there's little doubt that you would win if you chose the second opponent. But you'd probably choose the first opponent. This illustrates that the point of playing a game is not just winning – it's arranging an effort-payoff connection.

What's the point of this section?

A. It is possible that a 90 year old with arthritis could nevertheless be very good at tennis.
or

B. Games provide satisfaction not just if you win, but if you have a lot of effort-payoff connection.

233. Now suppose there are two children. Each of them wants some money with which to buy a fun toy. Each of them is also working on learning to type on a keyboard. The first parent just gives the money to the child and says, "Good luck in learning keyboarding."

The second parent says, "How about if you get a certain number of points for each of several milestones in learning keyboarding. For each milestone, you'll get a certain amount of money. When the last one is reached, you'll have enough to buy the thing you want. I'll test you for each milestone."

Which child do you think will enjoy learning keyboarding more? Which do you think will enjoy getting the prize more? And which parent is being "nicer" to the child: the one who gave free rewards, or the one who set up an effort-payoff connection?

The answer to each of these questions in the author's mind seems to be

A. the first,
or
B. the second?

234. Many of the things that we work for bring forth "external" rewards a long, long time after we do the work. For example, a first-year student in high school wants to become a doctor. The student works very hard in school to be able to get into college and medical school. But the actual reward of becoming a doctor probably won't come until at least a dozen years later.

Another person who is 25 years old puts money into a retirement account. The person doesn't plan to use that money until at least 40 years later. The work the person is doing for a secure retirement doesn't have its payoff until many years after the work is done.

What's the main point of this section?

A. If you want to have enough money when you get old, it's good to save when you are young.
or
B. Lots of the external rewards that we work for don't come until a very long time after the work is done.

235. Sometimes we work very hard and there are no external rewards at all. For example, a volunteer works very hard teaching someone. The student never says "Thank you." The volunteer teacher never gets any money or even a thank you card. Still, the volunteer experiences the effort-payoff connection. How can this be? One way is that the teacher delivers rewards to herself. We can call these internal rewards. She says things to herself like, "Hooray! I know I'm doing a good job! I'm accomplishing my goal!" This illustrates that often the most important rewards for our work are what we say to ourselves, or what we think about our work. We supply ourselves our own rewards.

What's the main point of this section?

A. Often very important rewards are the ones that we supply to ourselves, in the form of the congratulations we give ourselves for a job well done.
or
B. If someone receives a lot of service from a teacher, that person should say "Thank you" to the teacher, very often.

236. The congratulations we give ourselves are called "internal" rewards. They are very important. Things like food, the chance to play games, chances to socialize, permission to buy something, the chance to do some fun activity, and so forth are called "external" rewards.

This chapter is about how to rig up external rewards for yourself, in a way that lets you give yourself more of the effort-payoff connection. Everything in this chapter so far has been meant to help you understand more about the effort-payoff connection, so that you can be more motivated to set it up for yourself.

What's a summary of this section?

A. Although internal rewards are very important, the purpose of this chapter is to tell you how to use external rewards to set up for yourself an effort-payoff connection.
or
B. The condition we call "depression" is usually one where the person does not experience enough of an effort-payoff connection.

237. Here's how you save a reward for after you've used self-discipline. Let's give some examples.

A man has to do some unpleasant work getting tax information ready. He has the urge to put off the work by taking a walk and playing a game on the computer. He also has the urge to put off the work by eating a few squares of chocolate candy.

But then he decides that the game and the chocolate are rewards that he will use to help him work. He breaks off the squares of chocolate, puts them in a bowl, and puts a plate over the bowl. He writes on his to do list: "One hour of tax work. Reward: three squares of chocolate." He also

writes, "After the second hour of tax work, reward: go for a walk, then play chess against the computer."

What are the external rewards the man plans to use for doing the tax work?

A. The thought, "I am doing an important piece of work, and I am using self-discipline!"
or
B. The chocolate, getting to take a walk, and getting to play the game.

238. After the man makes this plan, he has to use self-discipline in two ways. First, he has to do the tax work. Second, he has to hold himself back from "stealing" the rewards before he has earned them. It's also his job to really enjoy his rewards when he earns them – to think, "Hooray! I have earned this chocolate!" or "Congrats to me! I get to take my walk and play my game!"

If he can carry out these self-discipline triumphs and joyousness triumphs, he probably will enjoy his work more, because he has more of an effort-payoff connection. Plus, he might find that the work gets done, whereas without the rewards he might have put it off.

This section describes the desired ending for the exercise of saving a reward for after self-discipline. That ending is:

A. That the person stays away from the rewards until earning them, works to earn them, and enjoys them when they are earned.
or
B. That the person decides to keep working and not waste time on the reward activities.

239. If you do this exercise, one choice is how big a reward to give yourself. If the man in our example had promised himself one tiny speck of chocolate, the reward wouldn't have been big enough to motivate him. If he had promised himself ten huge chocolate bars, the reward would have been too big: either he couldn't use chocolate as a reward again for a good while, or else he would encourage himself to have a chocolate-eating binge. So one of the tricks is to make the reward big enough, but not too big.

The main point of this section is which?

A. It's important not to get the reward before you've earned it.
or
B. It's important to pick a reward that is not too big, not too little, but just right.

240. A crucial part of this exercise is that you plan the self-discipline task and the reward beforehand, and you write down the plan in your to do book or file or assignment book before you start. This keeps you honest about what your own rules are. If you're like most people, you need that when you are making rules for yourself. It's very easy to change the rules at any time when you are the one making them.

For example, Liam has written in his assignment book, "Work on writing history paper for one hour. Reward: 5 minutes of running outside, followed by 20 minutes of video game." He gets a lot of work done, and he gets the urge to claim his reward. But then he checks with what he has written, and sees that the rule was 1 hour; he has only worked for 45 minutes. So he puts in the 15 minutes more and celebrates greatly when he follows his own rule and earns the reward.

The advice in this section is what?

A. Choose a self-discipline task that is not too big, not too little, but just right for a success.
or
B. Write down your plan before starting the self-discipline task.

241. Just as you want to choose a reward that is just the right size, you

also want to choose a task to do that is the right size.

If you are just starting out with this exercise and you haven't developed the skill of following your own rules much yet, you will want to pick a very small task. For example: "I will do math homework problems (which probably will take about 15 minutes). Reward: get to watch a 30 minute TV program I recorded earlier." As you develop more and more skill at this exercise, you can make the tasks bigger and the rewards smaller.

It's better to choose a task that is too little than one that is too big. If the task is too big, people tend to give up on the whole program or to "steal" the reward without earning it.

What's the message of this section?

A. Make sure the self-discipline task is big enough, and especially that it isn't too big.
or
B. Whenever you give yourself external rewards, practice giving yourself lots of internal rewards at the same time – for example by thinking, "Hooray! I did it!"

242. There are three ways that a tutor and a student can do this exercise together. First, they can do a small version of it right in the session. For example, the student gets a few potato chips. Then the student, with the tutor, does maybe 15 minutes of hard work: lots of fantasy rehearsals one after another, lots of math facts practice, lots of reading of difficult material. Only after the 15 minutes of hard work are done, does the student eat the potato chips.

The second and third ways that tutor and student can make this something they do together are fantasy rehearsals and the celebrations exercise. They can take turns imagining saving a reward until after self-discipline, and describing out loud what they are imagining – this is fantasy rehearsal. Or they tell each other about how they used this technique in life. This is the celebrations exercise.

What's a summary of this section?

A. The author recommends using video games and television only as rewards for self-discipline tasks, and never as unearned rewards.
or
B. There are three ways for a tutor and student to do this exercise together: in the tutoring session itself, in fantasy rehearsal, and in the celebrations exercise.

243. Here's what it might sound like if a student does a fantasy rehearsal of

saving a reward for after self-discipline.

"I have some homework to do. I also want to play a computer game. I make a plan. I divide my homework into two parts; the first is the bigger part. I write down in my assignment book: 'When I finish the first part, I get to play the computer game for 20 minutes, and then walk around some. When I finish the second part, I get to play for 20 more minutes.'

"I have the urge to go ahead and play the game first, but I resist it. I feel good about my self-discipline as I go ahead and get started on the homework. I work carefully, not just to get it out of the way.... Hooray! I'm done with the first part! Now I get to play the game. I set a timer for 20 minutes. This is the hardest part of all, pausing the game after 20 minutes, but I do it!

"Now I walk around just a bit and then I start the second half. I'm feeling good that I'm really going to pull this off.... Now I'm done! I get to play the game another 20 minutes! I do it, and again I push pause when the time is up! I feel great about my self-discipline triumphs!"

In this example, what did the person plan to do to avoid the problem of having to stay seated for too long?

A. The person did the game while standing up and running in place.
or
B. The person built in a walk outside between the two halves of the homework.

244. Here's what it might sound like if the tutor mentions saving a reward for after self-discipline when doing the celebrations exercise.

"Last night, I was going to mindlessly stick some chewing gum into my mouth. But then I thought, 'Here's a chance for me to do the saving a reward for after self-discipline exercise!' I needed to clean up my room and get my stuff organized. So I wrote on my to do file, '15 minutes of organizing my room. Reward: chewing gum.' So I took the stick of chewing gum and put it out where I could see it. I started timing. I got lots of cleaning up done in 15 minutes, even though it was not totally perfect. It was lots better! When the 15 minutes were up, I thought, 'Hooray for me! I did it!' and I chewed the gum happily. And this is a self-discipline celebration, because it took self-discipline to keep from chewing the gum before I earned it! "

This celebration should count as what kind of triumph as well as one in self-discipline?

A. productivity,
or
B. kindness?

245. Some people worry that if people get external rewards for doing a certain activity, they will be less able to do those activities for internal rewards alone. In other words, if you reward yourself for schoolwork, will you become unwilling to do the schoolwork without some external reward at stake? My own experiments have led me to the opposite belief. Getting external rewards, for me, tends to make an activity more fun for the future, even if those external rewards go away.

The author draws on his own experience to make the point that

A. Getting external rewards doesn't take away your internal reward system.
or
B. It's very hard to avoid the rewards until you have earned them.

246. The danger that you will weaken your internal reward system is probably even less if you "program" or "hypnotize" yourself by strongly wishing that your internal reward system will grow. In other words, you remind yourself often that you want to feel great about celebrating your own choice when you do things that advance you toward very worthy goals. When you earn external rewards that you have set up for yourself, you try to feel good, not only about getting the reward, but also about advancing toward the goal.

What's a summary of this section?

A. Wish and work for a strong internal reward system, while using external rewards.
or
B. The wish for rewards and the fear of punishment can both provide strong motivation, but the first is more fun.

247. People in the developed world spend many hours watching television, playing video games, and doing pleasant but not productive things on the Internet. They also consume an extremely large number of calories of "junk food": cake, candy, pop, chips, pie, sugar, and so forth. They devote many hours to watching movies and listening to music. They buy lots of things they don't need. What if people learned from an early age to use these rewards, in carefully measured amounts, to create an effort-payoff connection for the self-discipline tasks they most wanted to do? The world would be greatly changed. You have the opportunity to experiment with

developing the skill of self-reward. You have the opportunity to be a pioneer in discovering how well this can work, by experimenting with yourself.

In this section the author describes a vision in which

A. people have ceased to hurt and kill one another and be cruel to one another,
or
B. people learn early in life to use pleasurable rewards to help them do good things that require self-discipline?

248. Some people recommend that you not use junk food, or any type of food, as a reward for self-discipline. They argue that this may cause problems of overeating or binge eating or overuse of junk food. If you try using food as a reward, you can keep track of what effects it has on you, and stop it if there are bad effects. My own experience suggests to me that the self-discipline involved in not "stealing" the reward before you've earned it is the same sort of self-discipline you use if you decide to avoid junk food altogether or to restrict it to very small amounts.

A summary of this section is that

A. Some people advise not using food as a reward; the author advises that you make your own choice based on how it seems to affect you.
or
B. It is true that the things that we use as rewards may seem more valuable to us than if we enjoy them whenever we feel like it.

Mastery for Saving a Reward for After Self-Discipline

1. At the first level, you make a plan, at least once, to save a reward for after you complete a self-discipline task. Carry out the plan.

2. At the second level, you make a plan to postpone a reward till after self-discipline, and you carry out such a plan at least 5 times.

3. At the third level, you have made a routine practice of saving a certain reward until after a certain act of self-discipline, and you do this routine regularly, and have done it many times.

Chapter 21: The To Do List

249. In this exercise, you write down one or more things that you want to do. You also number the different items according to what you want to do first, second, third and so forth. You put the number 1 by the thing you want to do first, which may or may not be the most important thing. Sometimes you may want to start out with a shorter or easier task to get yourself moving. As a general rule, though, you want to "put first things first": plan the most important things to be done sooner.

When you get some time where you can choose what to do, you do the thing on your list that has the lowest number. When you have finished, you check that thing off the list, and celebrate that you have done it.

What's a summary of this section?

A. The to do list is a way of freeing up your memory so that you can concentrate on doing things.
or
B. In this exercise, you write down what you want to do, do it, and celebrate when you're done.

250. People who achieve and accomplish a lot tend to make daily to do lists. When you take a few minutes to make a to do list, you can devote your full attention to the questions, "What do I want to accomplish?" and "Of all the things that I could do, how would I arrange them in order of priority?" Without making a to do list, people tend not to spend much time thinking about these questions. They are very important questions.

What's a summary of this section?

A. One of the benefits of making a to do list is that it directs your attention to the questions of what you want to do, and how you rank different actions in order of importance.
or
B. A to do list can include relaxing and playful activities as well as work that needs to get done.

251. Here's an example of someone's to do list.

2. Spend one hour organizing my papers, objects, and tasks.
3. Succeed at not eating between meals.

1. Call up my grandmother and chat with her some.
4. Take my dog for a long run or walk, with someone else if possible.

The numbers are out of order to illustrate that you write down things in the order that they come to mind; then you go back and put numbers by them to tell yourself what order you want to do them in.

The items the person listed included

A. Working, socializing, exercising, and keeping a resolution.
or
B. Only work.

252. Here's another to do list that someone else might make.

3. Start reading chemistry book, for at least an hour, to get ready for my course.
2. Invite people to picnic on Saturday afternoon.
1. Deposit check in bank account.
4. Make appointment to get my teeth cleaned.
5. Practice singing, any length of time I want.

For the items on this to do list,

A. Some had a time (such as an hour) included in the item, and some did not.

or
B. Every item specified how long the person should spend doing it.

253. If you're doing this exercise with a tutor or mental fitness trainer, what do you do? You get something you can write with, and you say aloud the things you want to accomplish in the next day, and both you and the trainer write them down. After you have listed some things you want to do, you say aloud and write down numbers by them according to their priority. Then, after the session, you try to do the things you listed, and you check them off as you do them.

Then, the next day, you talk again, and you both get out your to do lists. You say which of the things you put on your list you were able to actually carry out. You celebrate together any that you were able to do.

The purpose of this section was to

A. Tell you to make the things on your to do list not too hard, not too easy, but just right.
or
B. Describe how you would do this exercise together with a tutor.

254. If you want, the tutor can also make a to do list. You can share them with each other, and the next day, you

can both let each other know which items you were able to do.

The to do list is a very simple method of making life lots more organized and lots better. It takes self-discipline to do it regularly. It greatly increases people's productivity.

It's great to do this exercise a few times. It's even greater to get into the habit of making a to do list just about every day.

The author believes that the to do list

A. should be done when things get too overwhelming to try to remember and keep in your head,
or
B. should be done nearly every day?

Mastery of the To Do List

1. At the first level, at least once you write down some things you want to do today. You do at least one of them. You take pleasure in referring to the list to check off the completed items.

2. At the second level, on several occasions you have made a to do list, have ordered the items on it, and have done at least some of the items on it in roughly the order that you numbered. You have noted which items you've done, and have felt good to check them as done.

3. At the third level, you have made a daily habit of the to do list and the ordering of the items. Daily, you do at least some of the items on the list, being guided by the ordering you have made, and feel good about checking them off when completed. You have used the to do list habit to increase your productivity.

Chapter 22: Listing Important Variables for a Decision

255. A *variable* is something that may be different between one individual and another. Suppose you were doing the divergent thinking exercise, and the question was, "There's something about a certain person that may not be the same as it is in some other people. What is it?"

We could think of lots of answers to this question, such as: the person's height. The person's weight. How old the person is. Whether the person is male or female. How much the person likes to smell daffodils, on a scale of 0 to 10. How many pounds of cabbage the person has eaten in his or her life. How happy the person has felt over the last week, on a scale of 0 to 10. How many paper clips the person owns. How many times per minute the person says the word "like" when he or she has a certain conversation. All these things are *variables* we could measure or estimate about that person.

Is the person's age another variable?

A. yes,
or
B. no?

256. Variables can apply to anything, not just people. Suppose the question for the divergent thinking exercise was, "What are things about a certain car, that may be different from other cars?"

We could think of a very long list. How much does it cost? How well do its airbags work? Does it use gasoline or electricity, or is it a hybrid? How far can it go on a gallon of gasoline? How badly does it pollute the air? How comfortably can a person 6 feet tall fit into it? How many miles has it already been driven? How many miles can this type of car usually go before it gets junked? All of these are variables about cars. Furthermore, they are variables that someone who is buying a car might want to think about when making a choice.

Which of the following two variables do you think is more worth thinking about for someone buying a car?

A. How much it costs,
or
B. How many letters are in the name of the model?

257. In the listing important variables exercise, you list the important and useful variables to consider when you're making a certain decision. The variables are the things about the

options you're considering that may be advantages or disadvantages.

What's a summary of this section?

A. The listing important variables exercise is thinking of important things to take into account for a certain decision.
or
B. When, once you make a decision, you become ever more convinced that it is right, that is called bolstering.

258. Suppose a first person is picking a babysitter for his children. Suppose he picks on the basis of what color hair the person has, how good the person is at a certain videogame, and how much the person can eat in an eating contest. Suppose a second person picks a babysitter on the basis of how honest and dependable the person is, how careful the person is about safety issues, how kind the person is to children, and whether the person is fun-loving and pleasant to be around.

      The second person is likely to make a better decision, because he has chosen more important and useful variables to consider.

What was the purpose of this section?

A. To illustrate how estimating the probabilities of certain outcomes is important in decision-making.
or
B. To illustrate how we are likely to make better decisions when we first pick the right variables to consider.

259. To do the listing important variables exercise, you pick a type of decision that is being made, and you take turns listing the most important variables. Here's what it might sound like.

First person: Time for the listing important variables exercise.

Second person: OK!

First person: The person is trying to decide where to live – what house or apartment. I'll go first: How safe the neighborhood is.

Second person: That's an important one. My turn: How much it costs to live there, and whether the person can afford it.

First person: That's a good one. Whether the house or apartment is in good repair, and doesn't have a lot of things that are broken.

Second person: If the person has kids, whether the school that they would be going to is good.

First person: Whether the place has enough space and room for everybody that is going to live there.

Second person: How pretty the place is.

First person: If the person has pets, and they're renting, whether pets are allowed or not.

Second person: Whether the neighbors are loud or not.

First person: Congrats, we've thought of eight good variables!

Which of the following variables did they not name?

A. Whether the neighborhood was violent, or whether it was safe.
or
B. Whether the neighbors are nice?

260. Here's another example of the listing important variables exercise.

First person: Time for the listing important variables exercise.

Second person: Sounds good!

First person: The person is deciding on an extracurricular activity to do in addition to schoolwork, like a sport or musical instrument or tutoring or helping people build houses or a chess club or hiking group or acting. I'll go first: how dangerous or safe the activity is.

Second person: How fun for the person the activity is likely to be.

First person: How much good the activity does for somebody else.

Second person: How good the activity is for the person's health, for example whether it gets the person in shape.

First person: How naturally good the person is at doing the activity.

Second person: Whether the activity is one that the person is likely to want to keep doing for the rest of her life.

First person: How much the activity brings the person into the company of other people the person might like.

Second person: How much other people value that activity.

First person: How much time the activity takes.

Second person: Whether the person would learn and practice important skills while doing the activity.

First person: Wow, we have thought of 10 good variables! Congrats!

Which variable, of the following two, did the two persons not think of?

A. How expensive the activity is to do.
or
B. Whether the person is likely to enjoy the activity.

261. When you've thought of the important variables for a certain decision, you can rate how favorable each of those variables is on a 0 to 10 scale and add up the ratings, to get a total score for each option you're considering. The option with the best total score has a good chance of being the best option to pick, if you've listed variables well and measured them well. A list of variables that you can rate and add up the score to get a total score is called a rating scale.

What's a conclusion you could draw from this section?

A. We could have called the "listing important variables for a decision" exercise the "making a rating scale for a decision" exercise.
or

B. If you measure the same variable several times, how much you get the same answer is called the *reliability* of the measurement.

262. Here's another example of the listing important variables exercise. Suppose that Madison is deciding upon a musical instrument to try to learn to play. Here's what it sounds like when the two people list important variables for this decision.

First person: How much you like the sound of the music played with that instrument.

Second person: Whether you can play the instrument in a band, if you want to be in a band.

First person: Whether you can play the instrument by yourself, if you want to put on solo performances.

Second person: How hard it is to learn to play the instrument.

First person: How much the instrument costs.

Second person: Whether you seem to have natural ability to play that instrument.

First person: Whether you can accompany singing with the instrument, if you like to sing.

Second person: How easy it is to take the instrument with you where you want to go.

First person: How many different styles of music you can play on the instrument.

What's a variable that they did NOT list?

A. How loud the music is that you play with that instrument, and whether it will damage your hearing.
or
B. How pleasant the sound of the music made with the instrument is to you.

263. If Madison wanted to use a rating scale to make the decision, here's what it might look like:

0=least favorable
10=most favorable

____1. Like the sound?
____2. Play in a band?
____3. Play solo?
____4. Inexpensiveness (0=high cost, 10 is low cost)
____5. My ability?
____6. Accompany singing?

____7. Take it places?
____8. Many different styles?

Let's suppose Madison has narrowed the choice down to the tuba versus guitar. She gives the tuba an 8 for liking the sound, a 10 for playing in a band, a 2 for playing solo, a 4 for inexpensiveness, an 8 for natural ability, a 0 for accompanying singing, a 5 for taking places, and a 2 for many styles. The total score for the tuba is 39. The guitar gets ratings of 9 for liking the sound, 7 for playing in a band, 10 for playing solo, 5 for inexpensiveness, 5 for natural ability, 10 for accompanying singing, 8 for taking it places, and 7 for many different styles. The total score for the guitar is 65. By 65 to 39, the guitar wins, so Madison decides to take up the guitar.

What's the better summary of what this section is trying to illustrate?

A. You can make up a rating scale, rate each of the options, and pick the option with the best rating; this is a way to make a decision.
or
B. Some people may be interested in a marching band, others in a rock and roll band, and others in no band at all; this is part of the reasons why ratings vary from person to person.

264. Sometimes it doesn't make sense to just add up the ratings, because some variables are much more important than others. Sometimes we should *weight* the variables according to how important they are.

Suppose that someone gets the chance to steal a lot of money. The person lists the important variables:

1. How good or bad my action would be. 0=bad, 10=good
2. Effect on my life if people knew what I did. 0=totally wrecked, 10=made lots better.
3. Whether I could afford to quit the very unpleasant job I have. 0=no, 10=yes
4. Whether I could afford to get a very fast computer. 0=no, 10=yes

The person first rates for the option of stealing the money. The first two questions get 0, but the second two get 10. So the sum is 20.

Then the person rates for the option of not stealing the money. The first two questions get 10, but the second two get 0. So the sum is 20.

Using just the ratings that the person has gotten with this method,

A. The option of not stealing the money wins,
or
B. the two options are in a tie?

265. But then the person thinks some more. He decides that the first two questions on the checklist are at least 10 times more important than the next two. So he will multiply the scores of the first two items by 10. Now, not stealing the money gets a score of 200. (10 x 10 plus 10 x 10 plus 0 plus 0) Stealing the money gets a score of 20. (10 x 0 plus 10 x 0 plus 1x10 plus 1x10)

After multiplying the scores according to how important they are,

A. the scores for the options are tied, or
B. not stealing the money wins by a very large amount.

266. Your decisions about which variables are more important than others are what make up your *values*. Imagine two people, Person A and Person B. In many decisions, Person A tends to list the following variables and consider them very important:

1. How much will the people around me be impressed?
2. How much excitement will get stirred up?
3. How much will I win out over someone else?

Person B tends to list the following variables and to consider them important:

1. Does the option make the world a better place?
2. Does the option increase people's happiness and decrease unhappiness?
3. Does the option tend to create harmony between people and reduce violent and hateful conflict?

Which of the two people values kindness more and probably creates less drama in relationships with others?

A. Person A,
or
B. Person B?

267. Let's give another example of what the listing important variables exercise might sound like.

First person: Time for the listing important variables exercise. This time the person is choosing what type of job the person wants to try to get.

Second person: OK! How much chance the person has to help people in that job.

First person: How much the person gets paid in that job.

Second person: Whether the person can decide what to do, versus whether the person gets bossed around all the time.

First person: How stressful the job is.

Second person: Whether the person is talented at the skills the job requires.

First person: Whether the work done is good for the environment of the planet.

Second person: Whether there is lots of need for people to do the job, or whether only a few people are needed for it.

First person: How long you have to go to school to work in that job.

Second person: Whether what you do in the job is fun or not.

First person: Whether what you do in the job is not too hard or too easy, but just right.

Second person: Whether you have to move often in the job, or whether you can stay in one place if you want to.

First person: How many hours a day you would work at that job.

A variable they did NOT list was

A. How much you get paid for the job, or

B. How much the government is likely to make you a criminal if you don't fill out the right forms on the job?

268. Here's one more example of the listing important variables exercise.

First person: For the listing important variables exercise, this time the choice is whom someone wants to get married to.

Second person: Whether the person is attractive to you.

First person: Whether you seem attractive to the other person.

Second person: Whether the person is hard working versus lazy.

First person: Whether the person is cheerful and upbeat and fun.

Second person: Whether the person is nice and considerate of other people, versus selfish.

First person: Whether the person is honest.

Second person: Whether the person can handle it when things go wrong.

First person: Whether the person is a good decision-maker.

Second person: Whether the person has the same preferences about whether to have children, and how many to have, that you do.

First person: Whether the person agrees with you on religion, and on what religion if any to teach children.

Second person: How smart the person is.

First person: How rich the person is.

Which of the following two variables did they not list yet?

A. the person's honesty, or

B. whether the person is addicted to alcohol or another drug?

269. Person 1 and person 2 continue the Listing Important Variables exercise with the decision of whom to marry.

Second person: Whether the person seems to really enjoy talking with you.

First person: Whether the person is a good listener.

Second person: Whether you have been happy in the time you have spent with this person so far, and whether you feel you really like the person.

First person: Whether the person is good with children and would probably be a good parent.

Second person: Whether the person has the same philosophy that you do about saving money versus spending it.

First person: Whether the person likes to do some things for fun that you also like, that you can do together.

Second person: How little the person criticizes, commands, and contradicts you and other people.

First person: How healthy the person is.

Second person: Whether the person has hereditary diseases in the family.

What's a variable that they have NOT listed so far?

A. whether the person wants to live in the city or the country,
or
B. the person's skills as a listener.

Mastery for Listing Important Variables

1. At the first level, you are able to grasp what is meant by listing important variables, versus listing options or listing pros and cons. You are able to take turns with a trainer in listing important variables for two or three decisions.

2. At the second level, you are able to think, by yourself, of most of the important variables for at least 4 test decisions we have prepared.

3. At the third level, you are able to think, by yourself, of most of the important variables for 10 more decisions we have prepared, and in addition, decide on appropriate ways to weight the variables when making a rating scale.

Chapter 23: The Joint Decision Role Play

270. Suppose two people are spending some time together. One of the people strongly wishes that the two of them play a video game together. The other strongly wishes not to do that, but to take a walk outside. But they both want to be with each other. They have a *conflict* of wishes. Suppose they decide to first take a walk and then play the game. Or, they decide to play basketball instead. Or, they decide that they will spend time together some other time but today each will do what he prefers by himself. If any of these solutions works out so that both of them are happy, they have come to a *resolution* of their conflict.

What was the purpose of this section?

A. To list and explain the steps of conflict-resolution.
or
B. To give an example of *conflict* and of *resolution* of conflict.

271. When people have conflicts, they can talk and think in ways that try to come up with resolutions that are just and good and make people happy. Or, they can scream at each other, say insulting things to each other, or hurt or kill each other. Or, they can say

nothing while they get more and more angry. Good conflict-resolution between people leads to happiness and peace; bad conflict-resolution leads to misery and fear of violence.

What's a summary of this section?

A. If people do conflict-resolution well, they have a much greater chance of being happy and at peace.
or
B. An example of a conflict is that one person wants the room temperature hotter and the other wants it colder.

272. Here is why I use another phrase, *joint decisions*, to name the very important situations this exercise helps you deal with:

Sometimes people make decisions together, without having disagreed about anything first. For example, two people get together, and they decide what to do together. A couple decides where to live together. Parents decide how they want their children to be educated. These sorts of situations, as well as conflict situations, are those where *joint decisions* are useful. Joint decisions are any decisions that people make together, that affect both of them, whether they start out disagreeing or not. If people can do joint decisions well enough and soon enough, fewer situations feel like conflict.

Suppose that two family members have some time to spend with each other. They think of playing a game, having a "study party," and taking a walk, and they both instantly realize they'd like to get some exercise and chat with each other. So they take a walk.

What would the author call this?

A. A joint decision that didn't become a conflict.
or
B. An example of how all conflicts are situations where joint decision would be useful.

273. How important is the skill of joint decision and conflict resolution for life? I once read in the newspaper that two men got into an argument over who would get to park a car in a certain parking place. Screaming and insulting and shoving quickly turned into deadly violence – one of the men killed the other. If both men had been had been very skilled in joint decision making, this incident wouldn't have happened. How important was the skill of joint decision for these men?

About as important as anything can be.

What's the main point of this section?

A. A very important part of good conflict-resolution is walking away from one another once the level of anger gets too high.
or
B. Joint decision making skill is extremely important – indeed, it can be a matter of life or death.

274. If you have a job, the joint decision skill of your boss or the people you're the boss of can make the difference between a pleasant work life and a miserable one. If you're in a family, the way that you and your fellow family members resolve conflict and make joint decisions can make the difference between love and hate. And conflict resolution between nations determines whether or not millions of people die in wars.

The newspapers are full of stories about bad things that people have done to each other. Most of these could have been avoided if people had enough conflict-resolution skill.

The purpose of this section was to

A. Persuade or remind the reader that joint decision and conflict-resolution skill is crucial for both happiness and survival.

or

B. Persuade the reader that when people are very angry, they need to spend time alone before attempting conflict resolution.

275. In the joint decision role play exercise, you take a pretend joint decision and talk it out. Two people can each play a part, or one person can play both parts.

There are seven things that you have each character do in the conversation. These seven things can be remembered by the name, "Dr. L.W. Aap." Each of the letters in the doctor's name stands for one of the seven things you do in the exercise.

Who or what is Dr. L.W.Aap?

A. The doctor who discovered that when people use these seven steps, conflict-resolution goes better.

or

B. A made-up name that is meant to help you remember the seven things to do in the conflict resolution role play exercise.

276. Some of the seven parts of joint decision making have their own exercises that have been described already in this book. The R is for reflections, as in the reflections

exercise. The L is for listing options, as in the brainstorming options exercise. The first A is for advantages and disadvantages, as in the pros and cons exercise. Thus the role play combines several skills that you may have already thoroughly practiced in previous exercises.

What's a summary of this section?

A. The joint decision role play draws upon skills that we have already practiced in exercises on reflections, brainstorming options, and listing pros and cons.

or

B. In conflict situations, people tend to fall back on commanding, criticizing, and contradicting each other unless they train themselves not to do these things.

277. Here are the 7 parts of the conflict resolution role play, that start with the letters Dr. L.W. Aap.

1. Defining. Each person defines the problem, without commanding or criticizing the other person.

2. Reflecting. Each person does a reflection to make sure he or she understands the other person's point of view about the problem.

3. Listing. Together, they list options for what to do. They list a total of at least four options.

4. Waiting. They wait until they are finished listing options before starting to talk about their disadvantages.

5. Advantages and disadvantages. After they are finished listing options, they talk about the advantages and disadvantages of the options that seem best (and not the bad characteristics of the other person).

6. Agreeing. They agree on something, even if they can agree on nothing more than the plan to continue to think about the problem and resume the discussion later.

7. Politeness. They do not interrupt each other, raise their voices, or insult each other.

What does the D in Dr. L.W. Aap stand for?

A. Discussion of information
or
B. Defining the problem.

278. Here's what the conflict-resolution role play may sounds like, when a tutor does it with a student.

Tutor: Let's do the conflict-resolution role play exercise, also known as Dr. L.W. Aap. Here's the problem. Pat and Lee live together. Pat leaves things lying around on the floor or on tables or chairs or couches that Lee wishes were put away. How about you be Lee, and I'll be Pat?

Student: OK. Pat, could I talk with you about a problem? I seem to want things neater than you do. When things are left out on the floor or couch or on chairs, it bothers me, even though it doesn't seem to bother you much, or maybe not at all.

Tutor: Lee, thanks for mentioning this problem to me. So you're saying that you'd be happier with things put away a lot more than I put them away.

Student: That's right, Pat.

Tutor: Well to tell you my point of view, you're exactly right that it doesn't bother me to have things lying around and not put away. I guess it just isn't as important to me as it is to you. But I want to see what we can do so that we are both happy.

Student: If I understand you right, you're saying that it doesn't bother you to have things not put away, but that you're wanting to see what we

can come up with that will make
things work out.

Tutor: That's right.

So far in this role play, what has
happened?

A. Both people have defined the
problem from their point of view, and
both have reflected their hearing of the
other person's point of view.
or
B. They have listed an option for
solving the problem.

279. The role play continues.

Tutor: One option is that I could just
try to put things away more often. It
would probably help me to be more
organized.

Student: Or, I could just try to get used
to having things less neat than I like.

Tutor: Another option is that we could
have a little cleaning up party at a
regular time each day, where we made
the place neater, together.

Student: Another option is that we
could get a big cardboard box. When I
find something of yours lying around,
I could put it in the box.

While the two people listed their four
options, did they wait until later to talk
about the advantages and
disadvantages of them?

A. Yes,
or
B. No?

280. The role play continues.

Tutor: Do you have more options, or
would you like to think about the pros
and cons?

Student: Let's go ahead to pros and
cons. Having a work party together
might be a fun way to solve the
problem, but it also might cause
resentment if one of us wants to do it
and the other isn't in the mood, and if
one wants to do it and the other is in
the middle of something else.

Tutor: An advantage of the big box
option is that you wouldn't have to put
up with things lying around, because
you could put them in the box very
quickly. I would always know where
to look if something wasn't where I
left it. The only disadvantage I can
think of is that you might resent
having to put my things in the box.

Student: Having to put things in the
box wouldn't be a big con for me. It
would be much more pleasant to do

that and get it over with than to put up with things lying around.

Have they spoken of advantages and disadvantages for

A. each of the options they listed, or
B. just the options that they thought were the most promising?

281. The role play continues.

Tutor: Then do you want to try the big box option?

Student: Yes. We could give it a try for a while and see if it works, and talk about it again soon.

Tutor: I think I know where to get a big cardboard box.

Student: Sounds great. Thanks for problem-solving with me on this.

Tutor: Thank you.

By now, the two people have done

A. six of the seven steps in Dr. L.W. Aap, or
B. All seven of the steps in Dr. L.W. Aap?

282. Some people read or hear models of Dr. L.W. Aap conversations, and say, in a critical tone of voice, "But that's not how people really talk, in real life." This is often true. But it's not a criticism, because in "real life," every day people make each other miserable, insult each other, come to hate each other, physically hurt one another, and kill each other as a result of the way "people really talk."

"What people usually do" is not a valid test for what is right and good. We should admire behaviors that bring happiness, even if people don't do them very often.

The point of this section is that

A. The fact that people do the things on the Dr. L.W. Aap list fairly rarely does not mean that the things on the list aren't good. or
B. The murder rate in the U.S. is a good bit higher than in most other developed countries.

283. Some other people may say, "But the people in the example were so calm and cool. Where's the emotion? How do they get their anger out?"

Lots of research has taught us that the point of conflict-resolution and joint decision making is not to "get anger out." In fact, the more calm and cool people can stay during a joint decision, the more likely they are to come to a good decision. And coming to a decision that they can both feel OK about is what reduces anger the most in the long run.

What's a summary of this section?

A. Joint decision goes best when people stay calm and are not trying to get their anger out.
or
B. When we predict a positive consequence of an option, we call it an advantage, and an unwanted consequence is called a disadvantage.

284. In fact, when people are talking about a conflict and they get mad enough at each other to even feel like yelling, I recommend that they politely call a time out in the conversation, go away from each other, stay alone for a while, and cool off. During this time, they can exercise, rest, read, or just think. They can tackle the joint decision again when they have gotten cool and calm. I recommend that family members make this plan: if either of them gets angry enough that the conversation feels like a battle rather than cooperation, they postpone the conversation. If people in families always followed this rule, huge amounts of violence and unhappiness could be prevented.

In this section the author recommends that

A. People use relaxation techniques to practice getting themselves calm and cool.
or
B. People in families plan ahead to go into separate places and cool off when a joint decision conversation starts feeling too much like a cutthroat competition.

285. Some people may say, "I understand how it may be good to stay calm and cool during conflict-resolution talks. But I just don't think I can do it. I always get very mad."

This is one of several good reasons for doing the role-play this chapter describes. It's easier not to get mad with pretend conflicts than with real ones. When you've practiced many times with pretend conflicts, you are more able to stay cool and think clearly when real conflicts come up.

What's the main point of this section?

A. The author thinks that one of the best ways to learn to stay cool in real conflict situations is to practice a lot with imaginary conflict situations.
or

B. Exercise may be a good thing to do while cooling off from anger, because exercise is what the flight or fight response prepares our bodies for.

286. Let's look at another example of the joint decision role-play.

Tutor: Let's do the joint decision role-play exercise.

Student: OK!

Tutor: Here's the situation. One person in a family often wants to work on homework, but another person in the family wants company and interrupts that person.

Student: OK. I'll be the person that's interrupted.
   May I talk with you some about a problem, please?

Tutor: Sure.

Student: I often want to work on my homework, and you often say things to me while I'm working, to have some company. Sometimes I find the interruptions interfere with my work.

Tutor: So if I understand you right, sometimes my interrupting you when you're working is something you don't like, and you're interested in

finding a way to reduce unwanted interruptions?

Student: That's right.

Tutor: I'm glad you told me about that. My point of view is that sometimes you do like to talk and do things other and work, and I often don't know, or maybe I forget to think about, whether you're needing to concentrate on serious work or just doing something like surfing the Internet.

Student: What I'm hearing is that you're interested in not making unwanted interruptions, and that one problem in doing that is knowing whether I'm really needing to concentrate or whether I'm basically goofing off.

Tutor: That's right.

What has happened so far?

A. They have both listed and waited.
or
B. They have both defined and reflected.

287. The role-play continues.

Student: Ready to list some options?

Tutor: Sure. One option is that you could put up a Do Not Disturb sign when you don't want to be interrupted.

Student: Or you could just watch for a minute to try to figure out whether I'm concentrating or not.

Tutor: Or we could have the custom be that the person who walks in asks, "Would you mind being interrupted now?"

Student: Or when I really don't want to be interrupted I can go into my room and lock the door.

Tutor: Think we have enough?

Student: Yes. Let's go to pros and cons.

What happened in this part of the role play?

A. They discussed the advantages and disadvantages of some options.
or
B. They each listed two options, without discussing advantages and disadvantages of any of them.

288. The role play continues.

Tutor: The disadvantage of my looking to see what you're doing first is that you might feel like I'm invading your privacy by coming and reading what's on your computer screen and so forth.

Student: Good point. The disadvantage of my locking the door is that it's nice not to be closed up, and another is that if there were some sort of emergency and I needed help, I'd be locked in.

Tutor: Having a Do Not Disturb sign sounds like a good plan. The only disadvantage of that is that you might forget to put it up.

Student: We could combine that with asking, "Do you mind if I interrupt?" Those two could both be done. That's an advantage of both of them: they could be done with the other.

What did they do in this part of the role-play?

A. Talk about pros and cons of options?
or
B. Define the problem further and reflect the other's point of view?

289. The role play continues.

Tutor: So do you want to try the Do Not Disturb sign, combined with asking whether someone minds being interrupted?

Student: That would be great. We could each do it, so that I won't interrupt you when you don't want it, either.

Tutor: Let's try it for a few days and then talk about how it's worked.

Student: OK! Thanks for doing this joint decision-making with me!

Tutor: Thank you for doing it with me!

What did they do in this part?

A. They thought about the probabilities that different consequences would occur.
or
B. They agreed upon something, and they continued to be polite to each other.

290. What do people naturally do instead of Dr. L.W. Aap when they have a disagreement? Too often, the answer is commands, criticisms, contradictions, and threats. For example:
First person: Quit interrupting me so much! (command)
Second person: I don't "interrupt you so much!" (contradiction) You are so spoiled, you think that people should be with you whenever you want and leave you alone when you don't want, without your even asking them! (criticism)
First person: If you call me spoiled again, you will wish you hadn't! (threat)

If people want to avoid commands, criticisms, contradictions, and threats, they need to carefully practice talking through conflicts and other joint decisions in non-blaming ways. The joint decision role play gives a chance to practice this.

What's a summary of this section?

A. When people have a conflict, they naturally tend to command, criticize, and contradict each other. The joint decision role-play lets them practice not doing these things.
or
B. The word *contradict* means to tell someone that what he or she said is not correct or not true.

291. Let's go through Dr. L.W. Aap and talk about some of the fine points of how to do it well.
When you define the problem, try very hard to avoid commanding or criticizing or threatening the other person. Tell what the problem is and how it affects you, and invite the other to try to solve it with you.

Which of these is a good example of what this section advises?

A. Turn that stupid music down. You have no consideration for other people.
or
B. Could we talk about a problem? You like to play the music loudly, but it distracts me and is unpleasant for me to hear.

292. People have written about various ways of communicating problems to people (that is, defining the problem) without insulting them or bossing them around. One of these is an "I feel statement": When you do ____, I feel ____, because ____." A variation of this is, "I don't like it when ____, for this reason: ____." For example, "When you leave a lot of food out on the kitchen counter at night, I feel uneasy, because the food attracts mice and rats and insects." Or, "I don't like it when you scream loudly, because it hurts my ears and makes it harder to think calmly. Can we talk about this?"

The main thing you want to do when defining the problem is to give the other person information about what you're concerned about, and how it affects you. You stay away from pointing out the bad things about the other person.

What's a summary of this section?

A. Statements like "I feel statements" can sometimes help people to define problems without insulting the other person.
or
B. People who study conflict resolution use the phrase *your interest* to speak about what you have to gain or lose, and why it makes a difference to you.

293. When you do a reflection of the other person's point of view, you want to avoid trying to make the other person's viewpoint look silly. You want to reflect to the other the other's point of view, in such a way that the other will agree, "Yes, that's what I'm saying."

Which of these two follows the advice of this section?

A. So you think that everyone in this house has to keep quiet all the time just so that you can study and show everyone how smart you are, huh.
or
B. So you'd like for it to be quieter, partly so that you will be able to concentrate better, and partly just because the quietness is more pleasant. Is that right?

294. When you list options, try to come up with at least four reasonable, good options. I recommend not wasting your time thinking of options that are obviously unreasonable or violent or silly.

Which of the following follows the advice of this section?

A. You could listen to the music with ear buds…. I could just turn it down, whenever you want…. You could move farther away in the house to play the music…. I could take the music player outside, now that the weather is warmer….
or
B. I could just have a tantrum whenever the music is too loud…. Or we have a fight and if I win I get to have the music loud….

295. While you are listing, it's particularly important to wait and keep listing before you criticize the options. It's OK to make a brief comment of positive feedback about an option.

Which of the following goes against the advice of this section, if it's said right after the first option is listed?

A. That's a good option. Or, we could….
or

B. I don't think that would work, because it's too complicated to keep track of.

296. When you talk about advantages and disadvantages, try to talk some about the advantages of some of the options the other person mentioned and some of the disadvantages of the ones you named.

   If you list, say, 6 or 8 options, it would take quite a while to do the pros and cons exercise with all those options. Thus I recommend just listing advantages and disadvantages of the best options – the top choices.

Which of the following is correct?

A. The author recommends listing at least 4 advantages and disadvantages for each option.
or
B. The author recommends talking about advantages and disadvantages of the options the two people like the best.

297. How do you do the "agreeing" part of Dr. L.W. Aap if the two people aren't ready to agree on one of the options? Isn't it unrealistic to expect that people would agree so quickly on every issue?

   If they can't agree on the final solution, at least they can agree on the next step. The agreement can be,

"Let's agree to think about this some more and talk about it later." Or, it can be, "Let's read about this and inform ourselves better, and talk about it more when we've done that."

What's an example of what the author is suggesting, for when people aren't ready to agree on a final solution?

A. We agree that any music played in the house will be only with ear buds and not over speakers.
or
B. We agree that we'll both do some more thinking about options, and talk again in two days.

298. What does politeness mean? Don't interrupt. Don't keep talking so long that the other person is tempted to interrupt. Don't raise your voices – don't yell. Don't insult the other person. Try to save your criticism for options rather than the qualities of the other person. Say *please* and *thank you* when appropriate.

Which of the following would the author tend to agree with?

A. People should let out their feelings when they talk about conflicts, by screaming or beating on pillows.
or

B. When people talk about conflicts, they should if possible use respectful speech that is not very loud.

Mastery for the Joint Decision Role Play

1. At the first level, you have done two or three joint decision role plays with a trainer; the trainer can prompt you as to what comes next in the sequence.

2. At the second level, you have done at least 15 joint decision role plays with a trainer, with no need for prompting, meeting all 7 of the Dr. L.W. Aap criteria.

3. At the third level, you can fluently do a joint decision role play for any joint decision a tester gives you, playing both parts yourself, meeting all 7 criteria.

Chapter 24: The Decisions Exercise

299. When you make an important decision, you can go through several steps that you can remember by the mnemonic SOIL ADDLE.

Situation: You describe the situation you're in, trying to include what's most relevant to the decision.

Objectives: You set your goals or objectives for this decision. What are you trying to bring about? What do you want the outcome to be?

Information: What can you look up or find out that will help you in the decision?

Listing options: What possible courses of action can you take?

Advantages and disadvantages: For the best options, what are the pros and cons? How likely are these to happen?

Deciding: You pick an option, or a set of them, based on what you have considered so far.

Doing: You carry out the option.

Learning from Experience: You see what happened. Was it as you had predicted, or did something else occur? You try to learn from what happened, for use in future decisions.

What would be a good a title for this section?

A. Why decision-making is an important skill.
or
B. Steps in decision-making.

300. When you do the decisions exercise, you take a choice point (perhaps one you generated in the listing choice points exercise). You pretend that you are in that situation. You describe the situation, describe your objectives, talk about what information would help you, maybe imagine yourself getting that information, list options, list advantages and disadvantages for the main options, and decide. Then you imagine yourself doing what you've decided and learning from the experience.

What's the point of this section?

A. The decisions exercise involves doing many of the steps of actual decision making, using your imagination to make up what is missing.
or
B. There is real benefit in doing the decisions exercise with pretend

situations before you use it with real situations from your life.

301. Here's what it might sound like when someone does the decisions exercise.

Situation: A couple of friends invite me to go with them to jump off a cliff into the river. I know this is a pretty dangerous spot, and that someone was hurt really badly at just the spot they are going to.

Objectives: I want to protect myself. I want to help my friends be safe if I can. I want not to lose my friendship with them.

Information: I wonder if their parents know that they are going to do this. They say they do. I wonder if they know that someone was hurt really badly there. They say they know that too, but that they'll be more careful. I wonder if it's legal to do this; I look it up and I don't see a law against it.

Listing options: I could just say no, I have something else to do. I could say no and advise them not to do it because I think it's too dangerous. I could go along so that I could help out if someone gets hurt, but not jump myself. I could call up their parents and let them know I don't think this is a good idea.

So far, which of the steps of decision making has the person done?

A. Situation, objectives, information, listing options.
or
B. Situation, objectives, and information.

302. The example of the decisions exercise continues.

Advantages and Disadvantages: The advantage of trying to persuade their parents not to let them go is that I could save a life. The disadvantage is that I might lose them as friends, and that the parents might not even listen to me. The advantage of just saying "No, I have something else to do," is that I don't offend them; the disadvantage is that I'd feel super guilty if anyone got hurt. The disadvantage of saying no and advising them that I think it's too dangerous is that they would think I'm a wimp; the advantage is that I might influence them to be careful and at least I know I've done something to prevent injury.

Decision: I decide to tell them I don't want to, and to advise that they don't do it because of the danger.

Doing: I do what I decided. They don't take my warning seriously; they just say something a little insulting and go on.

Learning from the experience: It turns out that they go, they have fun, and none of them gets hurt. And they stay friends with me. But a month later, someone else gets hurt really badly at the same place. I learn from this that my cautiousness was justified. If people hadn't gone, maybe this most recent person wouldn't have gotten hurt.

Which of the following is true about Learning from the Experience in this example?

A. The person doing the exercise made up an outcome that he or she could learn something from.
or
B. The learning that the person came up with was the only possible one that could have been arrived at.

303. Here's another example of the decisions exercise.

Situation: It's afternoon, and I'm done with school and classes, and I'm at home alone. My choice is what to do.

Objective: I want to use my time well. I want to either do something really

fun, or accomplish something very useful.

Information: I look at my assignments for tomorrow. I won't be in a huge rush to finish. I can take some time now to do something else.

Listing Options: I could do what most people default to, which is to play a video game or watch TV. I could organize the stuff in my room. I could get to work on my homework. I could do some exercising. I could call up a friend and chat on the phone some. I could take some time out and read my science textbook.

Which of the following two options did the person NOT consider?

A. Going over and visiting a friend at the friend's house.
or
B. Reading a science textbook.

304. The decisions exercise continues.

Advantages and disadvantages: Exercising is always good for me, but I've already had a good walk up a long hill back from class. I really don't want to waste my time on video games or TV. I've gotten to spend some time chatting with friends already today. If I organize the stuff in my room, it will help me to get more accomplished and have less trouble finding things. Reading my science book would really help me understand what is going on, and I think it might actually be fun.

Deciding: I think I'll work on organizing the stuff in my room for 20 minutes, and then sit on the couch and read my science book for about 45 minutes or so.

Doing: I'm now doing exactly what I decided.

Learning from Experience: It really feels good to be able to walk into my room without stuff all over everywhere; I got a lot done in 20 minutes and I feel good about it. And I actually enjoyed reading the science textbook. I understand things lots better than just by going to class and doing homework. I feel good about the decisions I made.

Which skill did the person seem to value highly when making this decision?

A. Productivity,
or
B. Friendship-building?

305. Here's another example of the decisions exercise.

Situation: I'm in a park in the city, and I see a man who starts to get up from a bench, and then falls over onto the ground. He seems to be in a daze.

Objective: I want to help him if I can.

Information: I think back over what I know about first aid. He could have a fainting spell from low blood pressure. He could be having a heart attack. He could be diabetic and be passing out from eating too little relative to his insulin, and getting low blood sugar. I go up to him and ask him if he is diabetic, and he nods yes. I ask if he feels low on his blood sugar, and he nods yes again.

Listing options: I want to get him something that will raise his blood sugar, before he passes out altogether. I could check his pockets to see if he has any food with him. I could run to a store and buy something. Or I could just grab something and run out and pay later. I could run to where people are eating very close by in outdoor seating for a restaurant and grab some lemonade or soda or a packet or two of sugar or something right off the table.

Which option, of the following, did the person NOT list?

A. Seeing if any of the people walking around in the park had a cup of soda or juice in their hands.
or
B. Grabbing sugar packets off the restaurant table?

306. The decisions exercise continues.

Advantages and disadvantages: I might get in lots of trouble by grabbing something without paying. But the man might be in big trouble if he goes totally unconscious, because then he wouldn't be able to eat or drink without choking.

Deciding: I feel his pockets and don't find anything. There's not a store nearby, but the people eating lunch outside will hopefully understand. I'm going to grab a soda right off their table.

Doing: I run over and yell to the people, as I'm coming, I'm sorry, this is an emergency, the man is about to pass out from low blood sugar, and I grab the cup of soda right off the table and run back and give it to the man to sip.

Learning from the experience: He is able to sip it, and he quickly revives. I learned from this that what I was taught in first aid class really is good stuff, and it works.

New situation: Now what do I do to make sure he'll stay OK? And what do I do about the people I stole this drink from?

What does the end of this exercise illustrate?

A. As soon as you finish one decision, you're usually in a new situation that requires still another decision.
or
B. It's helpful to relax your muscles when you want to turn down your level of excitement.

Mastery for the Decisions Exercise

1. At the first level, with prompting by the trainer, you go through the steps of SOIL ADDLE with two or three pretend decisions.

2. At the second level, you can go through the SOIL ADDLE steps on your own, without prompting, on test situations, setting good objectives, thinking of several good options, thinking of high quality advantages and disadvantages, making a reasonable choice, imagining a plausible outcome, and learning from the outcome.

3. At the third level, you can do all
that is described in the second level,
very fluently and very well, for at least
10 test situations and at least 3
situations that you make up yourself.

Chapter 25: The Choice Points Exercise

307. If you have done the twelve-thought exercise, the four-thought exercise, brainstorming options, pros and cons, listing important variables, joint decision role play, the decisions exercise, or fantasy rehearsals, you know that these all start with a situation – a choice point.

Life consists of one choice point after another. At any given moment, we are faced with a decision of what to do in that moment. In a sense, every moment of our lives is a choice point.

Yet if you ask untrained people to think of the choice points they have run into lately, or to list choice points that anyone could face, most will probably have a hard time with this question. Getting skilled at this is the aim of the choice points exercise.

What's an idea expressed in this section?

A. Even though almost every moment of life represents a choice point, it's hard for untrained people to list choice points.
or
B. Listing choice points can be thought of as a special case of the divergent thinking exercise.

308. Why is it good to be able to list choice points? First, it gives you lots of situations to practice with, using the other exercises! But more importantly, skill in this exercise helps you to be aware that you are at a choice point, and to be aware of your power to choose.

For example: a person is somewhat overweight. He is in the habit of wandering into the kitchen and eating a few hundred calories of snacks without even thinking about what he is doing. But suppose that, before he starts to eat, he thinks, "I'm at a choice point. I ate a couple of hours ago, and even though food would taste good now, I'm not particularly hungry. What do I want to do?" Then the person can make a conscious choice rather than just acting mindlessly, by habit.

What's the main idea of this section?

A. Making up choice points is a good exercise for fiction writers, because putting your characters into interesting choice points is what story-creation is about.
or
B. Making up choice points helps you to recognize the choice points you get

into in life, and to make conscious choices rather than automatic, mindless choices.

309. When you make up choice points, you can think of those for individual decisions and those for joint decisions; the second of these are situations that can be used for the joint decision role play. You can think of choice points that are best for the brainstorming options exercise, where thinking up lots of options would be very useful. Or you can think of situations that would be best for the pros and cons exercise, where there is one major option that needs to be accepted or rejected. You can think of choice points that are good for UCAC fantasy rehearsals, where someone has an urge to do some option that may not be the best idea.

What's the point of this section?

A. When you make up choice points, you can think back over both the celebration-worthy things you and others have done, and you can also think of mistakes you and others have made.
or
B. Some choice points are more useful for one sort of psychological skills exercise than others; you can think of all types.

310. When you do this exercise with someone else, you simply take turns thinking of choice points, of any sort. Here's what it might sound like.

First person: Let's do the choice points exercise. I'll go first, OK?

Second person: OK!

First person: Someone is taking guitar lessons, but the person finds that he or she isn't practicing much.

Second person: Sounds like a good one. My turn: Someone finds $800 in cash lying on the ground in a park.

First person: That's a choice point I'd like to have. Someone is asked by a friend to take the friend's pet hamster when the friend goes off to college.

Second person: Someone has some free time on a Sunday afternoon and wants to decide how to spend that time.

First person: OK! Someone has something really cool to say at school in a class discussion, and has to decide whether to hold up a hand and wait, or just go ahead and say it.

Second person: Some people are trying to decide whether to go out to eat, or eat the leftovers in the refrigerator.

Which of the above choice points would be a better one for the brainstorming options exercise? (The other would be better for pros and cons.)

A. The one about whether or not to go out to eat.
or
B. The one about what to do with free time on Sunday afternoon.

311. Here are more examples of what people might come up with while doing the choice points exercise.

Person 1: Someone sees someone who has been cut really badly.

Person 2: Someone sees a cat about to pounce on a chipmunk.

1 Someone finds that the light on the ceiling in their room makes their eyes and head hurt.

2 Someone is very poor, and the person sees someone from a restaurant dump a bunch of food into a dumpster.

1 Someone is walking along in the city and sees two guys who are about to get into a fight.

2 Someone needs to travel from one place in the country to a place several hundred miles away.

1 A student in school sees another student cheating on a test.

2 A person can sign up for an easy course that the person would enjoy a lot, or a hard course the person wouldn't enjoy but would look better on the person's record.

Which of the following choice points did the two people NOT list?

A. Someone gets invited to go for a hike lasting several days.
or
B. Someone has to pick between an easier course or a harder course at school.

312. Sometimes you can change a choice point just a little to make it more suitable for a different exercise. For example:

A person is deciding what career to try for.

This choice point is well suited for brainstorming options. Let's change it a little:

A person is deciding whether or not to try to go to medical school.

167

Now it's better suited for pros and cons.

Let's change it some more:

A person's mother wants him to become a doctor. But the person is interested in teaching philosophy.

Now it's more suitable for the joint decision role-play.

Here's another change:

A person decides to try to get into medical school, and finds out about all the very hard schoolwork that he would have to do to accomplish that goal.

This is good for the 12 thought exercise or the 4 thought exercise.

One more change:

A person is faced with a choice of playing video games versus studying his science courses so he can get into medical school.

This could work for STEBC fantasy rehearsal or UCAC fantasy rehearsal.

What's the author's point in these examples?

A. Listing important variables is good to do at the beginning of a choice point in real life, and fantasy rehearsals are good when you've made the decision of what's best to do.
or
B. Once you have a choice point that is suitable for one of our exercises, you can usually change it around to make it suitable for the others as well.

Mastery for the Choice Points Exercise

1. At the first level, you grasp what is meant by choice points and have thought of three or four of them.

2. At the second level, you have thought of at least 20 choice points, that you or your trainer has written down.

3. At the third level, you have thought of at least 50 choice points, that you or your trainer has written down. These should include situations suitable for various types of exercises: Brainstorming options, pros and cons, 12 thought, 4 thought, STEBC rehearsals, UCAC rehearsals, joint decision role play, decision exercise, listing important variables. You also know how to change choice points so as to make them more suitable for different exercises.

Chapter 26: A Guessing Game

313. In this chapter we look at an exercise that's a game. But it's meant to give a workout to psychological skills, just the same.

In this game, the first person thinks of something for the second to guess. It could be a cat, George Washington, the crowning of a king, self-esteem, an electron, or anything else. Then the first person gives a clue, of any sort that she wants. The second person takes his first guess. If the second person doesn't guess it on the first guess, the first person gives another clue, about the same thing, and the second person guesses again. They keep on until the second person gets it, or until the second person gives up.

What was the purpose of this section?

A. To describe which psychological skills the guessing game gives practice in.
or
B. To describe how to do the guessing game.

314. We live in a very competitive world. Therefore, many people, when they think of something for the other to guess, assume that the goal of this exercise is to stump the guesser. They assume that when the guesser gives up, they have won and the guesser has lost. They automatically try to beat the other person. But that's not the way this game works.

This is a cooperative game, rather than a competitive one. That means that both people have the same goal. The object, if you are thinking up the thing and giving clues for it, is to make the process of guessing as fun for your partner as you can possibly make it. To do this, you think of something to guess that is hard enough to be challenging, but not so hard as to be frustrating. Likewise, as you make up clues, you try to make the guessing challenging enough to be fun, but not so impossible as to be frustrating. After any given round, the guesser can say whether he would like it harder or easier next time.

When there has been a guessing challenge that is really fun for the guesser, both people win the game!

What's a summary of this section?

A. This exercise helps you understand how one goes about defining a word.
or
B. This is a game where people don't play against each other – both of them are trying to make the game just the

right level of difficulty to be the most fun.

315. Here's what the game might sound like.

Person 1: Let's do the guessing game! I've got one for you. The first clue is: It's white.

Person 2: Snow!

1: Good guess but not it yet. Here's the second clue. People put it on or in food.

2: Sugar!

1: Good but not yet. There's a lot of this in sea water.

2: Salt!

1: Yes! You got it. Harder, easier, or the same next time?

2: How about harder?

1: OK!

True or false: The clue-giver made it so that it would take a lot of luck to guess this after the first clue, but would not take luck to guess after all three clues.

A. True

or
B. False

316. Here's another example.

Person 2: Now it's time for me to do one for you. It's a quality that people can have.

Person 1: Honesty.

Person 2: Good guess, but keep going. Second clue: It's a quality that action and adventure heroes in movies usually have lots of.

Person 1. Let's see, not nonviolence. Violence?

2. Third clue: This quality comes in handy if you need to walk across a narrow plank joining one high place to another, where you could fall down a long way.

1: Good coordination!

2: That guess goes with all 3 clues so far, but it's not it. It's the quality that the cowardly lion in the Wizard of Oz wished for.

1: Courage!

2: You got it!

1: About the same difficulty next time?

2: OK!

How do imagine the clue-giver felt when the guesser got the right answer?

A. Bad, because he lost,
or
B. Good, because they both won?

317. Here's a third example.

Person 1: I've got one for you. First clue: This is a state of mind.

Person 2: Happiness.

Person 1: Good guess. Second clue: It's usually unpleasant.

Person 2: Fear.

1: Another good guess. It's a state of mind people get when everything is all mixed up.

2: Bewilderment?

1: That means almost the same thing. Next clue: it sort of rhymes with the word illusion.

2: Confusion!

1: You got it!

The last clue that the clue-giver gave in this example had to do with

A. The meaning of the word,
or
B. The sound of the word?

318. What psychological skills does this game exercise? First, whenever you are learning something, teaching something, choosing what jobs to try, choosing what courses to take, or getting ready to do almost any sort of work, it's very important to be able to take on challenges that are not too hard, not too easy, but just right. The proverb, "Don't bite off more than you can chew," means, "Don't choose challenges that are too difficult for you." Many people do commit themselves to more than they can do.

Studies in psychology have found that lower-achieving people tend to choose levels of difficulty for themselves that are either impossibly high or very low. High achievers tend to choose challenges that they have a chance to succeed at with skill and effort, challenges in the "right" range of difficulty.

What's a summary of this section?

A. One of the points of this exercise is to let you practice setting the right level of difficulty for tasks.

or
B. One of the points of this exercise is getting out of the competitive state of mind and into the cooperative state of mind.

319. Another skill that this exercise lets you practice is seeing things from another person's point of view. This has been called the skill of empathy, or of perspective-taking. You put yourself in the other's place to try to figure out what will make the other person have the most fun.

If I know my partner knows very much about space and the solar system, and if I pick, as my answer to guess, the name of one of the moons of the planet Jupiter, I am using good empathy skills. If I make the same choice because I'm into space exploration and my partner knows and cares little about it, I'm not using as good empathy skills.

What's the better summary of this section?

A. This exercise lets you practice a certain type of logical thinking, where you start out with a large number of possibilities and gradually narrow them down.
or
B. You practice empathy when you pick, as your answer to guess, something your partner knows about and would be interested in.

320. You also practice empathy as you choose your clues. When you feel that the other person is getting tired of making incorrect guesses, you start making your clues more informative. You try to sense when to make things more difficult and when to make them easier, to help your partner have the most fun.

What's the better summary of this section?

A. This game is sort of like the game "20 Questions," which is also a challenge to logical thinking.
or
B. You also put yourself in the other person's place to decide how much or little to give away in the clues.

Mastery for the Guessing Exercise

1. At the first level, you have done the exercise two or three times as both the guesser and the clue-giver. You "get" the idea that you're not trying to play against the other person, but that you're trying to make it as fun as possible.

2. At the second level, you have done the game enough that you are able to home in on a good level of difficulty when you are the clue-giver, and you are able to help the other person find a good level of difficulty when you are the guesser.

3. At the third level, you have done this enough that you and the other person feel that over time you have gotten better and better at all aspects of this exercise, and you also know your partner better from doing it.

Chapter 27: Breathe and Relax

321. One of the most important goals of psychological skills training is to learn to think carefully about what to do, even when you are in situations that might get you very scared, very angry, or very emotional in some other way. We've already talked about one way to achieve this goal, when we studied the 12 thought exercise and the 4 thought exercise. Not awfulizing, goal-setting, and listing options and choosing usually help you make calm decisions better than awfulizing and blaming someone else.

This chapter talks about another way of calming down, in which you get your muscles to relax.

What's a summary of this section?

A. We've talked about using thoughts to calm yourself; now we're going to talk about muscle relaxation.
or
B. For the last several decades, medicines that are supposed to help people get less anxious and stressed have been the biggest sellers in the U.S.

322. Learning to get your body very relaxed is useful in many different ways. Getting good sleep helps you in lots of ways; getting to sleep is very difficult for many, many people. The skill of relaxing often helps greatly in getting good sleep. Relaxing helps you to get rid of certain headaches and belly aches. Relaxing the muscles of the jaw can cure or prevent pain in the joint that connects the jaw to the rest of the skull. Relaxing can help you perform better in stressful situations.

What appears to be the purpose of this section?

A. To describe exactly how to go about relaxing your muscles.
or
B. To persuade the reader to value the skill of relaxation.

323. When we feel scared or angry, our muscles tend to tighten up. Probably this helps us to respond quickly if we need to fight or flee. When we calm down, our muscles naturally relax.

But the converse is also true: when our muscles relax, we usually feel calmer. When our brains perceive that our muscles are soft, loose, and relaxed, we usually conclude that things are all right, that there is not a need to fight or flee.

What is this section about?

A. The connection between muscle relaxation and a peaceful state of mind.
or
B. The reasons why skill in fighting and fleeing helped our ancestors to survive.

324. If you have been cooped up sitting at a desk all day long without being able to run and exercise enough, the breathe and relax exercise won't be very successful. If you are restless from lack of exercise, get some exercise first. Do jumping jacks, jump rope, practice dance moves, run, or exercise in any other way until you feel comfortably tired.

What does the author recommend in this section?

A. Bring to your mind images of a very safe place, in order to help you relax.
or
B. If you're restless, work out some before trying to breathe and relax.

325. Here's another activity to prepare you for the breathe and relax exercise; it's called tense and relax. You focus your attention on a certain group of muscles in your body, and first you make them hard and tense and tight. You tense your muscles as if you were

a body builder trying to make the muscles look as big as possible. Then you relax them. You pay attention to the feeling of tension, and you notice how relaxation feels different. At first you tense your muscles hard. Then you tense them very lightly, and you notice the difference between a small amount of tension and great relaxation. You want to teach your brain to be very sensitive to different degrees of muscle tension and relaxation.

What's the point of this section?

A. Practicing relaxing the muscles many times each day for very short periods of time works best for some people.
or
B. To get ready to breathe and relax, purposely tense and relax your muscles, and teach your brain to recognize different degrees of relaxation.

326. Here's how to do the breathe and relax exercise. Sit or lie down. Close your eyes. Notice the rhythm of your breathing, without trying to breathe faster or slower or deeper or shallower than whatever comes naturally. Each time you breathe out, try to make some muscles in your body more relaxed than they were before. With each breath out, you try to make some

muscles less tense. If you notice that your mind has wandered from this, gently bring your focus back to this goal. Do this for however long you have decided to do it.

What's a summary of this section?

A. It's important not to get down on yourself if you find that your attention has wandered from relaxing the muscles each time you exhale.
or
B. The breathe and relax exercise consists in trying to get some muscles a little more relaxed each time you breathe out.

327. I have done this exercise for as short as a few seconds and as long as 20 minutes. I find that both short relaxations twenty or thirty times a day, and one or two longer relaxations per day, are both useful.

      I recommend NOT saving this exercise just for the times that you feel scared or angry or tense. If you do that, you might come to associate efforts to relax the muscles with tense feelings, and find that the exercise starts to bring on feelings of stress and tension. Instead, do the exercise to practice relaxation regularly. If you want to use it every once in a while as the remedy to too much fear, anger, or tension, that's fine as long as most of the practice comes at other times.

What's a summary of this section?

A. Do the breathe and relax exercise for both short and long periods, and do it regularly, not just when you are tense or scared or angry.
or
B. The most important part of the exercise is relaxing the muscles; tying this to the rhythm of breathing is an extra twist that may or may not make it more effective.

328. If a tutor and a student are doing this exercise together, I recommend doing it for one or two minutes. The tutor looks at a watch or clock and says when to start and stop. During the time that they do it, they are both silent. After the exercise, they can share with each other the answer to questions like these:
How pleasant was it?
How relaxed were you when you started, and when you finished? (You can use a scale of 10 where 0 is not at all relaxed and 10 is totally relaxed.)
Did your mind drift off the breathing and relaxing, and if so did you gently bring it back without getting down on yourself?
In which muscle groups did you find the most tension? Were you able to get those muscles very relaxed?

What's a summary of this section?

A. There are often benefits to meditating or relaxing with someone else rather than doing it all alone.
or
B. When a preceptor and student do the exercise together, they are silent for one or two minutes while doing it, and then they review with each other how it went.

Mastery for Breathe and Relax

1. At the first level, you have used this technique for a couple of minutes, and it looks as though your muscles are very relaxed while you are doing it – you're not fidgeting or looking tense. Plus, you report being able to keep your mind on the muscle relaxation most of the time, and that the activity was pleasant and relaxing for you.

2. At the second level, you have used this technique for 10 minutes on at least 3 occasions, for 2 minutes on at least 5 occasions, and for 2 or 3 seconds on at least 30 occasions. On each of these, you succeed at getting your muscles very relaxed, you keep your mind on the muscle relaxation efforts most of the time, and the experience is pleasant and relaxing for you.

3. At the third level, you have done everything in the previous two levels. In addition, you have made a habit of using Breathe and Relax in one of its forms daily in your life, and you report that it is pleasant and useful for you.

Chapter 28: Mind-Watching

329. Mind-watching is one of many ways of meditating. When you do it, you don't necessarily try to think of any particular thing. You just save some of your attention to observe what the rest of your mind is doing. You try to have a kind attitude toward yourself as you watch whatever your mind comes up with. Often you sit with eyes closed while doing this. Perhaps images, memories, worries, melodies of songs, decisions, dream-like fantasies, or any other thoughts come into your mind. You just notice what comes in and out of your mind.

What's a summary of this section?

A. To meditate with a mantra, you say to yourself a word like the word *one*, over and over, and pull your attention back to this if it drifts away.
or
B. The meditation taught in this chapter is to sit, close your eyes, and observe whatever thoughts come into your mind.

330. There are several reasons why this form of meditation is useful. First, it's often very relaxing just to let your mind do whatever it naturally tends to do, with your blessings. I sometimes feel an "unwinding" with this form of meditation, when the thoughts that had been held back get to come to mind and be aired. Second, it helps you learn to focus your attention better, if you practice noticing what you are paying attention to at any moment. And third, if some of the thoughts that come to mind are frightening or worrisome, they often become less scary when you calmly observe them for a while.

The three advantages this section lists for mind-watching are which of the following?

A. Relaxation, attention, and fear-reduction.
or
B. Productivity, lightheartedness, and a feeling of optimism.

331. Here's what a session of mind-watching might be like.
  I sit and close my eyes. I try to have a peaceful feeling, and a curious feeling, wondering what will come into my mind.
  I see myself at a swimming pool, and there is someone on a fairly high diving board, doing some very beautiful dives, making them look very easy. I see someone sitting at the side of the pool, someone I recognize.

I feel good to see this friend. All of a sudden this image leaves me, and I remember that I wanted to call someone today and invite the person to get together with me. But I don't know the person well, and I feel nervous about making this invitation. I just watch that thought, and then I hear some actual music coming from outside where someone is playing it loudly in his car. I let myself listen to it.

When the person in this example did some mind-watching, what types of thoughts came into his or her mind?

A. Imagining a lifelike scene, worrying about something the person wants to do in real life, and hearing an actual sound.
or
B. A religious thought, a memory of a school assignment, and a wish for something good that may happen.

332. When a tutor and a student do this exercise together, they just sit silently for a minute, or for two minutes, and let whatever comes to mind come to mind. At the end of that time, if they want to tell each other about any of the things that came to mind, they can do so. If everything that came to mind is private, they are free to be silent about what went through the mind.

What's an aspect of mind-watching that was written about in this section?

A. The part of the self that does the watching tries to be calm, accepting, and compassionate to oneself and others.
or
B. When two people do this together, they can tell each other afterwards as much or little as they want about which thoughts went through their minds.

Mastery for Mind-Watching

1. At the first level, you have used this technique for a couple of minutes. You are able to remember, afterward, some of the things that went through your mind. Plus, you report being able to maintain your observation of your mind's activity most of the time, and that the activity was pleasant and relaxing for you.

2. At the second level, you have used this technique for 10 minutes on at least 3 occasions, and for 2 minutes on at least 5 occasions. On each of these, you succeed at observing what your mind is doing most of the time, keeping a peaceful attitude toward your own thoughts, and making the

179

experience pleasant and relaxing for yourself.

3. At the third level, you have done everything in the previous two levels. In addition, you have made a habit of using mind-watching daily in your life, and you report that it is pleasant and useful for you.

Chapter 29: Other Ways of Relaxing or Meditating

333. The previous two chapters described two big ways of relaxing or meditating: one was relaxing your muscles each time you breathe out. The other was observing your own thoughts with a serene attitude toward what your mind does.

This chapter tells of several other ways of relaxing or meditating. You can use these for any of several purposes. One is to recuperate from stress – to settle your nerves. Another is to practice focusing your mind, rather than being scattered. Another is to prepare yourself for something you'll be doing later. And another is to practice a certain attitude or way of being that you think is good and worth doing more often.

What's a summary of this section?

A. The world is a very stressful place, and this is why people need special methods of calming their nerves.
or
B. This chapter will go over several different ways of relaxing or meditating; they can be used for several different purposes.

Repeating a mantra

334. A mantra is a word or an image or anything else you repeatedly focus on while meditating. For some reason, people often seem to pick mantras which are words with sounds made by the letters o and n and m. One researcher asked people to use the word *one* as a mantra.

To meditate with a mantra, you sit down and relax, close your eyes, and repeat to yourself silently, the word *one*, (or some other word that you choose) every few seconds. You keep going for some preset length of time (say, 1 to 20 minutes). As with other meditation methods, you don't "try hard" to keep focusing on the word; if you notice that your attention has strayed, (which most people do, naturally) you don't get down on yourself, but just gently bring your attention back to repeating the word *one*.

What's a point made in this section?

A. Having your attention stray from the mantra is natural and not something to get upset about.
or
B. The rhythm of your footsteps while walking has something in common with the rhythm of a mantra.

335. At first glance, it may seem silly to sit and repeat a word to yourself. Why is this not just a boring waste of time?

Thousands of people have used this technique not only to have some pleasant and restful moments, but to also to function better after meditating. Some of these people even have felt that such meditation had huge positive effects on their lives. Here are some guesses as to why. The neutral word gets your mind off the problems and worries of the day. The repetitive stimulus somehow tends to be relaxing. Being aware of your focus of attention, and focusing on one stimulus, gives practice in focusing your attention. Focusing on something that is not particularly exciting or interesting lets you practice breaking a dependence on ever increasing stimulation, that our world of electronic distractions tend to foster.

The purpose of this section is to

A. tell possible reasons why repeating a word like *one* to yourself could be not a boring waste of time, but very useful,
or
B. suggest ways that you can find the mantra that is best for your particular mental makeup?

Meditation with movement

336. Lots of forms of meditation involve something that is rhythmic and repetitive – such as the rhythmic repetition of breathing, or of saying a word. What about getting up and moving in a rhythmic and repetitive way? Doing this can achieve the positive effects of exercise and meditation at the same time. This form of meditation is particularly useful when you aren't tired from doing physical work, but you have pent-up energy from having to sit for a long time (such as sitting in classes at school or sitting at a desk at work).

What's the main point of this section?

A. If you meditate while moving, you can accomplish the benefits of exercise and meditation simultaneously.
or
B. One of the benefits of meditation using a repetitive stimulus is that you increase your resistance to boredom.

337. Almost any movement you can imagine works well for this meditation. If you've ever seen people do Tai Chi, you might imitate the slow and graceful movements of this form of meditation. You can do a slow version of "jumping jacks," where you lift the hands from the sides to

overhead, while stepping the legs apart and back together. You can march in place. If you've been sitting in the same position a long time, it's great to move your shoulders up and down and to move your head around to loosen up your neck and shoulder muscles. You can use any dance step. You can simply walk.

What's a summary of this section?

A. Sitting at a computer or doing homework tends to make people hold their heads in the same position, which leads to tight muscles and headaches.
or
B. To meditate with movement, you can use just about any movement pattern you can think of.

Visualizing relaxing scenes

338. Are there places, real or imaginary, that are associated in your mind with a feeling of peace and relaxation? If so, a useful technique is to go to one of those places in your imagination and enjoy the feelings connected with that place.

Here's a short catalogue of scenes – are any of them relaxing for you?

Being warm while snow gently falls

Being near a clear flowing mountain stream

Standing on a mountaintop

Lying on a beach, listening to ocean waves

Seeing a starry sky at night

Seeing the colors in autumn leaves

Lying in bed on a morning when you have no responsibilities

Someone patting you on the shoulder

The technique described in this section is to

A. take scenes that at first are not relaxing to you, and make them relaxing,
or
B. find scenes that are already associated with relaxation for you, and call them to mind when you relax?

Imagining acts of kindness

339. Just imagining acts of kindness has a soothing and calming effect for most people.

To use this technique, you get in mind (or on a piece of paper) a list of different types of acts of kindness, such as the one in the next section. Then you go through this list one by one, and for each type of act, you imagine someone doing a specific act of kindness of that sort for someone else. Thus you are making up very specific images that are examples of the general categories. The examples can be memories of your kind acts toward others, others' kind acts toward you, acts you have witnessed, acts you have read about, or acts you simply make up during the meditation session.

To use the technique described in the last section,

A. you remember or make up specific examples of several different types of kind acts,
or
B. you simply think about the general concept of kindness, without landing on specific images?

340. Below is an incomplete list of types of kind acts. Feel free to add to it.

Types of Kind Acts

1. Helping
2. Complimenting, congratulating
3. Expressing thanks
4. Being a good listener
5. Teaching, and learning from
6. Forgiving
7. Consoling
8. Spending time with, keeping company, inviting
9. Being cheerful, approving, funny, or fun-loving with someone
10. Being affectionate
11. Giving
12. Doing fun things with someone
13. Working together
14. Working to benefit someone else
15. Being assertive, not spoiling

How does the author recommend that you use this list in a meditation technique?

A. Look at the list, and visualize someone doing an example of each of these things with someone else,
or
B. read the phrases to yourself slowly, over and over?

341. How does the "visualizing acts of kindness" meditation help? Much fear, anger, and other bad feelings have their roots in cruel and hostile acts, either real or imagined. Thinking about people being kind, caring, and considerate to each other can create a safe, pleasant feeling.

In addition, the principle of "positive fantasy rehearsal" tells us that imagining acts of kindness probably helps us to be kinder.

The purpose of this section is

A. to point out that the more vividly and concretely you imagine, the more effective this technique is,
or

B. to explain that imagining acts of kindness both reduces bad feelings and helps us to be better people?

The good will meditation

342. This technique also uses the fact that kindness and good will between people bring about a feeling of calm and security.

 For this technique, you begin with yourself, and wish three good things for yourself:

1. May I become the best that I can become.
2. May I give and receive kindness.
3. May I live with compassion and peace.

 After this, you visualize another person – perhaps a family member or friend – or even an enemy! You wish the same three things for that person. You let your mind go from one person to another, wishing these things for each one of them.

A summary of the technique described here is that you

A. visualize beautiful and relaxing scenery,
or
B. wish for one person after another to do good things and have good things done to him or her?

The pleasant dreams technique

343. Can you imagine having a very pleasant dream – not one like an exciting action movie, but one filled with soothing images of peacefulness, kindness, beauty, safety, and security? This is the type of dream that would not wake you up, and you would not want to wake up from it. The pleasant dream technique is to make up for yourself such a fantasy, while you are awake, and let it continue to unfold for as long as you want.

The pleasant dreams technique is done by

A. sitting and letting any fantasies come to your mind that happen in, or
B. purposely constructing fantasies of peacefulness, kindness, and beauty?

344. Here's an example of what a pleasant dreams fantasy might sound like.

 "It's early morning, and it's cool and pleasant. I'm sitting in an outdoor amphitheater with many people, and we are all reading and meditating upon the most important ideas on how to live well. Each person is striving to make good decisions. Then there's a beautiful sunrise, and I watch it with a feeling of gratitude for the universe and for being able to live. Now I'm with three very good friends, and we are doing some physical work that is very useful and at the same time very good exercise, and at the same time we can talk and laugh with one another.

Now my friends and I are in a kitchen, cooking a great breakfast, and we each know what to do, and the jobs go totally smoothly, and we work together joyously. Now we're sitting and having breakfast together, very glad to be together, very much enjoying each other's company.

The person who is constructing this pleasant dream-like fantasy is keeping in mind that

A. stories that people enjoy tend to have some conflict in them,
or
B. in the pleasant dreams activity, you want to have a feeling of safety and security from start to finish?

345. The pleasant dreams narrative we began in the previous section continues.

"Now I go to a beautiful and simple room, where I think and write. I am doing my part to work in maintaining a world where all the needed work gets done, where there is work for everyone to do, where everyone has enough of what they need, and where there are incentives for everyone to be productive. I feel great pride in being able to contribute to this wonderful society.

"Now I go outside, and it is winter. There are no cars, and all the streets are covered with ice, and people ice skate to wherever they want to go. I put on my skates and feel that I can move almost effortlessly, fast but very safely. I see friends, and we skate together, drifting from side to side, feeling invigorated by the cold air but warm from the skating."

In this example of the pleasant dreams technique, there is

A. a great deal of suspense and danger,
or
B. not much suspense and no danger, but lots of positive feelings?

346. When you are using the pleasant dreams technique, you don't have to worry that things are consistent. The time, the setting, or the characters, or even who you are in the dream can shift whenever you want, just as in real dreams.

At first it may be difficult to make up stories like those you want to use in the pleasant dreams exercise. But composing for yourself these fantasies of beauty, peace, kindness, and security is an art that can improve with practice. And, I believe, the better you get at this skill, the greater an underlying feeling of calm and peace you can achieve.

I think that the pleasant dreams exercise is an especially good one to do while lying in bed waiting to go to sleep. This is especially true once you have practiced enough that it's very easy to come up with the pleasant fantasies. I recommend practicing this technique in the daytime, when you are fully awake and alert. It's another exercise whose results are good to write down and read.

The author feels that making up fantasies for the pleasant dreams technique is

A. effortless, from the beginning, or
B. a skill that takes practice to cultivate?

The psychological skills meditation

347. To use this technique, you get in mind (or find on paper or in a file, or on this page of this book) the following psychological skills:

Productivity
Joyousness
Kindness
Honesty
Fortitude
Good individual decisions
Good joint decisions or conflict-resolution
Nonviolence
Respectful talk

Friendship-building
Self-discipline
Loyalty
Conservation
Self-care
Compliance
Positive fantasy rehearsal
Courage

These are the psychological skill groups that form the outline for all the books in this series.

This section

A. tells how to do the psychological skills meditation, or
B. tells the psychological skills that you will use for the meditation, but does not yet tell how to do the meditation?

348. To do the meditation, you sit quietly and relax. Then you let the word "productivity" come to mind, and you imagine yourself or someone else working, and feeling good about

the work. You can remember real examples, or make them up. Then you let the word "joyousness" come to mind, and very vividly imagine some concrete, specific joyous behavior. Then on you go, through the complete list of skills.

A summary of this technique is that

A. you sit quietly with eyes closed, and observe whatever thoughts come into your mind,
or
B. you go through a list of psychological skills, visualizing a positive example of each and imagining celebrating it?

Simple rest

349. The last technique is simply taking a few minutes and resting, in whatever way you want. You don't try to do anything in particular, other than to take it easy! As when using the mind-watching method, you think or imagine whatever you want. Unlike when using that method, you don't even try to observe or notice what your mind does, unless you feel like it. You can avoid trying to do anything, or you can try to do anything you want. This is perhaps what most people usually do when they lie down at night to sleep.

What's a summary of this section?

A. Some meditative techniques require a long time to master.
or
B. In the simple rest technique, you just rest, defining the word *rest* in whatever way feels best for you.

350. Simple rest may be harder than it appears. For many people in today's technological society, an opportunity to rest gets translated into checking text messages and emails, turning on the television, plugging into a music player, starting up an electronic game, or looking at a movie trailer. This is not what is referred to as "simple rest!" Resting means stopping activity for a while rather than directing activity to the closest electronic device.

This section implies that

A. When people try to rest, many of them end up getting distracted by electronic technology,
or
B. resting is most useful when you have first done something productive?

351. When you meditate or relax, you usually don't want to fall asleep. A way not to fall asleep is do physical exercise very fast for a minute or so before relaxing. If you first get

yourself panting and get your heart pounding, it's much easier to sit with your eyes closed without falling asleep.

If you find yourself falling asleep very quickly when you try to meditate or relax, pay attention to the message your body is giving you. The message is, "You need to get more sleep at night!" Many people would function much better if they slept longer – sometimes even an hour or two longer.

In this section the author gives two pieces of advice about how not to fall asleep during your meditation or relaxation. They are:

A. Exercise before meditating, and get more sleep at night.
or
B. Sit up straight rather than slouching, and do not sit on something too soft and comfortable?

352. This chapter has explained several techniques of relaxation or meditation. I recommend that you try out each of them. Often as little as one minute is long enough to get the flavor of the technique. You can gradually work your way up to longer sessions.

There is one main reason why these techniques don't work: that people don't do them. If you want these to work, you will have to spend time practicing them, for an average of something more than zero minutes per day!

The author believes that the most common reason that techniques of relaxation and meditation don't work is that

A. some people just don't have the natural talent to learn to relax or meditate;
or
B. people don't invest the time it takes to benefit from these techniques?

Mastery for Other Ways of Relaxing

1. For any one of these techniques, at the first level you can tell someone else how to do the technique, and you have used the technique successfully at least once, in a way that is pleasant and relaxing for you.

2. For the second level, explain how to do the technique again, and use the technique at least ten times in pleasant and relaxing way.

3. For the third level, have used the technique at least 30 times, and have incorporated it into your life so that you use it at least once a week. Furthermore, be able to report on how

the use of the technique has helped
your conduct of life.

Chapter 30: Task-Switching

353. Imagine a certain type of brain challenge. Someone shows you numbers like the following. We're going to call each of them a *stimulus*.

2

111

3333

Suppose your task is to just say what numeral is in each number, regardless of how many times it's repeated. So the answer to the ones above would be 2, 1, and 3.

Now the task switches. Now you have to look at numbers like these, but say *how many digits* are presented. So you see stimuli like

33

4

2222

and the answers are now 2, 1, and 4 – because 33 has 2 digits, 4 has 1 digit, and 2222 has 4 digits.

Now suppose you have to go back and forth frequently between the two types of tasks – saying the numeral in the stimulus, or saying how many digits. This is called a *task-switching* exercise.

The purpose of this section was to

A. explain why task switching is a worthwhile thing to do, or
B. give an example of a task-switching challenge?

354. There are lots of task-switching challenges that people have made up. Here's another one.

For the letter-number pairs you see: ignore the number, and say whether the letter is a vowel or a consonant.

e6

j5

7i

So the answers are vowel, consonant, vowel.

Now the task switches, and the directions change, even though the stimuli are very similar. Now your task is to ignore the letter, and say whether the number is odd or even.

u8

2k

a9

So now the answers are even, even, odd.

These tasks may seem straightforward, but if you do them in a timed trial, as fast as you possibly can, while aiming for zero errors, while the task switches back and forth at unpredictable times, you will find your brain working very hard.

What does the challenge described in this section have in common with the one in the previous section?

A. Both have you deal with similar stimuli, but have you switch back and forth between different directions on what to do with them.
or
B. Both of them have you decide whether numbers are odd or even.

355. Here's another task-switching challenge that looks totally different. One person is the leader, and the other is the follower. The leader demonstrates two motions – for example, jumping jacks and knee bends. The leader switches back and forth between these two motions. If

the leader says "same," the follower's task is to do the same motion. If the leader says "opposite," the follower's task is to do the motion the leader is *not* doing. Thus the follower sees the same sorts of stimuli to respond to, but the directions change.

This section describes

A. task-switching with sounds,
or
B. task switching with motions?

356. Why should anyone practice task-switching? People who are good at task-switching tend to also be good at other skills called *executive functions*: making and carrying out plans, thinking before acting, organizing yourself, working toward goals without getting sidetracked, and making careful decisions. Of course, these skills are really important for success in life. There's also some evidence that all these skills, including task-switching, give a workout to a certain brain region – the prefrontal cortex.

What's a summary of this section?

A. People are interested in task-switching because it's one of several important skills called executive functions.
or

B. In task-switching, you have to hold in mind what you're supposed to be doing, as well as doing it.

357. What if the part of the brain that does these important executive skills is like a muscle? What if by practicing task-switching, you can strengthen your skill not only in other task-switching challenges, but also in much more important skills, such as careful planning and decision-making?

Although this idea makes some sense, it may or may not be true. People haven't done enough scientific research (at the time of this writing) to know for sure whether practicing task-switching will help your brain with things other than task-switching.

What is the main point of this section?

A. Practicing with task-switching could help you with lots of other important skills, but we don't know this for sure.
or
B. There are lots of task-switching challenges in real life, for example when worksheets at school have different directions at different points.

358. So at this time, we're not sure how many benefits come from doing lots of practice with task-switching. But what if we build task-switching practice into other drills that you should practice with anyway, like math facts or reading or other school challenges?

For example: The task is to add the following numbers.

7 9

4 4

8 7

Now the task becomes to subtract the second number from the first.

6 3

9 6

18 9

Do you see how this is a task-switching challenge, where you have the same sorts of stimuli, but the directions change? While you're practicing task-switching, you're also practicing math facts, and this may help you, even if the task-switching doesn't. There are other ways of practicing task-switching with math facts, math word problems, or reading words.

What's the strategy that this section recommends?

A. Practicing task-switching with drills that are useful, so that you'll get something useful out of it one way or another.

or

B. Just having faith that improving in any difficult task has to be good for your brain.

359. When straightforward math facts used in task-switching become easy, you can practice math facts with negative numbers. (You can skip this section if doing math facts with negative numbers is too hard or easy for where you are in math now.)

Here's a summary of the rules you use for math facts with negative numbers.

1. The absolute value of a number is the value it has if you ignore any minus sign. So the absolute value of -3 is 3. The absolute value of +3 is 3 (or +3) also. (+3 means the same as 3.)

2. To add numbers of like sign, add the absolute values and give the answer the sign of the two numbers you're adding. So to add –3 and –4, we get –7.

3. To add numbers of unlike sign, we subtract the absolute values and give the answer the sign of the number with the higher absolute value. So –7 plus 3 = -4. –2 plus 5=+3.

4. To subtract a second number from a first, change the sign of the second number and add. So 4 minus –2 is the same as 4 plus 2 or 6. –6 minus 4 is –6 plus –4, or –10.

5. When multiplying or dividing, go ahead and multiply and divide the absolute values; give a positive sign to the answer when the two numbers are of like sign, and a negative sign to the answer when the numbers are of unlike sign. So –3 times 2 = -6. –3 times –4 = 12. 10 divided by –2 is –5. –10 divided by 2 is also –5. –12 divided by –3 is +4.

Practicing enough to get very fast and accurate at using these rules gives you lots of task-switching workouts. Even if such practice doesn't help your executive functions, it will help you in math!

What's the purpose of this section?

A. For the author to explain the meaning of negative numbers, for example as temperatures below zero or when you owe money rather than owning it.

or

B. For the author to give the rules for combining numbers when one or more is negative, and to advise practice with using these rules as task-switching practice.

360. Are you interested in music? If so, here's another task-switching exercise for you. You look at a piece of music that has notes on both the bass and the treble clef. For the first measure, you name the notes on the treble clef. Then you name the notes for the first measure on the bass clef. Then it's back to the treble clef for the second measure, and so forth. As with other task-switching challenges, the stimuli look very similar, but the notes are read differently for the two clefs. You have to hold in mind which of two systems to use in responding to the stimuli, at the same time that you're responding to them.

What's a summary of this section?

A. Another useful task-switching activity is naming musical notes, switching between the treble clef and the bass clef.
or
B. The treble clef names the lines on the staff e, g, b, d, f from bottom to top, whereas the bass clef names similar lines g, b, d, f, and a from bottom to top.

361. If you are working with a tutor or mental fitness trainer, we may supply you with some drills that are meant to be right for wherever you are in your education, that you can use to give yourself a task-switching workout. Some of these are written in a book called *Manual for Task-Switching or Set-Shifting*. If you do such exercises, you can see for yourself whether practicing task-switching seems to help you with thinking before acting, making careful plans, making good decisions, and any other skills other than task-switching itself!

This section invites the reader to do which of the following?

A. Get into good physical condition, so that you can do task-switching with movements easily,
or
B. Work with a tutor on task-switching drills, and see if your ability to plan and organize and decide also improve.

Mastery for Task-Switching

1. At the first level, do at least 3 different types of task-switching activity, and see if you can feel the type of mental effort that they have in common.

2. At the second level, work on a task switching task until you have increased your accuracy and speed by a level specified by your trainer. You are aware of what "executive

functions" are, and you notice whether task-switching training seems to help with other executive functions.

3. At the third level, you work on one task further, or on several tasks further, until you have increased your accuracy and speed to a still higher level specified by your trainer. You notice further whether your increased proficiency in task switching seems to help with other executive functions.

Chapter 31: Biofeedback

362. Biofeedback means measuring something that your body is doing, and seeing if you can control it. For example, you can measure your muscle tension, your heart rate, your fingertip temperature, or the amount that your fingertips sweat. All of these variables give you information on how excited or relaxed you are. As you get more excited, your muscles get more tense, your heart rate goes up, your fingertip temperature gets colder, and your fingers sweat more. As you get more relaxed, your muscles get looser, your heart rate falls, and your fingertips get both warmer and less sweaty.

When you get more relaxed, your fingertip temperature tends to

A. go up,
or
B. go down?

363. What's the point of learning to control how excited or relaxed you are? Fear and anger can be very troublesome when their levels get too high. You can turn down the level of fear or anger simply by calming yourself – by making your body more relaxed. At other times, increasing

your excitement and enthusiasm helps you perform better than if you are drifty and dreamy. You want to reach whatever level of excitement or relaxation will help you perform best at whatever you're doing. Learning to control your body's excitement level helps in this very important goal.

What's a summary of this section?

A. Your degree of excitement is controlled by a part of your body called the autonomic nervous system.
or
B. Learning to relax or excite yourself helps to control fear and anger and to perform best at whatever you are doing.

364. You can measure your fingertip temperature with a thermometer such as "Doctor Lowenstein's Stress Thermometer" that is available over the Internet for about $30. The thermometer has a wire coming out of it with a tip called the probe. You hold the tip of the thermometer's probe between your fingertips, and wait about half a minute for the heat from your fingertips to go into the probe. You read your fingertip temperature from the display on the thermometer.

What was the purpose of this section?

A. To tell how to measure fingertip temperature,
or
B. To tell what fingertip temperatures to aim for?

365. The fingertip temperature is a measure of how relaxed you are only if the temperature of the room is in the region of 70 to 74 degrees Fahrenheit. If the room is too cold, your fingertips will get cold to save heat for your body; if the room is too hot, your fingertips will get warm to try to get rid of the excess heat. But in the region of about 72 degrees, fingertip temperature varies depending mostly on how relaxed or excited you are. So the first thing you do when you're doing temperature biofeedback is to measure the temperature of the air in the room. You just let the tip of the probe hang in the air for a minute or so, and see whether you're in the right range.

This section tells

A. why your fingertip temperature goes up when you get more relaxed,
or
B. why you should measure the temperature of the air in the room

before doing temperature biofeedback?

366. Here's a simple way of doing temperature biofeedback. First measure your fingertip temperature. Then relax, using the "breathe and relax" technique or any other technique you want. It also helps to imagine your hands becoming nice and warm. Watch your fingertip temperature as you do this. See if the fingertip temperature goes up, and see how much you can get the temperature to rise.

How did this section suggest doing temperature biofeedback?

A. See if you can get your fingertip temperature to go down by getting yourself excited.
or
B. Relax, and watch what happens to fingertip temperature as you do so.

367. There have been times that I have started with fingertip temperatures in the 70's and have ended up after about 10 minutes of relaxation with temperatures over 95. More often, the temperature starts in the 80's and goes up to somewhere over 90. Even making the temperature go up by two or three degrees can be a sign of relaxation. Where the temperature starts out and where it ends up depend

upon lots of things that vary from person to person. If over time, you find that you are learning to raise the temperature more and more, that is something to celebrate.

What's a summary of this section?

A. Celebrate any increases in temperature with relaxation, and celebrate if you are learning to raise the temperature more and more.
or
B. Learn to raise the fingertip temperature to over 95 degrees Fahrenheit.

368. It's fun to play with moving your state of excitement in both directions. You can get yourself excited or think about scary things and see if your fingertip temperature falls. But fingertip temperature takes several minutes to move very far. Fingertip sweat, on the other hand, responds to changes in excitement very quickly. If you have access to a machine that measures this, you can relax or startle yourself and see the changes within seconds. The biofeedback program called "Journey to Wild Devine" comes with a device that measures your fingertip sweat. Because it measures this by seeing how well the skin conducts tiny bits of electric current, this is called "skin conductance level." Learning to raise

and lower your skin conductance level, or SCL, is another way to learn to control how relaxed or excited you are.

The author thinks that the best way to measure quick changes in excitement and relaxation is

A. fingertip temperature,
or
B. fingertip sweat, also known as skin conductance level or SCL?

369. If you buy all the most advanced biofeedback equipment, you can end up spending thousands of dollars. But there's a way of doing biofeedback without spending anything, if you have a watch or other timepiece that measures seconds. You count your heart rate. Then you relax and measure your heart rate again. You see whether you are able to make your heart rate go down by relaxing.

What's an advantage of using heart rate biofeedback that is mentioned in this section?

A. Heart rate changes fairly quickly when you get more excited or relaxed.
or
B. You can measure heart rate without having to buy anything.

370. You measure your heart rate by feeling your pulse and counting the beats. A good place to feel your pulse is on your wrist, on the side that the palm of your hand is on, and on the side that is closer to your thumb than to your little finger. Feel around with your first three fingers until you feel a beat. Notice the time, start counting, and count until fifteen seconds have gone by; multiply by four to get your heart rate in beats per minute.

The purpose of this section was to

A. tell how to measure your heart rate, or
B. explain which nerves tell your heart to go faster or slower depending on how excited you are?

371. There's another measure that's even easier. You simply notice and rate how relaxed you feel. How tense are your muscles? How much do you feel either worried or restless or excited? How much do you feel either scared or angry or keyed up or wired? Versus: how much do you feel a nice, peaceful, calm, secure, relaxed feeling? If 0 is least relaxed, and 10 is most relaxed, how relaxed do you feel? To use this measure, you take a few seconds to look inside yourself, and rate how relaxed you feel. Then use some method of relaxation, and see how much your relaxation rating

rises. It can also be fun to see whether variables like your heart rate or skin temperature change in the predicted way as your relaxation rating does.

What's the point of this section?

A. Getting your muscles less tense is an important way to relax yourself.
or
B. Rather than measuring temperature or pulse or such things, you can simply rate how relaxed you feel before and after using some relaxation method.

Mastery for Biofeedback

1. At the first level, spend some enjoyable time seeing if you can make some measure go up or down. On at least one occasion, move the variable number in the direction you want it to go.

2. At the second level, be successful on at least 10 occasions at moving a measured variable into the goal region for relaxation that you would like it to go.

3. At the third level, be successful on at least 20 more occasions at moving a variable into the goal region for relaxation that you would like it to go. Plus, use the skill of affecting your

level of arousal on at least 5 occasions
in real life.

Chapter 32: Concentrate, Rate, and Concentrate

372. People have tried various ways of using biofeedback to help people learn to concentrate better. They have measured something that the brain is doing, and have had the person concentrate on a task, such as reading or doing math. The measure is supposed to tell how well the person is concentrating. The person works to improve concentration by improving the number a machine displays.

What was the purpose of this section?

A. To tell what the concentrate, rate, and concentrate exercise is.
or
B. To tell how some people have tried biofeedback to improve concentration skills.

373. At the time of this writing, however, I believe that we can measure your concentration more accurately than any machine that tries to tell what your brain is doing. We do this by having you perform some task that takes concentration, and measuring how well you do in it. For example, if you do a standard minute of math facts, or a minute of touch typing practice, or a minute of vocabulary exercises, how many do you get right and how many do you get wrong? We define better

concentration as getting better scores on the task. One way of getting a score is by figuring out the number you got right, minus the number you got wrong, divided by the number of minutes you worked. If you do these trials over and over, you probably improve your performance. You may improving your general skill in concentration, along with getting better at math or typing or vocabulary or whatever the task involves.

The author believes that the best measures of concentration are

A. brain waves as measured by a machine,
or
B. performance on tasks that require concentration?

374. I have written very simple computer programs for practice on math facts, touch typing, and vocabulary that will let you practice these skills while at the same time practicing concentration. The computer gives a measure of your performance. There are many other computer programs available that do similar tasks.

What's a summary of this section?

A. Vocabulary building is one of the major keys to success in academic work.
or
B. Computer programs are available, that will measure your performance on concentration tasks.

375. But there's another way of practicing and measuring concentration that requires no equipment. You pick any sort of concentration task that you need to work on for a while. For students, the most obvious choice is homework. You do the task for a while (this is trial 1), and rate how well you concentrated, using a scale from 0 to 10. 0 means you accomplished nothing; 10 means you got a lot done, very efficiently. Then you do the task some more (in trial 2), and rate your concentration again. The trials can be anywhere from a minute to half an hour long. You continue with more trials. When you notice that you have concentrated particularly well, you ask yourself, "How did I do that?" You congratulate yourself. And you try to use the same methods of concentrating, or even better ones, on the next trials. This is the concentrate, rate, and concentrate exercise.

How do you do the concentrate, rate, and concentrate exercise?

A. You alternate between doing work and rating how well you concentrated on it.
or
B. You meditate on a certain question, and you keep coming back to the central question when your mind gets off the subject.

376. Here's a scale that you can use to rate your concentration:

0=Very poor
2=Poor
4=Not very good, so-so
6=OK
8=Good
10=Very good

You can use odd numbers or numbers like 5.5 if you want. You can give any number from 0 to 10.

Suppose your mind wandered a lot and you didn't get much done, and you felt like you were mainly wasting time. But you did get a little something accomplished. You feel your concentration was poor. About what rating would you give yourself?

A. 4
or
B. 2?

377. How can you tell whether you concentrated well? You primarily look

at how much you got done, how fast you were able to do it, and how well you did it. How much your mind wandered from the subject is less easy to measure. If your mind wanders a lot, but you pull your focus back on task very quickly, you can still work efficiently; efficient work is the main purpose of concentration.

The author feels that the more reliable way to rate your concentration is by

A. the speed and accuracy of your work,
or
B. how many times your mind wanders off task?

378. It's good to keep some records as you do this exercise. Otherwise, it's hard to even remember whether you did it or not. The simplest way to keep records is with two columns, where one is the trial number and the other is the concentration rating. For example:

Trial Number	Concentration Rating
1	6
2	8
3	4
4	7

The trials don't even have to be the same length of time. They don't even have to be on the same task!

In this simple way of keeping records, how many numbers do you write down for each trial?

A. Two,
or
B. Four?

379. If you want to keep a little more detailed records, you can write down four things: the trial number, the time, the task you were doing, and your concentration rating. Here's a sample:

Trial: 1
Time: 630 to 645 pm
Task: Math homework
Rating: 6

Trial: 2
Time: 645 to 700 pm
Task: Math homework
Rating: 9

In going from two variables to a four variable system of recording, the two variables that were added were what?

A. The time of the trial and the task you were doing,
or
B. Whether you were writing during the trial, and how much persistence power you felt you had when the trial began?

380. If you want, you can set a kitchen timer or some other type of time to go off at regular intervals. This way you can keep the time of each trial the same. But I think that the simpler you can make this activity, the more likely you are to do it. It's not crucial that each trial last the same length of time. You can stop and rate your productivity whenever you feel like it.

What's a summary of this section?

A. If you do this activity often, you should notice that the task gets more and more efficiently done over time.
or
B. You can use a timer, but the author feels that having intervals of exactly the same length is not crucial to this exercise.

381. We try to figure out ways, for most of the exercises in this book, that two people can do them together, especially when the two people are a tutor and a student who are connected by phone. Here are two ways to do this for concentrate, rate, and concentrate.

    The first is by using brief trials, done out loud over the phone. The trainer gives the trainee math facts questions, such as 7+9, or touch typing questions such as what finger for q, what finger for k, or any other questions that require concentration

and speed. The trainee does these for 3 or 4 one-minute trials. The trainee rates his or her concentration after each trial. Then, the trainer lets the trainee know how many he or she got right and wrong during the minute. You see whether the trainee's ratings correspond to the actual (right-wrong)/minute that the trainer calculated.

What's a summary of this method?

A. The student does a fantasy rehearsal of doing the concentrate, rate, and concentrate exercise.
or
B. The tutor arranges 3 or 4 one-minute drills, that they do over the phone, and the student rates concentration; afterwards, the ratings are compared with the performance records.

382. Here's a second way that a tutor and student can do the exercise together. This is particularly good when the student has lots of pressing homework that must get done. They connect by phone as usual. But then they each get started on their work, and they work on it silently, still connected by phone. About every 5 or 10 minutes, the tutor ends the trial by speaking over the phone, and each of them rates himself or herself on concentration. The student briefly

explains why the rating is what it is. They do this for more trials, until the phone session is over.

In this method,

A. The tutor and student each do the concentrate, rate, and concentrate activity with their own work while connected by phone, in a session that is mostly silent.
or
B. The student does the concentrate, rate, and concentrate exercise on his or her own time, and reports this to the tutor in the next session.

383. Here are some techniques to help you concentrate; you can use the exercise to see whether they help.

1. Rather than just reading a textbook, jot down questions and answers over what you are reading; then go back and read the questions and see if you can get the answers – test yourself!

2. When you are studying anything, don't just passively take in information; look away from what you are reading and see if you can repeat to yourself the important things. Try doing the "reflections exercise" with each paragraph you read.

3. See if it helps to make vivid mental pictures of what you are studying.

4. When you are doing math, read every word of the textbook's explanations, and work the sample problems done in the text, before tackling homework problems.

5. Get into an environment with as few distractions as possible. Turn off phones, text messages, pop-up messages, music, and any other electronic distraction. Try to get away from human distractions.

What's one piece of advice the author gives in this section?

A. Rather than passively taking in information, frequently test yourself in some way to see if you have mastered it.
or
B. Let someone else observe you and point out to you if you are doing things other than focusing on your task.

Mastery for the Concentrate, Rate, and Concentrate Exercise

1. At the first level, you have done this exercise in some form for a total of at least 6 trials, some of which are done in the presence (counting the phone presence) of a trainer or tester.

2. At the second level, you have done this exercise on at least 5 different occasions, for a total of at least 20 trials, some of which have been in the presence (counting phone) of a trainer or tester. At this level you should have noticed more control over your concentration, and some improved concentration.

3. At the third level, you do this exercise regularly for at least a few weeks, for example every time you do homework. At this level your self-monitoring should have noticeably improved your concentration skill.

Chapter 33: Responding to Criticism

384. Criticism can range from immature name calling – for example, "You're a dork!" to helpful instruction – for example, "You could improve this section of your book by making this sentence clearer." Criticism attempts to point out to us that we are imperfect or that we need to improve something.

Being criticized is one of the toughest situations for most people to handle. It can lead people to do whatever the critic wants, trying to please the critic (and in the process, rewarding the critic for being critical). It can lead to lots of getting down on oneself. It can lead people to be very defensive and claim with great emotion that the critic is wrong. (This is sometimes just what the stimulus-seeking critic is wanting, and can also reward the critic for being critical!) Criticism can lead people to feel very bad, for a long time. It can lead them to try to get revenge. It can lead to violence. Many people respond to it in ways that harm themselves or others.

What's a summary of this section?

A. Criticism, which points out to us that we are imperfect, is often very difficult to handle well.
or

B. Handling criticism, like any other skill, can be improved with practice.

385. The key to handling criticism well is to cultivate a certain attitude toward criticism, a certain way of thinking about it. Here is what that attitude is NOT:

It's terrible that this person criticized me! The person is trying to dominate me! I can't let the person do that! I need to prove the person wrong, in order not to be defeated and humiliated! Or, I need to dominate the other person in some way. If I can't do that, that's terrible! I must save face, at all costs!

What's the main idea of this section?

A. It's good to be able to tell the difference between constructive criticism and nonconstructive criticism.
or
B. An attitude that makes criticism most difficult to handle is a great fear of being dominated, losing face, and being humiliated.

386. The attitude that makes criticism easier to handle well sounds more like this:

I know I'm imperfect, just as everyone else is. If the criticism gives me some information that is helpful to me, I want to use it. If it doesn't give me useful information, but the critic had good will to me, I want to be relaxed and polite. If it doesn't give me useful information, and the critic was just trying to hurt my feelings, I want to avoid rewarding the critic. People can think whatever they want, and I don't need to change this person's opinion.

What's the key attitude that the author thinks is central to handling criticism well?

A. I know I'm imperfect; I want to stay cool while deciding on the best response to this criticism.
or
B. Right back at you.

387. The responding to criticism exercise lets you practice several standard ways of answering a critic. These ways of responding are usually compatible with staying cool and not feeling an urgent need to defend yourself. You start with an imagined criticism, and you practice responding in any of several listed ways that are appropriate. Not all of the ways of responding on the list may be appropriate, for any one criticism. If so, you just say that you don't think that response applies here. There are 10 ways of responding on the list; they

can be remembered by the mnemonic TP-Paarisec.

What's a summary of this section?

A. Families that exchange a large amount of criticism tend to have more mental health problems.
or
B. To do the responding to criticism exercise, you listen to a criticism and then practice making up several different ways of responding to it.

388. Here are the 10 ways of responding to criticism on the TP-Paarisec list:

1. Thank you.
2. Permission-giving.
3. Planning to ponder or problem-solve.
4. Agreeing with part of criticism.
5. Asking for more specific criticism.
6. Reflection.
7. "I want" statement.
8. Silent eye contact.
9. Explaining the reason.
10. Criticizing the critic.

The purpose of this section was simply to

A. Defend the attitude of nondefensiveness.
or

B. List the ways of responding to criticism that the author feels are worth practicing.

389. Let's give an example of each of these. Suppose I just sang a song and accompanied it on the guitar. Someone who is not a teacher, but who is another performer, says, "You did that all wrong."
1. Thank you: Thanks for your interest in my performance.
2. Permission-giving: You have a right to your opinion.
3. Planning to ponder or problem-solve: I'll think about whatever suggestions you want to give me.
4. Agreeing with part of criticism: I'm sure my performance can be improved.
5. Asking for more specific criticism: What helpful tips can you give me?

Which of the responses to criticism, if used in a nonchalant tone of voice, most directly communicates the idea that "I know I'm imperfect, and I'm OK with that"?

A. productivity,
or
B. Agreeing with part of criticism?

390. We continue with examples of the responses to criticism.

6. Reflection: Sounds like you've got in mind lots of ways that it could be made better.
7. I want statement: I want to improve, but I also may want to play it differently from the way you like it.
8. Silent eye contact: (I raise my eyebrows and shrug and look at the person as if to say, "Whatever.")
9. Explaining the reason: (I'm imagining that the person said the song should have been in 4/4 time but I did it in 3/4.) It's been done both ways, and after trying it both ways, I happened to like it better the way I did it.
10. Criticizing the critic: You sound rude when you use words like "all wrong" in your suggestions.

Which do you think is the author's attitude toward these ways of responding?

A. It's good to have all these ways of responding in your repertoire, and that's what the exercise is for. But for any given real-life criticism, you have to pick and choose, and not use all of them.
or
B. When you are criticized in real life, you should respond with all of these?

391. Here's what it might sound like if a tutor and student do the responding to criticism exercise, taking turns.

Trainer: Let's do the responding to criticism exercise.

Trainee: OK!

Trainer: How about this is the criticism. Someone gives a book report at school, and someone else says "That was about the lamest book report I've heard in a long time."

Trainee: OK, I'll go first. I think if the person said, "Thank you for your interest in my book report," it would sound sarcastic. So I'll say not really useful here. I'll skip to permission-giving. You have a right to think whatever you want.

Trainer: Good. For planning to ponder or problem-solve: Well, if I get suggestions on how it could have been less lame, I'll ponder them.

Trainee: For agreeing with part of criticism: I'm sure it could have been better.

So far, which of the ways of responding to criticism have they practiced coming up with?

A. Explaining the reason, silent eye contact, criticizing the critic, and I want statement,
or

B. Thank you, permission-giving, planning to ponder or problem-solve, and agreeing with part of criticism?

392. The responding to criticism exercise continues.

Trainer: For asking for specific criticism: So in what specific ways could I have made it less lame?

Trainee: For a reflection: Sounds as if you feel like you know lots of ways it could be made better, huh?

Trainer: For an I want statement: I'd to focus on what's going on now and not think about the book report any more.

Trainee: For silent eye contact: I give a look that sort of seems to say, "Whatever; you have a right to your opinion."

Trainer: For explaining the reason: (I'm imagining that the person has gone on to say that I should have advertised the book and sold people on reading it more.) That would have been silly for me to do, because as I said in the report, I thought it was a bad book that I wouldn't recommend to anyone.

Trainee: For criticizing the critic: Why do you feel the need to tell me this in these sorts of words? Do you enjoy trying to make people feel bad?

Trainer: And that's all of them. Congratulations, we did it!

Which of the responses is closest to debating or arguing with the critic?

A. Permission-giving,
or
B. Explaining the reason?

393. Let's go through the responses to criticism with a rather rude and uncalled for criticism. The critic says, "You've got the ugliest face I've ever seen."

1. Thank you: Not applicable.

2. Permission-giving: You can think whatever you want!

3. Planning to ponder or problem-solve: Not really applicable, but just for the exercise: I'll think about that.

4. Agreeing with part of criticism: Maybe so.

5. Asking for more specific criticism: So what particular parts disgust you the most?

Is it possible for the person who is responding to use a fairly upbeat, cheerful manner, that communicates, "You did not succeed in making me feel bad?"

A. Yes, possible,
or
B. No, not possible.

394. The example continues.

6. Reflection: It sounds like looking at me is quite unpleasant for you, and maybe is something you'd like not to do, huh?

7. I want statement: I'd like for you to avoid saying insulting things like that, and to say nice things instead.

8. Silent eye contact: I give just the slightest glance at the person, barely interested, and return to what I'm doing.

9. Explaining the reason: Well, I guess this is just how I happened to turn out.
.

10. Criticizing the critic: When you say such things, you don't give a very beautiful impression of your own personality.

Do you think that the actual choice in real life would depend on lots of factors, such as the age and maturity level of the person who said this, whether the person really believed it or was just trying to drum up some excitement, and so forth?

A. Yes,
or
B. No?

395. Let's go through one more example, in which this time we're imagining that the critic gives the criticism in a spirit of helpfulness. The critic says, "I think you need to come to grips with the fact that you can't have your cake and eat it too. You need to make decisions and go forward, without getting so upset over the fact that no option gives you everything you want."

1. Thank you: Hmm. Thanks for that insight.

2. Permission-giving: You have a right to make conclusions when you observe me, and in this case I'm glad you did so.

3. Planning to ponder or problem-solve: I'm going to think more about what you said.

4. Agreeing with part of criticism: I think you've made a correct and helpful observation about me.

5. Asking for more specific criticism: Can you help me remember some of the examples of this?

Which of the following two would have been another example of one of the five responses already given, but a less enthusiastic and grateful example than the one given in this section?

A. I guess you can think whatever you want.
or
B. So you're saying that I get too spooked by the disadvantages of whatever options I'm thinking of deciding on?

396. The example continues.

6. Reflection: So if I understand you right, you think I just need to accept more that every option has disadvantages, and make my decisions without being so afraid of the negative consequences. Do I understand right?

7. I want statement: I do want to be able to make decisions with a lot less agonizing.

8. Silent eye contact: I nod and raise my eyebrows and look at the person as if to say, "Tell me more."

9. Explaining the reason: Sometimes being very careful to avoid bad

consequences has really paid off for me. It's sometimes quite useful.

10. Criticizing the critic: I appreciate your sharing this with me, but your conclusion may be a little premature. You may want to collect some more examples before generalizing.

Suppose the person had said, "You're right. I waste too much time and feel too much pain going back and forth on decisions. There comes a point where I have to take the plunge and get them over with." This would have been another example of

A. Explaining the reason,
or
B. Agreeing with part of criticism?

Mastery for the Responding to Criticism Exercise

0. At a preliminary level, you are able to recognize each of these responses when you read it or hear it.

1. At the first level, you are able to take turns with the trainer or a tester on at least two criticisms, coming up with examples of the responses.

2. At the second level, you can come up with all of the responses to at least 3 criticisms, when the tester prompts you for them. You've done at least 7 situations with your trainer, and two more with a tester.

3. At the third level, you remember what TP-Paarisec stands for and you don't need to be prompted. You have done at least 15 situations with your trainer, and at least 2 more with a tester. Furthermore, the responses you come up with not only are the types that are on the list, but also are very good examples of these.

Chapter 34: Self-Monitoring

397. Self-monitoring means keeping track of how you are doing – giving yourself your own report card regularly.

There is a saying among business people: "That which is measured gets improved." If you want to improve your profits, you had better keep track of what your profits are and see what makes them go up or down. If you want to improve how productive your employees are, you'll probably be more successful if you find some way of measuring how much work they do.

The same idea applies to psychological skills. All the exercises in this book are designed to improve your psychological skills. As you get better at these exercises, you should be able to do very important things better in real life. We need ways of measuring how well you're doing these skills in real life.

What's the main idea of this section?

A. With psychological skills, as well as with business, it's good to be able to measure how well you're doing.
or
B. It is sometimes possible in businesses to have worker productivity be too high – to the point where workers are unhappy and get "burned out" soon.

398. The more accurately you can rate your own performance in psychological skills, the more you'll be set up to improve these skills over your lifetime.

One very important way of measuring your psychological skills starts with simply remembering the things you've done lately – for example the last day, the last week, or the last month. What have been the good and bad examples for each skill, and how much do the good ones outweigh the bad ones? You give yourself a rating on a 0 to 10 scale, where 0 is worst and 10 is best, for each of the psychological skills, and for your overall psychological functioning.

What's the method of measuring skill performance that this section talks about?

A. Letting a tester test you on certain psychological skill challenges.
or
B. Remembering what you've done in real life, and deciding, on a scale of 0 to 10, how well you've done on the

various psychological skills, and overall.

399. There is a rating scale in an appendix of this book, called the Psychological Skills Inventory. It simply presents the psychological skills that you have become very familiar with (by doing the celebrations exercise, skills stories, affirmations, and the psychological skills meditation, as well as reading about these skills). You remember what you've done, and you give a rating for each skill on a scale of 0 to 10. Here's how the 0 to 10 scale goes:

0=Very poor
2=Poor
4=Not very good, so-so
6=OK
8=Good
10=Very good
n=Not applicable, not answerable, or not known

You can use any number from 0 to 10 for your ratings, including odd numbers or even numbers like 5.5 or 7.8.
    One of the problems of using a scale like this is deciding where to draw the lines. What sort of performance counts as a 6 on a scale of 10, and how much better does it have to be to get to a 7? This is a problem with all rating scales.

What's a summary of this section?

A. We can use a rating scale for psychological skills that's in an appendix, using a scale from 0 to 10. But deciding how to assign the numbers is a problem.
or
B. People have found that when you use rating scales, you get better information when you have more possible numbers that the person can answer with.

400. One of the hard parts of rating your behavior is remembering what you did! For this reason, if you want to be most accurate, you can give yourself a rating each day, when your memory is still fresh, rather than waiting and trying to rate a whole week or a month. If you've gotten into the habit of doing the celebrations exercise every day, you have probably improved your ability to remember things you've done.

What's a summary of this section?

A. The first task for accurately rating is remembering what you've done. For this reason, ratings of shorter time periods are better.
or

B. The celebrations exercise is meant to help you feel good about the good things you've done each day.

401. Here's a way of thinking about the 0 to 10 scale. Think of the best possible performance that you could see yourself doing, and call that a 10. Think of the worst possible performance for you, and call that a 0. Try to divide the region in between those into equal spaces, so that the difference between, say, 3 and 4, is the same as the difference between 6 and 7. It's hard to do this, but try.

Then, as you give yourself ratings over and over, think, for example, like this: "Today was better than that day I remember, where I gave myself a 6. It was almost, but not quite, as good as another day when I gave myself a 9. I think about 8 is right for today." In other words, you compare today to other days in the past that you remember.

In this section, what two principles does the author recommend when using rating scales?

A. Honesty and accurate memory.
or
B. Equal intervals and comparison to previous ratings.

402. The first person I know of who used daily self-monitoring to try to improve himself was Benjamin Franklin, who described his method in his *Autobiography*. Franklin was one of the most productive and creative individuals of history. At the age of 79, he looked back and wrote that he owed the constant happiness of his life to what he called the "little artifice" of monitoring himself daily. He judged himself on what he called virtues, and what I have called psychological skills.

What's the purpose of this section?

A. For the author to give credit to Benjamin Franklin as perhaps the first to write about daily self-monitoring, and to use Franklin as a model of successful self-monitoring.
or
B. To make the point that rating scales, though they are inexact, are better than no measurement at all.

403. Franklin listed 13 "virtues" that he wanted to strive for. Several of them are very similar to the skills and principles that organize this book and the others in the series. One of Franklin's virtues was "Industry," which he defined partly by the sentence, "Be always employed in something useful." This sounds a lot like the skill of productivity. Another of Franklin's virtues was "Frugality," partly defined by the command,

"Waste nothing." It's very similar to the skill of conservation. A third was "Sincerity," which is very similar to honesty, and a fourth was "Resolution," which is very much like self-discipline.

What's a main point of this section?

A. Benjamin Franklin made big discoveries in electricity, made important inventions, and was an important statesman.
or
B. Several of the virtues that Franklin chose to try to improve in are similar to the skills and principles you have studied in this book.

404. As Franklin monitored himself every day, he noticed his imperfections more, but he enjoyed improving them. In his words, "I was surprised to find myself so much fuller of faults than I had imagined, but I had the satisfaction of seeing them diminish."

Other people have found the same thing when they start to self-monitor. They get a more accurate picture of how they are doing, and sometimes they realize that they aren't doing as well as they thought they were. But over time, they do better and better.

What's a major point of this section?

A. Being honest with yourself in self-monitoring can open your eyes to your own faults, but it can also help you improve yourself.
or
B. In order to check how accurately you are self-monitoring, it's good to compare your ratings with those of someone else who has been with you during the day.

405. Let's think some about what 10 on a scale of 10 performance is for some psychological skills.

For productivity, to get a 10, you work really hard at very worthy goals. If you're a student, you put in enough time on your studies, and you use your time very efficiently. (The word *efficient* means that you choose how to work so as to get the most payoff from a certain amount of effort.) You concentrate well. If you work at a job, you devote yourself to doing a good job, and if possible, you learn more about how to do a better job. In addition, you work effectively at keeping yourself organized. What's more, you do your share or more for chores like putting things away, washing dishes, washing clothes, cooking, cleaning the place where you live, and other household chores. You work because things need to be done, and not just because someone commands you to do something. You take initiative in deciding what to work on – you don't passively wait for directions.

You don't work so hard that you get burned out or that you make yourself not enjoy life. You make sure you pace yourself and take care of yourself for the long term. It seems that many more people live on the "too lazy" side of the scale than the "too hard working" side.

What are goals mentioned in this section?

A. Writing down plans, revising the plans, and giving them to someone else for feedback.
or
B. Choosing worthy goals, spending enough time working at them, and working efficiently.

406. For a 10 on a scale of 10 rating in joyousness: You feel good about the work you accomplish, the kind acts you do, and anything you learn. (You celebrate your own choices.) You take some time to do things you really enjoy. You don't take for granted the things others do for you; you feel grateful. (You celebrate other people's choices.) You spend time recognizing the blessings that fate has given you, and you feel thankful for them. (You celebrate luck.) You appreciate any beauty around you. Even when you

are faced with bad things, you are able to feel good if you choose well how to handle them. Even when you are faced with decisions where no option is free of disadvantages, you feel good about making the best choice you can. Most of the time you act cheerful and enthusiastic with other people, unless there's a good reason not to. You appreciate the miraculous nature of being alive.

Which categories of things to feel good about does the author mention in this section?

A. Good things in the past, the present, and the future.
or
B. Things you've done, things other people have done for you, and blessings of fate.

407. What does 10 on a scale of 10 kindness look like? You make people feel good with friendly greeting and parting rituals. You help people when you get the chance, and often ask yourself the question, "How can I best make other people happy?" You watch for other people's good acts and you compliment and congratulate and thank people for them. You are a good listener, and if you get the chance to teach or learn from another person you do that. You are generally forgiving, and you console others when they are

upset. You give to others, not just of material goods, but your time and company and interest. You invite others to spend time with you. You are affectionate in appropriate ways; you let people know you like them. You work for the benefit of others, speak in kind tones of voice. and avoid unkind acts.

You do any of these you get the opportunity to do. But you avoid "enabling" bad habits of other people by rewarding their bad decisions with your kindness.

What are some categories of kindness the author mentioned in this section?

A. Helping other people, speaking in kind tones of voice, and giving people your time and interest.
or
B. Giving to charity, making medical discoveries, and not stealing.

408. What does 10 on a scale of 10 honesty consist of? You don't lie to people, you don't cheat, you don't steal things. As much as possible, you keep promises; you take promises very seriously. You avoid sneaking or deceiving or doing things behind someone's back.

You are also honest with yourself. You are able to be aware of your own shortcomings, and also of your own strengths.

What are some of the things this section mentioned as being part of the skill of honesty?

A. Not having secrets and not promising other people to keep secrets.
or
B. Not lying, cheating, stealing, or deceiving yourself about your strengths and weaknesses.

409. To get a high fortitude rating: You don't let yourself get upset by little things. When hardships come up, you try to make the best decision about what to do. Even when very bad things happen, you keep trying to make things better when you can, and you try to tolerate bad things if you can't make them better. Fortitude doesn't mean not having bad feelings; it means trying to make good decisions despite feeling bad. Sometimes the best decision is to lie down and let other people take care of you, for example when you're very sick. Sometimes the best decision is to cry out very loudly for help. Fortitude just means trying to do what's best, even when things go badly.

To get a high rating in fortitude,

A. Try to decide on the best thing to do and do it, even when things go wrong.
or
B. Don't waste time and money.

410. Regarding fortitude ratings: what if everything goes your way, and there are no bad things that happen to you during the time you're rating? Then you have two choices. You can rate fortitude as "not applicable" for that interval. Or you can give yourself a high score for feeling that all is going your way, and not being bothered by the hardships you may be facing without thinking about them. These are hardships like the fact that you will die someday, that there will be someday be lots of work to do that you don't feel like doing, that someone somewhere doesn't like you as much as you would want, that you have not been a total success in everything you've tried, that not everyone considers you the most beautiful person in the world, and so forth.

Which of the following would, according to this section, definitely not deserve a 10 on a scale of 10 rating for fortitude?

A. A day where things went well for you.
or

B. A day in which you had a temper tantrum that distressed other people unnecessarily, over something little.

411. In order to achieve a high rating for good decisions, you first decide well which decisions are important and which are not. For the important decisions, you use the SOIL ADDLE process described in the chapter on the Decisions exercise. You use the skills that you have practiced in many of the exercises of this book, including listing important variables, brainstorming options, pros and cons, and others. You are guided by worthy goals and good values as you make your choices.

In order to get a high rating on good decisions, not everything you choose has to come out right. There is such a thing as bad luck, and such a thing as unforeseeable events. For example: someone makes a very careful decision about what to study for a test. It turns out that the test covers other things that the person could not have predicted or found out about in any way. The person doesn't do well on the test, but that's more because of bad luck than bad decision-making.

Jim makes very careful choices about a hike. But on the hike, a tree branch suddenly and without warning happens to fall, just when Jim is under it, and he is hurt. Which would the author say?

A. Since there was a bad outcome, Jim made a bad choice.
or
B. The injury came because of bad luck rather than a bad decision-making skill.

412. To rate high in joint decision making or conflict resolution, you don't have to come to perfect agreement on every conflict or joint decision. Other people also have a role in producing that outcome, and you can't control what other people do, although you may be able to influence them.

The principle the author speaks of in this section is that

A. A high rating in joint decision skill doesn't depend on actions of other people that are beyond your control.
or
B. It's good to keep persisting at very important goals until you decide that the method you're using isn't likely to work.

413. To get a high score for joint decision, you do as many of the Dr. L.W. Aap guidelines as you can. You define the problem without accusing or commanding. You reflect to make sure you understand the other person's point of view. You list options. You talk about advantages and disadvantages of options rather than insulting the other person. You stay polite during the conversation. You are appropriately assertive, and you don't give in to an unjust option, just for the sake of agreement. But if there is a reasonable option that is wise to agree on, you can agree on it.

Even if you don't go through many of the Dr. L.W. Aap guidelines, you can still give yourself a high score on joint decision-making if you manage to make joint decisions in a calm way, taking into account both your own needs and those of the other person, and advocating just and wise options.

Which of the following would be less likely to result in a high score on joint decisions?

A. Conversations in which both people scream at each other.
or
B. Conversations in which the people can't agree on a final solution to the problem.

414. Nonviolence in many ways seems to be an easy skill to score high in. All you have to do is avoid the following: being physically violent to anyone, threatening violence, urging

anyone else to be violent, rewarding anyone else for violence, or rewarding anyone for modeling or urging violence. If you can take active steps to work toward a less violent community or world, that's even better.

But some of these are not easy. If you pay for a ticket to go to a mixed martial arts match, you're probably rewarding someone else for violence. If you buy a violent video game or movie, you are rewarding someone else for modeling violence.

The author counts for nonviolence skill

A. only those acts in which you physically harm someone else,
or
B. acts that either harm someone else or that encourage other people to be violent?

415. Respectful talk certainly does not mean that you have to agree with everyone, or act submissive. You can let people know that what they are doing is wrong. You can strongly command them to do something, or to stop doing something, if necessary. You can strongly disagree with people. But to get high ratings for respectful talk, you make your words and tones of voice as gentle as they

can while still accomplishing your purpose.

One of the skills of respectful talk is that when you disagree, you challenge the other person's choice of behavior or conclusions or ideas, but you avoid implying that the other person himself or herself is bad or worthless.

Which of the following should probably lower the rating for respectful talk?

A. I totally disagree with that, and I'd like to point out several reasons why.
or
B. You don't know what you're talking about. You aren't smart enough to understand this.

416. For friendship-building, keep in mind that family members can also be friends, and we can show good or bad friendship-building skills with them.

Almost every day you get to practice the skills used in the listening with four responses exercise and the social conversation role play. If you use these skills well, count them toward a higher rating for friendship-building.

Part of friendship-building is putting out the effort needed to spend time with a friend or possible friend. If you make an invitation that takes some gumption to make, count it toward your friendship-building rating.

Two types of behaviors mentioned in this section that increase the friendship-building rating are

A. sending greeting cards and remembering birthdays,
or
B. good social conversation and making invitations?

417. There are lots of things to do in a day that require self-discipline: getting ready for work or school on time, doing the work you need to do, eating a reasonable amount and choosing well what to eat, not wasting money, and so forth – making choices that achieve goals, even when they don't feel as good. When you rate yourself, think back over how you did in your self-discipline choice points.

 I call it "advanced self discipline" when you are able to actually enjoy the choices that achieve your goals. So you don't have to feel a lot of pain or deprivation to get a high self-discipline rating.

An example of an action which would raise the self-discipline rating would be

A. choosing not to watch a time-wasting TV show, but going for a run instead;
or
B. appreciating the beauty of a sunset?

418. If you carefully decide which people are the most important to you, and which you have obligations to, and you keep those commitments, score yourself high in loyalty. Lots of times this means not forgetting about people who mean something to you, but reaching out to be in touch with them. Sometimes it means sticking up for someone whom other people are against.

 Give yourself a high rating for conservation if you don't waste money, waste energy, waste the earth's resources, or waste your own time.

If you get the urge to buy a very expensive supper at a restaurant but eat something much less expensive at home, that would increase your rating of

A. Loyalty,
or
B. Conservation?

419. For a high self-care rating, you need to pay attention to lots of health and safety rules – getting enough sleep, eating right, exercising, no

abuse of drugs or alcohol, protecting your skin from the sun, protecting your ears from loud noises, wearing helmets, avoiding taking needless risks, adequately protecting yourself from your fellow human beings, and so forth.

For a high score in compliance, you obey authorities such as parents, teachers, or the law of your government, when they are reasonable authorities. When you are told to do something immoral or unwise, then the skill of compliance involves figuring out how to disobey in the best way.

If a child sneaks so as to drink alcohol after having been told not to by a parent, this should greatly lower the rating of which skills?

A. Courage, nonviolence, and productivity.
or
B. Self-care, compliance, and honesty.

420. Give yourself a high rating in positive fantasy rehearsal if you do two things: first, avoid entertaining yourself with displays of bad behavior, such as TV shows of violence or brattiness or violent videogames. Second, consciously practice in your imagination doing good things – for example, do STEBC fantasy rehearsals or UCAC fantasy

rehearsals, or any of most of the other exercises mentioned in this book. The more positive fantasy rehearsals you do, the higher the rating you deserve. You can decide how many rehearsals are your quota for a 10.

What two things does the author mention as requirements for a high rating in positive fantasy rehearsal?

A. Concentrating deeply, and imagining very vividly.
or
B. Avoiding being entertained by fantasies of bad behavior, and using the imagination to practice good behavior?

421. Give yourself a high rating for courage if anxiety, fear, worry, self-consciousness, and nervousness didn't hold you back from doing good things or enjoying yourself.

Some people are disposed to have more fears and worries than others, often because of genetics. If you tend to have lots of fears, and you do a good job of exposing yourself to and tolerating an unrealistically feared situation, count that as a courage triumph and give yourself a high rating for the day, even if you haven't gotten rid of all your fears.

Someone with fears of vomiting, spiders, and public speaking does a great job of giving a speech. The person is still afraid of all three things, but now somewhat less afraid of speaking. The author recommends, for the person's daily rating,

A. A low rating, because the person has fears.
or
B. A high, but not perfect rating, because today the person did something to lower one of the fears?

422. There's one more way of self-monitoring that we should talk about: a one-item rating scale. It takes a lot less time to rate yourself on this one question than it does to go through the whole Psychological Skills Inventory. To answer the question, use the same 0 to 10 scale that we talked about before. Here's the question:

_____ Please rate your overall functioning. Good functioning is the thoughts, feelings, and behaviors that tend to: produce happiness and well-being in both oneself and others; produce good social relations and positive achievement; and accomplish worthwhile goals. Please rate how good, overall, your functioning was.

What is the essence of high psychological functioning as defined by this item?

A. Getting good grades, being good at sports, and doing lots of extracurricular activities.
or
B. Being happy, causing others to be happy, having good relationships, and achieving worthwhile goals.

Mastery for Self-Monitoring

1. At the first level, you have rated your functioning over the last 24 hours of your life, using the Psychological Skills Inventory and the One-Item Functioning Rating, on at least one occasion, explaining in your own words what each question means.

2. At the second level, you have rated your functioning during the last 24 hours using both inventories at least 7 times total, recalling at least some positive or negative examples that explain why your rating is higher or lower.

3. At the third level, rate yourself over the last 24 hours using both scales, a total of at least 14 times. On three of those times, let someone else who has been with you at least part of the day also rate your functioning, and see how well you agree.

Chapter 35: Goal-Setting and Goal-Monitoring

423. The exercise of the last chapter had to do with self-monitoring how good you are getting at psychological skills. We assume that everyone needs to keep improving in all psychological skills. The idea was, "That which is measured gets improved."

This chapter presents a different approach to working toward goals. It has to do with forming specific, concrete goals that you can some day check off as accomplished. Over time, you keep track of progress, and when you accomplish your goal, you celebrate.

What's a summary of this section?

A. The exercise for this chapter is to form, and keep track of progress on, very specific and concrete goals that you can some day check off as done.
or
B. When you set goals, it's good to think about what the obstacles will be to achieving them, and to plan how to overcome those obstacles.

424. What do we mean by concrete and specific goals? We mean using words that allow us to tell, very clearly, whether the goal has been accomplished or not.

If I set a goal such as, "I want to be very productive in writing," that could mean that I get a lot accomplished in one day, or it could mean that in one lifetime I write a lot of good things. On the other hand, if I say, "I want to produce a finished, well-edited book on psychological skills exercises by the end of September, 2013," then that's more specific and concrete.

If I say, "I want to get into better shape," that could mean lots of things. On the other hand, if I say, "By the end of this year, I want to trim my waistline so that I can comfortably use the fourth hole of my belt rather than the third," that is more specific and concrete.

This section tries to provide

A. A list of techniques for reaching goals,
or
B. Two concrete and specific examples of what "concrete and specific" mean?

425. Here are some more examples. If I say, "I want my room to be more organized," that could mean lots of things. On the other hand, it's more concrete if I say that my goal is that "Every day for the next month, allowing only one or two exceptions, I want to spend 15 minutes every

morning putting the things in my room into their homes. I want to have nothing on the floor that has a home somewhere else."

Here's another example. I could set the goal of "having more respectful talk with family members." But it's more concrete and specific if I say, "I want to go for two weeks without raising my voice in anger at a family member. I want to have approving tones and statements outnumber the disapproving ones, for all family members, by a ratio of 4 to 1 for the next two weeks."

In each of these pairs of examples, it is much easier to decide whether you have reached

A. the less concrete one,
or
B. the more concrete one?

426. Many people are not driven or guided by their own goals. Many people go to work or school and do what they are commanded to do. When they get free time, they drift toward whatever grabs their attention first – a television show, a video game, a party, eating, drinking, or whatever. When you have your own goals, and these goals guide and drive your behavior, you have reached a higher level of functioning than many people ever reach.

In this section the author expresses the opinion that

A. Goals are most useful if they are concrete and specific.
or
B. People whose actions are guided by their own goals have reached a higher level of functioning than those who simply react to what grabs their attention.

427. It's not enough, though, that you have goals. You should have "worthy" goals – goals that help both you and someone else, goals that help you to help other people, goals that somehow make the world a better place.

Making lots of money by making up catchy advertisements for cigarettes is not a worthy goal. Making lots of money by figuring out an effective way for people to quit smoking is a worthy goal. Winning as many fist-fights as you can is not a worthy goal. Figuring out a way to prevent fights is a worthy goal. Owning more different pairs of shoes than you could wear in a lifetime is not a worthy goal. Providing jobs to people who otherwise could not buy shoes is a worthy goal.

Which of the following do you think the author believes to be the more worthy goal?

A. Injuring the quarterback of the other side in a football game so that your side can win the championship.
or
B. Figuring out ways of reducing sports injuries.

428. Here's a menu that may be helpful to you in choosing goals for yourself. If you choose any of these you can make more specific decisions about exactly what you want to accomplish by what date.

a. Personal development: Improve in certain psychological skills?
b. Relations with family: Get along better with any family member? Get to know a family member better? Spend more fun times with any family member?
c. Relations with friends: More friends? Become a better friend? Better activities with friends? Better relationship with a friend? Better anger control?
d. Fitness, health, athletics: Sports accomplishments? More exercise? Eating habits? Sleep habits? Other health habits?
e. School achievement: better grades? Specific subjects to get better in? Better organization? Higher fraction homework completion? More work capacity? Better test preparation? Better system for writing? Skills you want to improve? Subjects you are curious to find out more about? More self-directed learning or writing?
f. School behavior: Make life more pleasant for your teachers? Make life more pleasant for your classmates? Get a better reputation for behaving well? More self-direction in your study?
g. Service to humanity: Make the world a better place in some way? Learn more about how to serve humanity? Join a cause such as nonviolence, reducing poverty, tutoring, improving the environment?
h. Hobbies: Take up a new activity? Improve in an activity you're doing already? Spend less time on a certain hobby? More time?
i. Work: Earn certain amount of money? Learn certain job skills? Get more responsible position? Help people more? Be more successful?

What are some of the goals listed on the menu you just read?

A. More self-directed study, reducing poverty, better test preparation, getting along better with a family member,
or
B. Winning a competition, regardless of what the competition is in?

429. So how do you do the goal-setting and goal-monitoring exercise? Here's what it may sound like when two people are doing the goal-setting part of it.

Person 1: Let's do the Goal-Setting Exercise.

Person 2: OK!

Person 1: I have a goal. In two weeks I have an article that I'm supposed to write for school, on how to reduce the likelihood of nuclear war. I want to make this article good enough that I feel good about posting it on the Internet for anyone to read, and confident that the ideas may be helpful to those who read it.

Person 2: Sounds like a good goal. I want to make a goal of getting along better with my younger brother by two weeks from now. The specific part is that almost every day I want to spend some time playing with him, using lots of tones of approval, and continue for longer if he is nice, and just stop quietly and do something else if he is not nice.

Person 1: Sounds like a great goal. So you're going to spend some time just giving him undivided attention, using lots of approval, but just withdrawing

your attention if he starts being unpleasant to you, huh? In other words, using differential reinforcement?

Person 2: That's right. And I'll know I've accomplished this goal if at the end of the two weeks, he and I have fun with each other more often and get angry at each other lots less often.

Person 1: Sounds great.

When Person 2 set a goal, how did Person 1 respond?

A. By a facilitation.
or
B. By some positive feedback and a reflection?

430. Of course, it isn't good just to set goals and then forget about them. It's a good idea to write down the goals you've set, and to look at the written goals every day. But even that isn't enough: you need to put out some effort and work toward the goal every day, or nearly every day. Here's how it might sound if Person 1 and Person 2 do the Goal-Monitoring part of the exercise.

Person 1: Let's follow up on the goals we set the other day. I'll report first. I've spent at least an hour each day working on my article, since we talked about this last. I've made an outline, and I've read a bunch of things about the topic, and I've started to fill in my outline with ideas. The draft is about 5 pages long now, and it will eventually be about 15 pages.

Person 2: Congratulations! Sounds like some good productivity in working toward that goal! Just yesterday I invited my brother to throw a football back and forth in the yard with me, and we had a good time, with no arguing or fighting. And the day before that I sat with him while he did some math homework, and I congratulated him when he got the problems right, and gave him a tip now and then. When he argued with me once or twice, I just sat silently and didn't worry about it.

Person 1: Wow, great job! You're really moving toward that goal of a better relationship with him in a good way!

Person 2: Already he seems to seek my attention less by bugging me and more by inviting me to do something with him.

Person 1: Congratulations! Keep up the good work!

In this case, the Goal-Monitoring part of the exercise sounds a lot like the

A. celebrations exercise,
or
B. pros and cons exercise?

431. What if you set a goal and then forget all about doing anything to achieve it? You won't be alone! Lots of people do this. When you do goal-monitoring, just remind yourself of your goal, and think about a specific action you can take toward it very soon. Here's how that might sound.

Person 1: How about we do a little goal-monitoring? (Person 1 tells some progress toward the goal.)

Person 2: I'll have to be honest. I've been in a play, and I've forgotten all about my goal of improving my relationship with my brother for the last 3 or 4 days. But I want to get a little exercise this evening, and I can ask my brother if he wants to go out for a walk with me.

Person 1: Sounds like a good plan. Maybe tomorrow we can touch base on how it came out.

Person 2: Sounds like a good deal.

In this little conversation, Person 1 probably helped Person 2 with the goal by

A. mildly reprimanding Person 2 for not doing anything,
or
B. reminding Person 2 about the goal by bringing up the goal-monitoring activity?

432. When the deadline for goal achievement occurs, the two people should check and see whether the goal was achieved.

Person 2: Hey, it's two weeks from when we set those goals we wanted to achieve by now. We should do some goal-monitoring.

Person 1: You're right! Well, I wrote my article, and turned it in, and I think I'm going to get a good grade on it. But there is a lot more that I want to put into it. So I've decided to make the version that goes on the Internet longer than 15 pages. I think that will take me about one more week to finish.

Person 2: So you've gotten more ambitious about the goal you want to achieve, and you want to take another week to achieve it?

Person 1: Right!

Person 2: OK! Well, I spent some time with my brother, using differential reinforcement, nearly every day for the two weeks, and I think we get along lots better now. There is a lot less yelling in anger. He comes around to purposely bother me a lot less now. I think it's been a big success, and I want to think about the goal of how to maintain what I've got now.

Person 1: Congratulations to you!

Person 2: Thank you!

In this imaginary conversation, both people were not ready to just check the goal off the list and forget about it. One had expanded the goal, and one wanted to set a goal of maintaining the accomplishments already made.

What's a summary of the point made in this section?

A. Often, rather than just checking goals off the list and moving on, you want to expand them or figure out how to maintain what you've accomplished.
or
B. If you can't remember what your goals are, you are less likely to accomplish them.

433. A major self-discipline challenge is making what you do each day correspond to your most important goals.

For example: a man decides that his number one goal is to have a happy family. But because of habits of work and hobbies and television and so forth, the amount of time per day he actually devotes to any activity that promotes this goal is zero.

Someone has a very important goal of learning to play the guitar. But the daily practice time averages close to zero minutes.

Someone very strongly wishes to do well on a college admission test. But the person spends zero minutes per day actually studying or practicing for the test.

What are your most important goals? And how much time each day do you spend working toward them? The goal-setting and goal-monitoring exercise should help you choose daily activities that help you reach your goals. The exercise helps you avoid the situation where you have goals but spend no time trying to achieve them.

The major challenge this section talks about is

A. deciding upon which goals are more worthy than others,
or
B. devoting time to your most important goals?

Mastery for the Goal-Setting and Goal-Monitoring Exercise

1. At the first level, at least onee, you choose some worthy goals, make them specific, writte them down, and read them every day for a week.

2. At the second level, you have on at least three occasions chosen, written, and read daily some worthy goals, and you have also worked nearly daily to achieve those goals, and have made large progress as a result.

3. At the third level, you have maintained the habit of choosing and writing important goals, reading them daily, working nearly daily to achieve them, and often achieving them, for at least three months.

Chapter 36: Examples of Brainstorming Options

434. This chapter provides, not a new exercise, but some examples of how to do the brainstorming options exercise. When you are learning to think of lots of options for solving problems, it's really good just to read examples of options other people have thought of.

The first problem is that someone has traveled to a city he is not familiar with. In walking around, she has gotten lost. Her goal is to get back to the place where she's staying. Let's think of options for this situation.

1. If she has a cell phone that has a GPS, she could use that.
2. If she has a cell phone with Internet access, she could see where she is and get directions on how to get where she wants to go.
3. She could ask someone for directions on how to get to where she's staying.
4. If she knows a landmark, like a park or a bridge near where she's staying, she could ask someone directions to that.
5. She could use her sense of direction to just go in the direction she thinks is right and see if she sees something that looks familiar.

What sort of category of solution would you call the option of using a GPS on a cell phone?

A. Consulting a human helper category.
or
B. Technological solution category.

435. The options for the previous problem continue.

6. She could hail a cab or call a cab and hire the driver to take her back.
7. She could call up someone at the place where she's staying and get directions from that person.
8. If she's with someone else in the city, she could call that person and see if the other person can help out.
9. She could see if she can find a map in a bookstore, hotel, library, or anywhere else, and use the map.
10. She could just retrace her steps backwards from wherever she is.
11. She could look at the sun and the shadows and figure out which way north and south are, and try to use that to help her figure out which way is back.
12. If for example she was staying near the top of the hill of the city, she could try walking uphill.

13. If she can get to a phone but not to the Internet, she could call up anyone she knows and ask them to look up on the Internet directions on how to get back.

Which of the following two options falls into the category of "hiring someone to help?"

A. Finding a map in a library,
or
B. Getting a taxi cab back?

436. Here's the next problem. A person joins a baseball team. But he finds out that he is the worst player on the team, and it isn't fun for him.

1. Quit the team.
2. Transfer to a team or league that doesn't have such good players.
3. Pick a different sport that he is better at.
4. Pick a different activity other than sports, like a musical instrument, to get good at.
5. Practice a lot on his own, so that his skills improve.

What category does the option of practicing a lot on his own fall into?

A. The category of working toward skill-building.
or

B. The category of paying someone to help out.

437. The baseball team problem continues.

6. Use a mechanical pitcher at a batting cage to practice hitting.
7. Get a friend or family member or teammate to help him practice.
8. Practice throwing the ball at a brick wall and catching it when it bounces off.
9. Talk to the coach and see what the coach would advise.
10. Consult a book on how to be expert at baseball.
11. Just keep playing and try to enjoy it without worrying if the other people are better.

If we call an "information bank" something like a library, the Internet, or a bookstore, which of the following options listed above falls into the category of "consulting an information bank?"

A. Reading a book on how to be expert in baseball,
or
B. Using a mechanical pitcher at a batting cage to practice?

438. A kid has been sick for a long time and has missed school. When she comes back, the teachers expect her

not only to do the current work, but to make up all the past work.

1. She and her parents could have a conference with the principal, trying to figure out a better plan.
2. She could just start back where she left off, working independently as long as she can each day, and not worry if she can't do the current work.
3. She and her family could band together with the families of other people who have been sick to convince the school to make a better plan.
4. She and the school could agree that she would do the make up work first, and would listen in class, but would not have to do the current work or take the current tests until she caught up.
5. She and the school could figure out a lot of the past work that she should just not do, so that she can start back with the current work soon.

Which option falls into the category called "organizing a group of people who can work for change together?"

A. Starting back where she left off and working independently.
or
B. Banding with other families of kids who have been sick and working for a new way to handle this.

439. The missed schoolwork problem continues.

6. She could drop a course or two, so that she would have time to do the work for the other courses.
7. She could withdraw from school for the rest of the school year and be home schooled.
8. She could withdraw from school for the rest of the school year and take online courses.
9. She could get an individual tutor to work with her.
10. She and the school could agree to extend the deadline for her finishing up the year's work until sometime during the summer.

Which option falls into the category called "moving away from the problem situation?"

A. Home schooling for the rest of the year.
or
B. Working really hard to catch up?

440. The next problem is that a family doesn't have enough money. They are all afraid of running out of money and not being able to pay for things if some problem came up like a health problem or damage to house or car. What could kids in the family do?

1. They could work at jobs instead of spending time on sports.
2. They could study very hard so that some day they could get a job that pays a lot.
3. They could get information from libraries or the Internet or bookstores on which jobs do pay enough.
4. They could persuade the family to get food only at grocery stores and not waste money on restaurants.
5. They could get used clothes at thrift shops rather than spending money on new clothes.

Which of the options mentioned so far falls into the category of "consulting information banks?"

A. Finding out from library or Internet etc. what the high paying jobs are.
or
B. Avoiding restaurants.

441. The problem of too little money in the family continues.

6. If anyone in the family smokes or drinks alcohol or uses drugs, the family members could all ask that person to quit and save the money.
7. If kids are trying to get the family to get a dog or cat, they could stop doing that, so the family could save lots of money and have lots more time to be working.

8. People could persuade family members to open up a separate bank account and put money into it each paycheck, and not take money out of it except if there's a real emergency.
9. Each family member could get his or her own separate savings account, and people could have a friendly competition as to who could save the most.
10. People could persuade each other to have really healthy habits, so they will need less medical care.
11. They could read books about how to spend less money.

The options of buying used clothes and not spending money on cigarettes or pets all fall into the category of the skill of

A. conservation,
or
B. productivity?

442. One person likes to practice singing. The other person, who shares the same residence, is bothered by the sound because it distracts from that person's studying.

1. If the singer can go to a room, such as a basement, that is far away from the studier, the singer can go there to practice.

2. The singer can practice singing more softly.

3. The studier can go to a library.

4. The studier can go to a different part of the house or apartment such as the basement.

5. The studier can try some noise-canceling headphones.

6. The studier can go and study with a friend at the friend's place when the singer is practicing.

Which of these options falls into the category of a technological solution?

A. One of them going to the basement, or
B. The noise-canceling headphones?

443. Options for the singer and the studier continue.

7. They could not live with each other any more; one or both of them could move out.

8. The singer could schedule practicing when the studier has to be gone anyway.

9. If they have a car, the singer could go out to the car to practice.

10. If there are some woods nearby, the singer could practice there.

11. The studier could try regular ear plugs.

12. The studier could just practice concentrating even with the singing going on.

13. The singer could not practice when the studier is studying; this would result in the singer's practicing a lot less than he or she otherwise would.

The last two options fall into which of the two options?

A. One person sacrificing for the sake of the other.
or
B. A compromise solution where each person gets some but not all of what the person wants?

444. A man and a woman are thinking of getting married. But the man likes to do risky things, like cliff climbing, hang-gliding, parachute jumping, and so forth. The woman doesn't want her husband and the father of her kids to get killed or badly injured.

1. They could split up and not get married.

2. The risk-taker could climb cliffs only when there are ropes to catch him if he slips.

3. The risk-taker could hang glide not off cliffs, but on gently sloping sand dunes where he's never far off the ground.

4. The risk-taker could double and triple check that his parachute was packed correctly and always have a spare parachute and only go on days when there is almost no wind.

5. The risk-taker could promise to stop doing such risky activities if they have a child.

Which of the options falls into the category of "calling off the deal?"

A. The risk-taker's taking extra precautions.
or
B. The two deciding to split up and not get married.

445. The options regarding the risky activities continue.

6. The woman could just put up with the risky activities and hope for the best.

7. The man could stop doing the risky activities altogether.

8. The man could look for thrilling and exciting activities that are not dangerous, for example putting on performances in front of lots of people, or being an emergency doctor.

9. If they get married and have kids, the woman could stay very close to extended family such as grandparents or aunts and uncles, in case the man gets killed.

10. The risk-taker could do the activities a lot less frequently than he would like, but more frequently than the woman would like.

Which of the options falls into the category of a compromise, where each person gives up some of what they want?

A. The man's doing the activities less often than he wants but more often than she wants,
or
B. The man's giving up the risky activities altogether?

Chapter 37: Examples of Pros and Cons

446. This chapter also introduces no new exercise, but gives examples of how to do the pros and cons exercise.

A town has a tight budget. The mayor considers getting rid of the Fourth of July fireworks display that the town has traditionally put on.

1. A disadvantage is that some of the residents of the town may get mad because they expect this entertainment.

2. A disadvantage is that if enough people are upset enough, the mayor may not get re-elected.

3. A disadvantage is that if the mayor becomes less popular, he or she may have a harder time getting people to agree to other good ideas.

4. An advantage is that the town would save money.

5. An advantage is that the chemicals used to make the fireworks wouldn't pollute the air, water, and ground.

Which of the ones we've named is a consequence having to do with the environment?

A. The polluting effect of the fireworks.
or
B. The mayor's possibly becoming less popular.

447. The pros and cons of eliminating fireworks continue.

6. An advantage is that there wouldn't be so much noise.

7. An advantage is that if the mayor is able to persuade people that saving the money and avoiding the pollution is a good idea, the mayor may become more popular, not less.

8. An advantage is that if there are no fireworks there is no possibility of someone's getting hurt by them.

9. An advantage is that the people of the town could figure out better ways of enjoying themselves on the holiday.

10. A disadvantage is that the people could get into worse ways of using their free time on the holiday, such as getting drunk and getting into fights.

11. An advantage is that the town's tax rate may be lower than if it spent the money on the fireworks.

12. An advantage is that people could start thinking about other ways of saving money also.

Which psychological skill or principle is the advantage of preventing any injuries from the fireworks most related to?

A. Honesty,
or
B. Self-care?

448. Someone who can type medium fast considers learning to use the correct fingers for the correct keys so that he or she can type lots faster.

1. For a little time, while learning, the person will probably type even more slowly than before. (a con)

2. After learning, the person will probably save a very large amount of time, for the rest of his or her life, especially if he or she writes a lot. (a pro)

3. After learning, the person will type more automatically, and be able to think more about what he or she is writing. This may make the person a better writer. (a pro)

4. It will take time and effort to teach himself or herself this skill. (a con)

5. The person may be able to find games and computer exercises that make learning to be a fast typist fun. (a pro)

Having a disadvantage of having to invest time and effort in the short run, but probable bigger payoffs in the long run, make this choice point have to do with

A. joyousness,
or
B. self-discipline?

449. The pros and cons exercise with learning touch-typing skills continues.

6. If the person does learn to be a better and faster writer, the person will probably be more successful at school. (a pro)

7. If the person is more successful at school, the person will enjoy school more. (a pro)

8. If the person is more successful at school, the person may get a better job and enjoy life more. (a pro)

9. If the person is a better writer, it could turn out that the person would write something that would help people. (a pro)

10. If the person is a better writer, it could turn out that the person could make some money from writing something. (a pro)

11. It could turn out that voice recognition software will get so good so soon that people don't really need to type any more, and the person will consider that he or she wasted time in learning to be an expert typist. (a con)

Which of the following advantages or disadvantages has NOT been listed for the option of learning touch typing well?

A. Being able to think lots more about what you are writing and having to think less about how to type. (a pro)
or
B. Getting so good at typing that you do a huge amount of it and your fingers or hands get injured by the repeated stress. (a con)

450. A person considers studying to become a doctor.

1. The person could study a long time and still not get into medical school. (a con)

2. If the person doesn't get into medical school, the person could possibly get into a training program

for another type of health career. (a pro)

3. The person would be able to help a lot of people. (pro)

4. The person would be able to make a good income. (pro)

5. It would be very unlikely that the person would be unemployed. (pro)

6. The person would have to be waked up in the middle of the night to take care of sick people, at least at some point in training. (con)

Helping people and making a good income are advantages that have to do with which two psychological skills?

A. Kindness and self-care,
or
B. Honesty and nonviolence?

451. The pros and cons for studying to become a doctor continue.

7. If the person doesn't enjoy science such as organic chemistry, the person would have to spend a lot of time doing it anyway. (con)

8. If the person does enjoy sciences, the person might have fun taking the courses that would get him or her into medical school. (pro)

9. The person would have to be in school for a large number of years before earning a living. (con)

10. College and medical school are expensive, and the person might finish medical school with lots of debt. (con)

11. The person would probably get lots of respect from other people for what he or she does. (pro)

12. The person would have to worry that every patient he or she ever saw might sue him or her. (con)

13. The person might have to spend lots of hours on record-keeping and paperwork. (con)

14. The person would get to study lots of very interesting subjects. (pro)

15. The person would get to be with lots of interesting people. (pro)

The advantage of getting to study lots of interesting subjects throughout your life has to do with which psychological skill?

A. Fortitude
or
B. Pleasure from discovery, a skill in the joyousness group?

Chapter 38: Examples of Listing Important Variables for a Decision

452. This chapter provides examples of what you get when you do the exercise on listing important variables for a decision.

A person is deciding on an item of clothing to buy or not buy. Important variables listed:

1. Whether it feels good to wear.

2. How expensive it is.

3. Whether it fits in with what's expected wherever I'm going to wear it, for example at a certain workplace or school.

4. Whether it is too "revealing" versus whether it covers up what it's supposed to.

5. Whether it looks attractive on me.

6. Whether it fits me well.

7. Whether it's warm or cool enough for the season and place I want to wear it in.

8. Whether it attracts attention, if I want to attract attention, or fails to attract attention, if that's what I want.

9. Whether it's associated with a certain group of people whose values I admire.

Which variable was not listed above?

A. How much the clothing cost.
or
B. Whether any words written on the clothing are words I agree with.

453. The next decision has to do with whether or not to buy a video game, or which game to get.

1. Whether it's possible to play the game on the hardware I already have.

2. Whether it's fun.

3. Whether it's so much fun that it will lead me to waste a lot of time.

4. Whether it's violent and therefore does a little bit to encourage a more violent world.

5. Whether it causes me to get exercise (as for example with a dancing video game) versus sit still.

6. How much it costs.

7. Whether my friends will like to play it with me.

8. Whether it will improve my mind to work at it.

9. Whether you do it just once or whether you can enjoy doing it many times.

Which variable was NOT t listed?

A. Whether it teaches me to drive a car.
or
B. Whether it leads people to practice violence.

454. The next decision has to do with how to spend my time on a day that I have free. What variables do I use to evaluate the activities I'm considering?

1. How much the activities help me accomplish an important goal.

2. How much fun the activities are.

3. How much I have a friendship strengthened with someone I'd like to strengthen a relationship with.

4. How much I help anyone else.

5. Whether I make money, and if so how much.

6. If I spend money, how much I have to spend.

7. How healthy and safe are the activities for me and others.

8. How much the activity improves my mind.

9. How much the activity gets me into better physical shape.

Which variable was NOT listed?

A. How much, if anything, the activities cost.
or
B. What effect the activities have on the earth's resources.

455. The next decision is: I have some time to read a book that hasn't been assigned to me, and I'm deciding what book to read.

1. Whether I think reading it will teach me something useful and good.

2. Whether it seems that it will be fun to read.

3. Whether other people with values like mine thought it was worthwhile.

4. How expensive it is.

5. Whether it's available in the format that I like better, for example ebook or book made of paper.

6. Whether the length of it suits me.

7. Whether it's not too hard for me to understand.

8. Whether it seems to motivate people to make the world better.

Which variable did the person NOT list?

A. Whether the author has written other good books.
or
B. Whether it seems that it will be pleasant to read.

Chapter 39: Examples of the Twelve Thought Exercise

456. The situation is that the first person is discussing with the second whether boxing is good or bad for society. The first person makes all sorts of really good points, but the second person argues back and isn't the least bit convinced by what the first person says. The twelve thought exercise is about this situation, from the first person's point of view.

1. Awfulizing: This is going to drive me nuts that I can't make this person see what should be so clear!

2. Getting down on myself: I'm failing. I must not be a persuasive person.

3. Blaming someone else: His whole way of thinking about this is stupid. Plus, he doesn't even want to think straight.

4. Not awfulizing: It almost always is true that when people debate, neither convinces the other, so it's not awful that I can't convince him.

5. Not getting down on myself: It's not my fault that he is choosing not to take seriously the points I'm making. So there's no need to punish myself.

6. Not blaming someone else: I don't like the way he thinks about this, but I don't want to waste energy blaming him for it.

When, in getting down on himself, the person says "I must not be a persuasive person," rather than "looks like I can't persuade this particular person." The first of these two statements gives an example of

A. overgeneralizing,
or
B. undergeneralizing?

457. The twelve thought exercise concerning the debate about boxing continues.

7. Goal-setting: I'm deciding that my goal is not to convince this person. My goals are to practice making the best points I can make, to stay cool and polite, and also not to waste too much time on this.

8. Listing options and choosing: I could go over the research about brain damage in boxers. I could point out the research about whether fighting drains off anger or makes it stronger.

Or, I could just say, "It looks like we're not going to agree on this one," and change the subject. I think I'll do the last one.

9. Learning from the experience: I am reminded by this that when people start debating, hardly ever does either of them get convinced that the other is right.

10. Celebrating luck: I'm really glad that there's no need for me to convince this other person.

11. Celebrating someone else's choice: I celebrate the people who have been able to look at the research and make a good decision.

12. Celebrating my own choice: I'm glad I chose to stay cool and not start yelling at the other person or anything like that.

When the person celebrates his own choice in this example, he celebrates using the skills of

A. fortitude and respectful talk, or
B. productivity and compliance?

458. Here's another example. Let's use an imaginary situation, and pretend that a space ship lands in someone's back yard, and some creatures that don't look human get out of the space ship.

1. Awfulizing: Oh, no! They're probably going to kill me or take over the whole Earth!

2. Getting down on yourself: I should have made a plan about what I was going to do if this ever happened. I was just too lazy to do it.

3. Blaming someone else: This is my yard! They have no right to land their spacecraft in it!

4. Not awfulizing: If they'd wanted to destroy us, they probably would have done that before they came. They don't necessarily want to do anything harmful.

5. Not getting down on myself: This is so unexpected, I certainly don't want to punish myself for not trying to prepare for this.

6. Not blaming someone else: They haven't done me any harm, and in fact it's a great privilege to see them, so I don't want to blame them for landing near me.

If the person had mainly done "blaming someone else" type thoughts in this situation, the person probably would feel

A. guilty,

or

B. angry?

459. The twelve thought exercise about the alien landing continues.

7. Goal-setting: If there's anything I can do to prevent any violence, either toward them or toward myself or other Earthlings, that's my main goal.

8. Listing options and choosing: I could go and show my parents. I could show my sister. I could go outside and try to meet the people I see. I could call the police. I could just watch them from here a little longer and see what they do. I could video record them with my cell phone.

　　I don't want to get a lot of other people and the police involved for fear that someone will hurt them. I don't want to just walk out, for fear that they might harm me. I think I'll watch them from here and record them with my cell phone for the time being, and see what they do next and what direction they go.

9: Learning from the experience: I learned that sometimes when you look out your window at night, you see amazing things!

You can tell particularly from the person's goal-setting and listing options and choosing that the person highly values the skill of

A. nonviolence

or

B. positive fantasy rehearsal?

460. The twelve-thought exercise about the visitors from space continues.

10. Celebrating luck: I'm so lucky to be able to see this!

11. Celebrating someone else's choice: They probably have the technology to do a lot of destruction to us. I'm so thankful that they haven't used it.

12. Celebrating my own choice: I'm glad that I'm keeping my head and deciding what to do!

When the person did "celebrating someone else's choice," it sounds like the thought was one that promoted the feeling of

A. pride,

or

B. gratitude?

461. In the next situation, some people have noticed a mouse in their kitchen.

A person sets a humane mouse trap that captures the mouse alive without hurting him. When the person gets up in the morning, she sees a little mouse in the trap, looking healthy but scared.

1. Awfulizing: Oh no, I'm in a hurry and now I have to do something with the mouse in addition to everything else I have to do.

2. Getting down on myself: I should have planned and left more time for myself, but I didn't.

3. Blaming someone else: Why did the mice have to pick my house to try to settle in?

4. Not awfulizing: It won't take me very long to take the mouse to a new home. I can handle this.

5. Not getting down on myself: It looks scared. I feel compassion for it, but I don't want to punish myself for that.

6. Not blaming someone else: No one did anything blameworthy in this whole event!

The person who set the trap caught the mouse, just as she wanted to. This situation illustrates that you can use the twelve thought exercise

A. with unwanted situations,
or
B. with any situation, wanted or unwanted?

462. The twelve thought exercise with the mouse capture situation continues.

7. Goal-setting: My goal is to give the little fellow a nice new home outside, and still be on time where I have to go.

8. Listing options and choosing: I could take him across the road and down the trail and let him loose by the creek. I could let him loose in the thicket at the end of our street. I could wait until I get back from school. I'm choosing the thicket at the end of the street, going there right now, hustling so I won't be late, and leaving some raisins for him to eat when he gets there.

9. Learning from the experience: This trap looks like a humane and effective way to remove a mouse from my kitchen.

10. Celebrating luck: Hooray, I'm glad I caught the mouse!

11. Celebrating someone else's choice: I'm glad that someone chose to design these humane traps.

12. Celebrating my own choice: I'm glad I chose to get the trap and use it, and I like my choice of where to take the mouse and turn him loose!

Sometimes "learning from the experience" involves learning, from a failure, to do something different the next time. Sometimes it involves learning, from a success, to do the same thing next time. Was the "learning from experience" done above an example of

A. learning from a failure,
or
B. learning from a success?

Chapter 40: Examples of STEBC Fantasy Rehearsals

463. This chapter gives more examples of STEBC fantasy rehearsals, which can be used to practice any psychological skill.

Situation: I'm at home, and there's nothing much going on. I'm getting the urge to watch TV or do a video game.

Thoughts: If I can set a goal and work toward that goal, I'll probably feel better about how I used my time than if I just goof off. What goal do I want to work toward? One option is getting better at math. I have the math book that will teach me how to do problems that I couldn't do before. What if I set the goal of learning how to do one problem that I couldn't do before? It will take self-discipline, but I think I can do it.

Emotions: I'm feeling determined to make a success of this.

Behaviors: I go and find the math book that I own. I look through and spend some time choosing the new type of problem to learn to do. I read the explanation in the book, and the sample problems. I get pen and paper and work the sample problems myself, right after reading how the book authors did them. I look at the problems like that that are in the book, and work them. I check the answers, and see that I got them right.

Celebration: I feel really good about myself. I did something productive, that will help me be successful, and I proved that I have the self-discipline to get work done when I start to feel bored!

Some of the psychological skills the person is practicing in this fantasy rehearsal are

A. compliance, honesty, and nonviolence.
or
B. productivity, self-discipline, and the part of joyousness that involves pleasure from learning.

464. The person in the next fantasy rehearsal is working on a fear of pain.

Situation: I have a blood test to get. I'm at the lab.

Thoughts: This is an opportunity for me to practice handling pain. My plan is to relax my muscles and to keep them as relaxed as I can during the whole thing. It doesn't matter what it feels like; the important thing is what I do. I already congratulate myself for just coming here. If I can sit still for the test, I'll really feel good.

Emotions: I feel nervous, but I feel very determined.

Behaviors: When my name is called, I go in and put out my arm, and they do the rest. Meanwhile I relax my muscles all over. I don't even flinch when they put the needle in. I hold still in a relaxed way until it's done.

Celebration: Hooray for me! I did it! My strategy of focusing on muscle relaxation really worked well!

The skills the person was practicing in this fantasy rehearsal were

A. courage and fortitude,
or
B. productivity and friendship-building?

465. The person doing the next fantasy rehearsal is working on social conversation skills.

Situation: I'm wanting to practice social conversation with family members, as a way of preparing myself to do it more comfortably with other people. I call up my grandmom on the phone, to chat.

Thoughts: I'm planning to ask her what's going on in her life, and to be a good listener with follow up questions, reflections, facilitations, and positive feedback. I'm planning to tell her what I've been studying in school, and what I've been reading about in history, when I get a chance. I want to have a cheerful and enthusiastic tone of voice.

Emotions: I feel a little bit nervous, even though I feel sure that she will enjoy hearing from me.

Behaviors: She answers the phone, and I tell her it's I, and tell her I just called up to see how she was doing and chat some! She sounds glad. I ask about what she's been up to. She tells me, and I say, "Oh, please tell me more about that!" We continue to have a good chat. I tell her about the things I'd planned to. After a while I say "It was really nice to talk with you," and we say good bye.

Celebration: Hooray! I helped her to feel good, and I had fun, and I got some good practice of social conversation also!

The person in this one was practicing

A. nonviolence,
or
B. friendship-building?

466. Fantasy rehearsals of situations that cause unwanted fear or anger or other unpleasant emotion can be "mastery" rehearsals if one imagines being totally comfortable, and "coping" rehearsals if one imagines feeling the bad feeling but doing the best thing anyway. Someone who fears going to bed in the dark does the following rehearsal.

Situation: It's bedtime.

Thoughts: I feel very safe. I'm in a safe neighborhood and a safe house. I look forward to resting.

Emotions: I feel secure and sleepy, not the slightest bit afraid, and happy that all my fear has gone. It's going to feel really good to go to bed.

Behaviors: I turn out the light and get into bed. It's pretty black, but that's fine with me. I close my eyes and relax and enjoy the feeling of resting. I have some pleasant fantasies for a while and then fall asleep.

Celebration: Hooray, it feels really good to be able to go to bed and sleep with total security!

Was this a

A. Coping rehearsal,

or
B. Mastery rehearsal?

467. In the following, someone works on a bad habit of "road rage."

Situation: I'm driving down the street, and someone pulls out from a side street, going the direction I'm going. They should have waited – they didn't have nearly enough time to get out. I have to slam on the brake instinctively and I feel a lot of anger rise up in me.

Thoughts: This is actually a good opportunity to practice. In the past I might have expressed lots of anger at the other driver, but I've decided I don't want to do that. It's not my job to improve other people's driving. I don't accomplish anything by giving them a loud horn honk or an angry gesture. By putting on the brake, I've done all that needs to be done. I want to live and let live and not insist that everyone else is perfect, because I'm not either.

Emotions: As I think these thoughts, I can feel my anger going down some. I still feel it, but not so strongly.

Behaviors: I continue going slowly for a few seconds to let the other driver put a safe distance between us. I don't honk or gesture or even give an angry face. I stay cool and concentrate on driving as well as I possibly can.

Celebration: I feel really good about the way I handled this! Acting as if I were not angry helped me to get less angry!

This is an example of a

A. Coping rehearsal,
or
B. Mastery rehearsal?

468. The next fantasy rehearsal has a middle school youth practicing "refusal skills."

Situation: I'm with some friends. They take out some cigarettes and light up. One of them offers one to me. I say no. Another of them says sarcastically, "Oh, you're such a good little kid. What's the matter, are you scared?" None of the others back me up.

Thoughts: The decision not to smoke is a no-brainer. But how do I want to respond to them? I could be meek and submissive and just laugh and shrug my shoulders. I could be pretty aggressive and say, "I said, NO! That's not hard to understand, now is it! Go harass somebody else if you want to." I could say, "Yes, I am scared of lung cancer and emphysema and bunches of other bad diseases, and

if you thought about it more you would be too." I could say very little and just walk away from these guys. Actually I kind of like the last one best, because no matter what I say, sitting here with them watching them smoke is going to feel awkward. Do I want to say, "See you around, losers," as I walk away? I think I'll decide that dominating them or reforming them is not my job.

Emotions: I feel angry at them for trying to get me to do something so stupid, but not so angry that I can't make good decisions.

Behaviors: I say, "I'll see you guys later," and walk away. I seek out some of my other friends to hang out with.

Celebration: I like the way I handled this. I think I made some good choices.

Do you think the anger the person felt in this rehearsal was

A. something the person was trying to get rid of,
or
B. an emotion that the person found useful, in moderate amounts, in this situation?

469. The person in the next example is working on a fear of getting dental work done.

Situation: I go to the dentist's office, and I sit in the chair. They adjust it for me and put a towel over me.

Thoughts: It's good that this is not a painful procedure. Even if it were, I feel confident that I could handle it. All I have to do is to relax my muscles, open my mouth, and not move my head away. That's easy. While they're working on me I get to do anything I want in my mind.

Emotions: I feel determined, and very confident. I have practiced this to the point where I feel very relaxed, almost sleepy.

Behaviors: I open my mouth, relax the muscles of my head and face, and remain still. I notice myself breathing slowly, as when I'm very sleepy. The dental work begins, but my mind drifts around to all sorts of other things. When they ask me to open or close more I do it, but otherwise I don't pay much attention to what's going on. Then they say they're done.

Celebration: Hooray for me! I not only did it, but I made it easy to do!

Was this a

A. mastery rehearsal,
or
B. coping rehearsal?

470. Here's another version of the same situation.

Situation: I go to the dentist's office and sit in the chair and they get ready to work.

Thoughts: I'm noticing that I'm really scared. My heart is pounding, and my hands are shaking. But I can still be successful at this. I want to concentrate on "doing, not feeling" as what makes it a success. All I have to do is open my mouth, be still, and relax my face muscles as much as I can.

Emotions: I'm feeling scared about 9 on a scale of 10.

Behaviors: Despite what I'm feeling, I am being successful! I'm holding my mouth open and I'm relaxing my face and head and neck and not flinching or pulling away! I keep doing this, and it gets a little easier over time. I keep going to the finish.

Celebration: Hooray for me! Despite the fact that I was so scared, I did what I needed to do! This is not only a big success – it proves to me for the future that I can feel fear and do what I need to do anyway!

This was a

A. mastery rehearsal,
or
B. coping rehearsal?

471. In the following, the person practices a certain type of fortitude known as "transitions": having to stop doing one thing to do something else.

Situation: I'm playing a video game. It's really exciting. I'm working toward a goal. My family member warns me that we will have to leave in 15 minutes to make our appointment. I keep going for about 5 minutes, and I meet my goal. But now there's something else I can take on!

Thoughts: I have a goal of doing a good transition. The time isn't up. But I know from past experience that if I try to keep going right up to the last minute, I'm going to have to interrupt myself right in the middle of trying to do something. It's better to pause now, when I've reached an OK stopping point. If I do, I can run around a bit and do a few push-ups and get a little bit of exercise before we go.

Emotion: I'm feeling determined to make this transition a good one. I feel a little frustrated to have to stop the game, but when I think of what worse things people put up with, I decide I don't want to feel bad, and I don't feel bad.

Behavior: I pause the game. I get ready to go to the appointment. I tell my family member I'll be outside and ready to go. I go out and do some running back and forth and some push-ups. My family member comes out, and I say, "Ready to go?" in a cheerful voice. Then I say, "Thanks for going with me to this appointment. And thanks for reminding me about it ahead of time!"

Celebration: Hooray, I handled this transition like a champ!

In this, the person said things to the family member that were practices not only of fortitude, but also of

A. kindness and joyousness and respectful talk,
or
B. conservation?

472. In the following fantasy rehearsal, the person is working on reducing a habit of picky eating.

Situation: I'm really hungry. I sit down and see my meal. There are two stews, each having a bunch of things mixed together, and I don't even know what some of them are. The two foods are touching each other on the plate, and starting to mix with each other. I look at what I have to drink, and it's some smoothie with blended fruits and also some vegetables like broccoli. It looks greenish-brown.

Thoughts: I know that there is nothing that will harm me. It's possible that I won't like this. But at any rate, if I eat this, I will have had a major triumph over my fear of eating unfamiliar foods. I want that triumph a lot. It will help me nourish myself better and help me feel more at ease around people if I'm not such a picky eater.

Emotions: I feel a little disgusted at the sight of the food, but I also feel hungry, and mostly I feel determined.

Behaviors: I start eating the food, right at the point where the two are mixing together. It turns out to be OK – not great, but good enough. I drink the smoothie, and it's actually pretty good. I say to myself, "You're doing it!" and I keep on eating until I've had enough and have had a reasonable meal.

Celebration: Hooray for me! I have eaten just the sort of food that has given me the most trouble in the past! I've made a really important step toward getting over my fear of unfamiliar foods!

In this fantasy rehearsal, the person practiced

A. courage and self-discipline skills, or
B. skills of social conversation?

473. In the next fantasy rehearsal, someone is practicing responding to the taunting of bullies.

Situation: I walk toward lunch, and a kid coming from the other direction looks at me with a sneering look and says, "Hi, Stupid-face."

Thoughts: In the past I've probably reinforced behavior like this by responding with excitement. I've learned not to do this. My goal is not to reinforce this behavior. My goal also is not to do anything that gets me in trouble or starts a fight. I want to practice the frame of mind that lets me handle this without getting upset. I'd like to end this sort of behavior one day, also.

I've decided to keep a log of these sorts of events, in case I want to use the rule of law, and I want to stick to that plan, also.

Emotions: I feel more cool and calculating than angry. I feel compassionate toward myself, and determined to handle this well.

Behaviors: I give the kid some silent eye contact. I don't smile or frown. I look at him a little puzzled. Then I look away and keep going. I notice the time. When I get a chance I open up my log and write down what happened as accurately as I possibly can.

Celebration: I feel really good about the way I handled this. I didn't reward the kid for taunting me by getting upset. Good job!

In this, the person is practicing

A. fortitude, nonviolence, and good decisions,
or
B. kindness, respectful talk, and loyalty?

Chapter 41: Examples of UCAC Fantasy Rehearsals

474. Someone has resolved to get working on some writing, starting at 8:30 in the morning. The person is reading the newspaper and lingering over breakfast, and notices that it is already 8:30.

Urge: I'm getting the urge to just keep reading the newspaper, get a little more breakfast, and take it easy for a while.

Celebration: I'm glad I became aware of this urge, and the fact that it's not what I resolved to do!

Alternative: I'm choosing to get up and start my writing without further delay.

Celebration: Hooray, I just did a self-discipline triumph!

The urge that the person didn't want to give in to, in this example, was

A. the urge to be lazy instead of working,
or
B. certainly the result of an additction?

475. The person in the next example has a habit of clenching his teeth and grinding them against each other. This is not good for the teeth or the jaw joint.

Urge: I'm getting the urge to grind my teeth.

Celebration: I'm so glad I caught that urge before I did it!

Alternative: My alternative is to relax the muscles of my face, head, neck, and shoulders for several seconds.

Celebration: Hooray! I did what is good for me rather than what's bad for me!

This fantasy rehearsal is meant to help the person with a skill of

A. self-care,
or
B. respectful talk?

476. In the next situation, a girl is trying to study in the living room, and her younger brother starts singing and dancing around to get her attention.

Urge: I'm getting the urge to scream at him something like, "Get out of here and shut up!"

Celebration: I'm so glad I caught that urge before acting on it.

Alternative: I say to my brother, "It's good to see you being joyous. I need to study now. I'm going to my room and close the door for a while, and when I get done, maybe we can play some then."

Celebration: Hooray, I took care of my own needs, and I was nice to him also! I feel good about myself!

This fantasy rehearsal was meant to help the person get into good habits of

A. respectful talk and kindness,
or
B. conservation and courage?

477. In the next situation, the person reads in the news about acts of senseless violence.

Urge: I get the urge to say to the people who are with me, "The human race is so savage. If they all kill each other off it will almost serve them right."

Celebration: I'm so glad I caught this while it was just an urge!

Alternative: I think a bit and say, "When I read about these acts of savage violence, it makes me so glad that we are doing some work toward nonviolence! It makes me feel

determined to work harder for nonviolence!"

Celebration: I'm so glad I celebrated our choices and set goals, instead of awfulizing and blaming!

The fantasy rehearsal that the person used helped him or her to say things that are more hopeful and optimistic. Thus this rehearsal contributed to the person's skill of

A. honesty,
or
B. joyousness?

478. A kid is on the playground at recess in winter. He sees another kid wearing a hat.

Urge: I get the urge to run up, grab the kid's hat, and run off with it.

Celebration: I'm glad I caught myself before doing that – I'm getting too old to do something that immature.

Alternative: I ask the other kid if he wants to throw a football back and forth with me. We go over and get one and throw some passes to each other.

Celebration: Hooray, I chose a good way to have fun with the other kid rather than annoy him!

This fantasy rehearsal will probably help the person with the skill of

A. compliance,
or
B. friendship-building?

479. The person in the next example has a problem with a hand-washing compulsion, and he has already washed his hands enough recently.

Urge: I'm getting the urge to wash my hands, not because it would accomplish anything, but just to get rid of a feeling of germiness or something.

Celebration: I'm glad I caught this urge and didn't just go and wash my hands automatically.

Alternative: Instead of washing my hands, I relax my muscles a few seconds, and then I ask myself what's my best use of time. It would do me good to look over something I've been studying. I'll do that instead. After that, I'll go for a run and get some exercise.

Celebration: Hooray, I've chosen good things to do, and I didn't give in to the compulsion!

If we think of the hand-washing as a behavior that temporarily reduces an unrealistic fear of being contaminated by germs, this fantasy rehearsal helped the person with the skills of

A. honesty,
or
B. courage?

480. The child in the next UCAC fantasy rehearsal sees his mom's credit card lying around.

Urge: I'm getting the urge to use the credit card to buy something on the Internet.

Celebration: I'm glad I didn't act on that urge! That would have been a very untrustworthy thing to do.

Alternative: I take the credit card to my mom and say, "This was on the table. You might want to put it away in a safe place so no one such as myself will be tempted to use it!

Celebration: I feel really good about communicating to her that it's a good idea not to leave me open to temptation with that sort of thing. But I also feel really good about resisting the temptation.

The person in this rehearsal was practicing

A. honesty and self-discipline,

or
B. productivity and nonviolence?

Chapter 42: Examples of the Social Conversation Role Play

Conversation 1: Two hikers

481. People are hiking in the wilderness. At a place where you can get water, two people going the opposite direction chat with each other.

1. So how is it up the trail in the direction you've come from. Is it steep walking?

2. It's steep, but it's very beautiful. There are some great views.

1. Sounds great. I'll take some pictures. It's a pretty gentle walk for a few miles in the direction you're going. But it's pretty, and there are no mosquitoes, even though it goes by marshes.

2. That's good news, thanks for letting me know. Is this your first time hiking this trail?

1. Yes, except that when I was only about one year old apparently my dad took me along part of this trail in a backpack.

2. How interesting! Do you get feelings of familiarity when you go along those parts?

When Person 2 said, "Do you get feelings of familiarity...," was that an

A. reflection,
or
B. follow-up question?

482. The conversation between hikers continues.

1. I wish I could say I did, but no. I don't think I remember a single thing from when I was that young, other than from people's telling me about it.

2. It sounds like you come from a family of hikers.

1. Yes, and my dad still likes it, although now he's into the short trips of two or three hours rather than the longer ones like this one. How about you, do you have family members who are into hiking also?

2. I do. In fact my sister is going along with me on this hike. She's not into the roughing it bit quite as much as I am, though. So I'm carrying most of her stuff in my backpack.

1. That's really nice of you. What do you do when you're not hiking?

When Person 1 said, "That's really nice of you," that was

A. a reflection,
or
B. positive feedback?

483. Conversation of hikers continues.

2. I'm in school, at Straywood College. I tried to get a job this summer but with the recession, there was nothing.

1. So hiking is a pretty inexpensive way to spend some time during the summer, and it sounds like that's a good thing for you, huh?

2. Yes. My family is renting out the house this week, to tourists, when the music festival is in town, trying to pick up a little extra money. My mom and dad are in a little campsite, and going to work from there this week.

1. Sounds really resourceful! How do you like going to Straywood College?

2. I like it a lot. They have some different philosophies there. They have each teacher of each course spell out exactly what you need to do to get

an A, or a B, or a C, and so forth. You get the grade you deserve regardless of what anyone else in the class does.

1. So if I understand you, you have a set of standards you're trying to match, and you're not trying to beat your classmates, huh?

The response that Person 1 just made was an

A. facilitation,
or
B. reflection?

484.

2. That's right. How about you, what do you do when you're not hiking?

1. I'm working on writing a book, and while I'm doing that, I make a living as a ballroom dancing instructor.

2. How interesting! Is the book on ballroom dancing?

1. No, it's on economics. It's on how we can set things up so that people are working more at more useful things, and less at less important things.

2. What a cool topic. I was just reading about demonstrations that people were having in Brazil. The people there were angry that money

was being spent on stadiums instead of things like health care and education.

1. That's exactly the type of thing I'm writing about. And one of the keys is that the voters in any countery have their priorities straight. I'm really impressed that the people in Brazil seem to value basic human needs more than sports.

2. And how did you get into ballroom dancing?

What Person 2 just said was an

A. follow-up question,
or
B. facilitation?

485.

1. I just saw an ad for help wanted. I got some books and some videos, and studied like crazy for about a week, and was able to get the job. I study really hard to keep ahead of my students!

2. I was in Quebec City recently, and there was a park with a little gazebo. I saw about 8 or 10 people doing ballroom dancing with each other, and they looked so good doing it, and they seemed to be enjoying it so much.

1. It is lots of fun. And it's a really cooperative thing, where people help each other. Maybe there's a ballroom dance club at Straywood College!

2. I'll have to look into that!

1. Well, looks like my group is getting ready to take off again. It's been really nice talking with you.

2. You too! Have a great rest of your hike!

1. You too! Bye bye.

When they said things like nice talking with you, have a great rest of your hike, and bye bye, they were using

A. facilitations,
or
B. parting rituals?

Conversation 2: The cleaning person and the hotel guest

486. The cleaning person, who is person 1, comes into the hotel room where person 2 is staying.

1. Hello, will I be disturbing you if I clean up the room now?

2. Not at all. Thanks very much for doing that. We don't need much done, but there is some garbage to take out. We've been eating here rather than eating out.

1. That's a smart thing to do, with how expensive the restaurants are around here. With a microwave and a fridge and a grocery store, you really don't need them, do you?

When Person 1 says, "That's a smart thing to do," that's an example of

A. a facilitation,
or
B. positive feedback?

487.

2. That's our plan; you called it exactly.

1. Looks like you're getting some work done here.

2. We are getting ready for a sales presentation. We have a business that tutors kids in reading, and we're trying to convince a school district to contract with us.

1. Sounds interesting! How do you teach them, better than they do in school?

2. We try to rig it up so that each child is working at just the level that is not too hard, not too easy, but just right. If you can find that magic level, it becomes fun to learn rather than frustrating.

1. That sounds like the sort of thing that you can do with one-on-one instruction and not in a large group, is that right?

2. Exactly. The tutor is constantly trying to figure out the right level for the individual student.

1. I'm doing some tutoring in math, in addition to this job. The idea that you just said is really important for math, also. If it's too hard, the student gets frustrated, and if it's too easy, the student gets bored.

2. Isn't that a coincidence, that you work in tutoring also! Do you do it on your own, or are you with an organization?

The last sentence that Person 2 said so far is an example of

A. a follow-up question,
or
B. a facilitation?

488.

1. I work for the Farmingdale Learning Center. The people that run it are nice, but they don't pay much.

2. And what level of math do you teach?

1. Mainly algebra 2 and precalculus. Those seem to be really hard for a lot of people. I've always thought they were fun, particularly the trigonometry.

2. Wow, I'd like to hear more about your experiences some time. Here's my card, if you'd like to get in touch.

1. That would be really nice. I'll let you keep preparing, and I'll get on to the other rooms. Nice talking with you.

2. You too, and thanks again for helping us out today.

1. You're most welcome. Bye bye.

2. Bye.

When Person 2 said, "Thanks again for helping us out today," that was

A. positive feedback,
or
B. a reflection?

Conversation 3: Two young children at a playground

489.

1. Hi!

2. Hi! Want to throw the ball with me?

1. Sure, thanks!

2. You're good at throwing and catching.

1. Thank you. You're nice to say that.

2. Who are these people whose pictures are on the ball?

1. They're Joompka and Snook. They're on television.

2. I've never seen them. What kind of things do they do?

When Person 2 says "What kind of things do they do," that's an example of

A. a reflection,
or
B. a follow-up question?

490.

1. Joompka has the power to see through things and go through walls.

And Snook can turn him and Joompka invisible.

2. Are they good or bad?

1. They're good. They usually save people. One time Joompka saw someone locked up in a bank vault, and he saved the person. But the police thought they were robbers. Lots of people chased after them. Snook turned them invisible so they could get away.

2. Thanks for telling me that story! Do you live near here?

When Person 2 says, "Thanks for telling me that story," that's

A. a reflection,
or
B. positive feedback?

491.

1. Yes. I walked here from my house. It's over that way.

2. I can walk to this park from my house too. Mine is over that way.

1. My name's Pat; what's yours?

2. I'm Lee. Glad to meet you, Pat.

1. You too.

2. Want to go out onto that field and kick the ball some?

1. Yeah! Do you like soccer? We could pass it back and forth as we go down the field.

2. I don't play soccer much. But let's give it a try.

1. If you kick it with the inside of your foot, you may be able to aim it better.

2. I'll try it that way too.

1. You aim it well.

2. Look at that dog over there.

1. I know that dog. He belongs to some people in my neighborhood.

2. What kind is he?

When Person 2 says, "What kind is he," that's

A. a follow-up question,
or
B. a reflection?

492.

1. He's a mix between a collie and something else. I don't know what. Want to go over and pet him?

2. Sure. What's his name?

1. His name's Pedro.

2. Oh, my mom is calling me. Looks like I've got to go.

1. Thanks for playing with me, Lee.

2. Thank you, Pat. Hope to see you again later.

1. You too! Bye bye.

2. Bye.

Thanks for playing, hope to see you later, and bye bye are all

A. parting rituals,
or
B. greeting rituals?

Conversation 4: The speaker and the audience member

493. One person has just given a speech. The other was in the audience, and chats with the speaker afterward.

1. I very much enjoyed your speech. I think your ideas on reducing bullying should really help people.

2. Thanks very much for saying that. I'm not really sure we should call them my ideas, since so many other people have put them forth.

1. Right, and you gave lots of credit to those others. I'm a guidance counselor at a school, and a wealthy person has actually offered to install surveillance cameras all around the school, to try to reduce bullying. Do you think we should do it?

2. Wow, that's an interesting idea. But in addition to cameras, you would pretty much have to install microphones too, since a lot of bullying is hostile talk. And it's really hard to record everything that goes on.

1. So if I understand you, the technology of recording bullying is more complicated than just putting video cameras all around.

What Person 1 just said is an example of

A. a reflection,
or
B. a facilitation?

494.

2. Yes. Plus a lot of bullying goes on in bathrooms, and there are problems with putting cameras there.

1. That's a good point.

2. But if you do it, I hope you'll try to measure how much good it does. Does your school give a questionnaire to students, asking how much bullying they give and receive?

1. We haven't so far. That would be a really important thing to do, and I appreciate your making the point in your speech about how that itself can reduce bullying some.

2. Thanks for saying that. Which school do you work at?

1. It's called the Alfred Adler School, in the Finchburg School District.

When Person 2 says, "Which school do you work at," that's

A. a reflection,
or
B. a follow-up question?

495.

2. Do you think that a lot of bullying goes on in your school?

1. There sure are a lot of students who talk with me about how they've been mistreated by other students. And there are probably lots of others that I don't know about.

2. There sure are lots of students who are afraid to talk about it, for fear of being thought wimpy. But lots of them can find it easier to say something about it on a survey than actually talking to someone.

1. We should definitely try that. And the idea of having discussions among students about how to reduce bullying, that you mentioned in your speech, sounds like something else to try.

2. Just measuring it and getting people talking about how to solve the problem is a really great first step, I think.

1. But part of the problem is that teachers are so busy trying to improve standardized test scores that they don't feel they have time to spend on things like how students treat each other.

2. I know what you mean. In your school, do teachers feel scared that they will be scolded or fired if students don't do well enough?

The sentence that Person 2 has just said is

A. a reflection,
or

B. a follow-up question?

496.

1. Yes, they do feel that fear, and it creates a feeling of anxiety that goes through the whole school.

2. I'm sorry that the push for test scores makes it harder to spend time reducing bullying. But I guess we just do the best we can, huh?

1. Yes. And I'll not take up any more of your time. Thanks again for talking with us today!

2. You are most welcome, and I'm honored that you came.

When Person 2 says, "I'm honored that you came," that's

A. a facilitation,
or
B. positive feedback?

Conversation 5: The spelling bee winner and the chess tournament winner, continued

497. This is a continuation of the chat between the two characters who talked in the chapter on the Social Conversation Role Play.

1. So tell me about how you got good at chess.

2. Well, first of all, I'm not that good. I just won a little tournament. You get higher and higher ratings the more you win, and there are many, many people out there with higher ratings than I.

1. Sounds like you're not claiming greatness, and I admire that.

2. I'm certainly not, and thank you. But to answer your question, a lot of people think that you get better at chess by just playing a lot. What really helped me the most was studying books.

1. Really. I wouldn't have guessed that.

When Person 1 says, "Really," that's an example of

A. a facilitation,
or
B. a follow-up question?

498.

2. There are all sorts of books out there that explain how to win in chess. And also, lots of them give you positions on the chess board and ask you to make the best choice. If you practice with those enough, you start

finding the same sorts of positions coming up in actual games.

1. So it sounds like chess is something you can study like math.

2. That's exactly right. You read the explanations and then you do practice problems. Another thing that helps people get better in chess is the computer. You can always have an opponent that is just a little bit better than you, any time you want it, with the computer. In fact, if you enjoy it, you have to watch yourself that you don't waste too much time on it.

1. Computers have changed so much. I used a computer program to get myself ready for the spelling bee. The computer would display on the screen and pronounce the word, and I'd type it, looking at it, and then type it again not looking at it.

2. I see. So you practiced in a way that kept testing yourself, like I did.

The last sentence that Person 2 said is

A. a follow-up question,
or
B. a reflection?

499.

1. That's right.

2. So what did you think of the speech we heard?

1. I had thought about the fact that technology is progressing so much faster than people's ability to get along with each other, but the speaker had some great facts to give us on that.

2. I really enjoyed hearing it too. It sort of had to do with what we had been talking about before, the idea that people are so busy competing with each other, when what they need to be doing is figuring out how not to blow up the world.

1. Huh. That sounds like a good title for a book: "How Not to Blow Up the World."

2. Really, I think it seriously might be! Well, I guess it's time to go. Thanks very much for chatting with me.

1. Thank you for chatting with me! Let's be in touch.

2. Sounds great. Bye.

1. Bye.

When Person 1 says, "Huh," that's

A. a facilitation,
or

B. a parting ritual?

Conversation 6: A Chat with Superman

500. You can get as whimsical as you want in the social conversation role play. In this one, a student has won a chance to chat with Superman.

1. Hi Superman, I'm glad to meet you; my name is Daniel Beck.

2. Hi Daniel. Glad to meet you too. My official name is Clark Kent, as you probably know.

1. I do know that, but don't worry, I won't give away your secret to anybody.

2. Thank you. Tell me about yourself, Daniel, please.

1. I'm 10 years old and in the fifth grade. I live just in one of the suburbs of Metropolis. I've never needed to get saved from any great danger by someone like you, because I'm pretty careful and stay away from bad guys.

2. Sounds like you know how to look out for yourself, huh Daniel? I like that. Are there many bad guys in your suburb?

What Superman just said was

A. A reflection, positive feedback, and a follow-up question, in that order.
or
B. A facilitation, a greeting ritual, and a parting ritual, in that order.

501. It's Daniel's turn to speak.

1. I read in our local paper about people's doing bad stuff pretty often. But I guess it doesn't happen nearly as much as it does in downtown Metropolis.

2. Wow, I'm impressed that you read the newspaper, Daniel. Do you also read the Daily Planet?

1. I sure do, and I'll have to say, the articles and news stories written by Clark Kent are some of the best ones. If you ever lose your superpowers you can continue to make a good living, because you're a good reporter.

2. Thanks very much, Daniel. Not many people compliment me about that, with all the flying around and saving people and so forth. But I appreciate that.

1. You're most welcome, Superman. Do you mind if I ask some things I'm really curious about?

2. I wouldn't mind at all, please do.

1. Do you think that if you and Lois Lane ever got married and settled down and had some kids, that your kids would have superpowers, or maybe would be just a little super, or not super at all?

2. Well Daniel, that's a smart question. So you're wondering what the kids would be like if I had them with a human rather than a resident of Krypton. Nobody knows for sure, but the scientists I talk with tell me that they might be sort of super, but not quite as super as I am. For example, they would still be faster than a speeding bullet, but not as fast as light. They could leap tall buildings at a single bound, but they couldn't leap to other planets.

When Superman says, "That's a smart question," he's giving

A. a reflection,
or
B. positive feedback?

502.

1. Hmm. Sounds like this is a question you've considered and that you're interested in, if you've talked with scientists about it.

2. I'm curious about a lot of things. But yes, I've been curious about this. It sometimes gets lonesome in my Fortress of Solitude.

1. Thanks for sharing that with me. If you ever get lonesome, you're welcome to visit my family. It's a big family, and there are lots of nice people.

2. Thank you for that invitation, Daniel. The question you ask about superpowers in my children is an important one. I've wondered, how could a mom from Earth keep control over a two year old child, if the two year old for example got the urge to throw her a few hundred meters into the air just for fun.

1. I see what you mean, Superman: it could be downright dangerous for a mom.

What Daniel just said was

A. a reflection,
or
B. a follow-up question?

503.

2. Exactly.

1. Here's another question, Superman, if you please. How can just a pair of

glasses keep people from recognizing you when you're Clark Kent? I've got lots of friends who wear glasses sometimes and not others, and I've always recognized them either way.

2. Good question, Daniel. The glasses themselves are not ordinary glasses. They send out waves that interfere with people's ability to recognize my face. If you want to know how they could do that without interfering with anything else, I'm afraid it's too complicated for me to explain.

1. So you're saying it's the special glasses themselves. Huh. I had always thought they were just ordinary glasses. Well, I guess it's really important for you not to lose them, isn't it? In the summer I wear sunglasses a lot, and I lose them all the time.

When Daniel says, "So you're saying it's the special glasses themselves," that's

A. a reflection,
or
B. a facilitation?

504.

2. I have lots of that type of glasses, just in case they get broken. But with my x-ray vision and super speed, I can

usually find them quickly if I lose them.

1. I would ask you to help find my sunglasses when I lose them, but I wouldn't want to take you away from more important things like keeping trains from wrecking into each other and keeping asteroids from hitting the planet and all that kind of stuff.

2. Thanks for that, Daniel. I have to have priorities, and it sounds as if you have a good sense of what's important.

When Superman says, "You have a good sense of what's important," that's

A. a facilitation,
or
B. positive feedback?

505.

1. Do you ever get tired of rescuing people and getting people out of bad jams?

2. No, I'll have to say it's a lot of fun being Superman. I am really lucky that helping people and making justice happen and all that kind of stuff never get old for me.

1. I'm glad you're lucky that way, too. Well, Superman, it's been really nice to be able to chat with you. I don't want to hold you back from doing more important things. Thanks for spending the time with me.

2. Thank you, Daniel, it's been a real pleasure. Would you like a lift home? I could fly you if you like.

1. Thanks, Superman, but I think I'll take the bus instead. I know you wouldn't drop me, but I'm not too fond of heights. I think I'll head on home in the usual way.

2. Bye, Daniel; please keep in touch with me.

1. I'll be happy to do that! Have a great day!

When Daniel says, "I'm glad you're lucky that way too," he's giving

A. a follow-up question,
or
B. positive feedback?

Chapter 43: Examples of the Joint Decision Role Play (Dr. L.W. Aap)

506. Two brothers are passengers in a car ride. There is one hand-held electronic device that they can use. (Remember that these examples are not meant to entertain with drama, and they are not meant to show how people usually talk with each other.)

1 (Defining) I'd be interested in using the Plexus GL on the car ride, and I imagine you would too, so we have to decide what we're going to do.

2 (Reflecting) So you're wanting to chat about how we can share the Plexus GL during this car ride.

1 That's right!

2 (Defining) You're right that I'm interested in using it too, and I appreciate your bringing the subject up.

1 (Reflecting) So you'd like to use it during the car ride also, and I appreciate your appreciating me!

2 (Listing) One option is that we could divide up the time in half, and you use it the first half of the trip and I use it the second half.

1 (Listing and waiting) Or you could use it the first half and I the second half. Or one of us could use it all the trip out, and the other the whole time the trip back.

2 (Listing and waiting) Another option is that we could not use it at all, but just chat with each other.

1 Another option is that we could use it to do something we could both listen to or watch, or do together, such as listen to a recording of a book.

2 We could flip a coin and let the person who wins use it.

1 Ready to start evaluating these options?

2 Yep.

Which parts of Dr. L.W. Aap have they done so far?

A. defining, reflecting, and listing only.
or
B. defining, reflecting, listing, and waiting also, because they didn't evaluate the options until they were through listing.

507. The Dr. L.W. Aap conversation continues.

1 (Advantages and disadvantages) The advantage of one using it on the way out and the other on the way back is that we wouldn't have any trouble deciding what half way is.

2 You're right. The disadvantage of each using it half the time is that when one is using it, the other doesn't have anything to do. The advantage of chatting with each other or listening to a recorded book is that we both have something we can do together.

1 An advantage of chatting with each other is that we would have a chance to catch up. Plus it gives us practice at interacting with a human being rather than a screen.

2 (Agreeing) I like that option too. Do you want to choose it, and if we get really bored, decide again?

1 (Agreeing) Sounds like a good plan to me. Let's give it a try!

Which of the Dr. L.W. Aap guidelines did they follow?

A. All seven of them, because they were polite to each other throughout the conversation,

or
B. Defining, reflecting, listing, waiting, advantages, and agreeing?

508. In the next joint decision role play, Pat, a child, is talking with his dad.

Pat: Dad, may I talk with you about something for a few minutes?

Dad: Sure.

Pat: (Defining) I think it's great that you're marrying Jennifer, and I like her. But after Mom died I got used to having time with you alone. Already there's lots less of that with Jennifer around. I'm worried that if I lose my time alone with you because of her, I'll start resenting her.

Dad: (Reflecting) Sounds like you've done some important thinking. You like her, but you don't want the loss of our one-on-one time to make you resent her, huh?

Pat: Yes.

Dad: (Defining) I'm glad you brought that up. I hadn't thought of that, but I can see how that would be a danger. I'm glad that you're thinking about how to prevent it.

Pat: (Reflecting) So even though you hadn't thought of that, now that I mention it you think that it isn't a bad idea to do some planning about it?

Dad: That's right.

Pat: (Listing) One option is that we could try to spend some time with just the two of us every week, go out for a walk or something like that.

Dad: (Listing and waiting) If something like going out for a walk will do, and not going out to someplace special, we could even do that more often, even every day. Another option is spending a little time before bedtime together.

Pat: (Listing and waiting) You could walk in to school with me in the morning, if that fits your schedule.

Dad: (Listing and waiting) A different option is that I could ask Jennifer to let us chat more often without interrupting us, even when she's around.

Pat: These sound like great options. Ready to start evaluating?

Dad: Yes.

About how many options did they list?

A. five,
or
B. two?

509. The joint decision continues.

Pat: (Advantages) I really like the idea of spending some time one-on-one almost every day. The advantage of our walking to school together is that I will be doing that every day anyway.

Dad: (Advantages) The disadvantage of that it's cutting it pretty close to the time I go to work, and sometimes I have to go in early. But I like to go for walks, and it's really good for my health, and it's good for being together, and we can do it in the evenings too. So there are lots of advantages for that.

Pat: (Advantages) Spending some time before bed is something we did more when I was younger. I wouldn't complain about that either. I wouldn't want to hurt Jennifer's feelings by your asking her not to interrupt so much.

Dad: (Advantages) I think she could handle it just fine. These are the sorts of things that when people get married, it's good for them to deal with openly. Actually an advantage is that it would help us get practice in that.

Pat: So really all these options sound good, except that usually you won't have time to walk in the morning.

Dad: (Agreeing) But I could do that when I get the chance, and do it in the evenings otherwise, plus a little time before bed, and just talk gently with Jennifer about the issue.

Pat: (Agreeing) Sounds great to me. So we're going to tray all of them! Thanks so much for understanding, Dad.

Dad: You're welcome, and thanks to you for talking about this with me!

As a result of this conversation, they agreed upon

A. one option,
or
B. a plan consisting of a set of options?

510. In the following example, the two characters are neighbors.

1 May I talk with you about a joint decision, please?

2 Sure.

1 I have a little pet rabbit that I saved after she got hit by a car. And I want to let her out in my yard sometimes to eat the clover. Her accident did enough damage that she can't run away. But I'm worried that your cat, who roams around outside, will kill her.

2 So if I understand you right, you'd like to let your rabbit have some outside time, but you fear that my cat will kill her.

1 Right.

2 I've let my cat run freely outside for a long time, and he does sometimes kill mice and birds. I've never seen him kill anything as big as a rabbit, but it's not impossible. But there are also other predators around other than my cat.

1 So you're saying that it's possible your cat could be a danger, but there are also other predators other than your cat.

2 Right.

1 To clarify a little bit, I would be out in the yard with the rabbit. Predators like foxes and coyotes and so forth probably wouldn't come with me there, because they're afraid of me. But your cat isn't.

2 So you go out into your yard with your rabbit, and you think that my cat is the main predator who would not be afraid to come into your yard with you there.

1 Yes.

2 I'm sorry that you have to worry about what my cat does in your own yard. But at the same time, he is an outdoor cat, and I can't control him once he's out.

1 I appreciate that. You're saying you don't feel that your cat owns the whole neighborhood, but on the other hand, you can't control him once he's out.

2 Right.

Which of the following does the conversation so far illustrate?

A. That when the people are defining the problem for each other and reflecting, they should do their defining by speaking only once.
or
B. When people define and reflect, they can speak twice or more, and sometimes they should go back and forth for a while before starting to list options.

511. The conversation continues.

2 Want to list some options? One is that you could call or text me when you want to let your rabbit out, and I can tell you whether my cat is in or out.

1 If there is some regular and predictable time that your cat is inside, I could take the rabbit out during those times.

2 We could look into getting some sort of fence or barrier that could be put up.

1 I could run toward your cat and chase him out if he comes into the yard when the rabbit is out there.

2 You could call me up if he comes into the yard when the rabbit is there, and I could come and bring him inside.

1 The most drastic option is that one of us could keep the pet inside all the time.

Have they "waited" at the same time they were listing options?

A. Yes, because they didn't say anything yet about the pros or cons of the options.
or

282

B. No, because they didn't wait to list another option when the other person had finished listing one.

512. The conversation continues.

2 Ready to think of advantages and disadvantages?

1 Yes.

2 Unfortunately there is no regular and predictable time the cat is inside. He comes in and goes out at totally random times. Texting to find out whether he's in or out has the disadvantage that I'm in and out a lot too, and lots of times I don't know whether one of my family members has let him in or out.

1 The disadvantage of my running at him and chasing him away is that it just doesn't seem like a nice and neighborly thing to do.

2 It probably would work, though, and since we've talked about it, I wouldn't be offended. I also wouldn't mind if you called up for one of us to come and get him, but we may not be home. And he may run away from us too – he has a mind of his own.

1 A physical barrier like a fence would have the advantage of keeping out other predators too. I don't want a

permanent fence in my yard, but maybe there is something that you can put up and take down.

2 Why don't we both look around, maybe on the Internet, and see if there is a type of fence you can easily put up and take down, and in the meantime, feel free to chase the cat away or call us up to try to take him away?

1 That sounds like a good plan. Thanks a lot for talking with me about this.

2 Thank you.

Did they do

A. All 7 of the Dr. L.W. Aap guidelines,
or
B. All but one of the Dr. L.W. Aap guidelines?

513. In Brazil, there is an Indian who lives in the jungle by himself. Two people who are with the government bureau of Indian affairs are talking with each other.

1 He's the last surviving member of a tribe; the rest were probably killed by ranchers and miners. For that reason he's scared of human beings and runs away or shoots arrows when anyone

tries to get close to him. But it's up to us to recommend what to do with him.

2 You point out that he perhaps stays alone because of fear of human beings, and that he's got good reason to be afraid, and that we are the ones to recommend how to deal with him.

1 Exactly.

2 And there are laws that apply. For example, members of an Indian tribe have a right to live on their land undisturbed, even if the tribe consists of only one person.

1 You're reminding us that the law gives him certain rights to stay where he is and be left alone.

2 Yes.

The sentence that person 1 spoke that started with, "You're reminding us that..." is an example of

A. A reflection,
or
B. Agreeing on an option?

514. The conversation continues.

1 Shall we think about the options? One option is to try to communicate with him in some way, to let him know that people don't want to harm

him and that he doesn't have to live all by himself if he doesn't want to.

2 To expand on that, if there is any written language he understands, we could leave a letter for him.

1 If he understands speech but not writing, and if anyone can speak that language, we can maybe try to leave him a portable phone and talk with him that way.

2 Or we could leave him a recording that just gives the message.

1 Another option is that we could just keep the land he lives on off limits to developers, and let him stay there by himself.

2 Ready to talk about the pros and cons of these options?

So far, have they listed at least four options?

A. Yes,
or
B. No?

515. The conversation continues.

1 Yes. A disadvantage of just keeping people out and leaving him alone is that he may be very unhappy and

lonely, and just staying alone because he's scared.

2 Another disadvantage in the eyes of some is that valuable land isn't used.

1 But that's an advantage too, because too much of the jungle has been cleared already, and lots of the cleared land is just going to waste.

2 An advantage of leaving him alone is that trying to get him to be with other people may just scare him more. Any electronic device may just scare him. Another is that he may be happy. He may enjoy being with animals who keep him from being lonely, for example.

1 Another disadvantage of trying to communicate with him is that it is expensive trying to find a language expert who can talk with him. People can argue, why spend the money on him; why not spend money on someone who wants help, like a little child who needs an operation for example.

2 Another disadvantage of trying to communicate with him is that there is some danger. He's shot an arrow at one person who was trying to communicate with him, already.

1 I think that the most humane and the cheapest and easiest thing to do is to let him alone and deal with him only if he wants to come to us.

2 I agree, except if his tribe did have a written language, it would not be hard at all to leave a note for him where he could find it. Why don't we recommend that people try this, and leave him alone if this doesn't work?

1 That sounds like a good plan to me. Thanks for talking with me about this.

The solution the two agreed to recommend was

A. to try one option, and then try another if the first didn't work, or
B. to try one option only?

516. The next situation is one described in a newspaper. Two people had a dispute about a parking place. The newspaper story had a violent and unhappy ending. But in this role-play, the same situation will end happily.

1 Hi. I see you just pulled your car into that parking place. I just worked really hard shoveling snow out of that place so I could park there. I just went to get my car, and found you there.

285

2 So what I hear you saying is that you feel you should be able to park here, because you're the one who did the work shoveling the snow.

1 Yes.

2 I understand how you feel. From my point of view, you're someone I've never seen before, and you could be perfectly honest, but it's hard for me to know whether to trust you when you tell me that.

1 I understand. You don't want to be a sucker who leaves a good parking place because someone tells you they cleared it out when they didn't.

2 Yes.

So far, would you say that the people have been

A. less polite than people usually are in real life,
or
B. more polite than people usually are?

517. The conversation about the parking place continues.

1 I could show you my snow shovel, which is in the trunk of my car, which is probably wet from shoveling.

2 You could perhaps lend me your snow shovel for just a few minutes so that I can shovel out a different parking place.

1 I could see if the man in the barbershop saw me shoveling and would confirm that for you.

2 I see footprints in the snow; we could match them with your shoes.

1 These sound like some good options. Ready to evaluate them?

2 Yes.

Did they wait until they were through listing, before talking about advantages and disadvantages of options?

A. Yes,
or
B. No?

518. The conversation about the parking place continues.

1 I would love to show you the bottom of my shoes and match them with the footprints in the snow here. And I'd also be happy to lend you my snow shovel for a few minutes.

2 Those would solve the problem beautifully. Thank you so much.

It turns out that the footprints match, and Person 2 quickly shovels out another parking place. The two people become friends – unlike in the newspaper story, where one of the men killed the other.

This example illustrates that

A. Practicing the divergent thinking exercise helps you list options during the joint decision role play.
or
B. Doing joint decisions well can save people lots of grief, loss, and misery.

Appendix 1: Questions for Divergent Thinking Practice

A person forgot something. What did he or she forget?

A person is really happy. Why?

A person had something he or she liked for lunch. What was it?

A person is really tired. Why?

A person says, "Oh, that's awesome!" What did the person think was so awesome?

A person needs to use some fortitude skills. What has happened?

A person can't drive a car to a certain place. Why not?

A person found a box on the ocean floor. What was in it?

A person passionately believes in a certain cause. What is it?

A person wants to get to know someone else. The person walks up and says an "opening line" to try to get a conversation started. What does the person say?

Someone sees something that's tall. What is it?

Someone wants to get divorced from his or her spouse. Why?

Someone compliments someone else. What does the person say?

Someone is grateful. For what?

Something is growing. What is it?

Someone likes someone else a lot. Why?

Someone has failed at something. What is it?

Someone says, "How beautiful!" Why did the person say that?

Someone wants something really badly. What does the person want?

Someone asks someone a question, and the person doesn't reply. Why not?

Someone doesn't do well in a certain subject in school. Why not?

Someone says, "That's the type of person I want to hire to work for my company!" Why?

Someone is laughing. Why?

Someone uses a rock for something. How does he or she use it?

Two people have a conflict with each other. What is it?

Someone has a problem to solve. What is the person's problem?

Someone sets a goal for himself. What is that goal?

Someone gets a peace prize. What did the person do to deserve it?

A fish is swimming really fast. Why is it doing so?

Someone has an unrealistic fear of something. What is it?

Two people are having a good time playing. What are they playing?

Someone is worried about something. What's the person worried about?

Someone does something to protect his or her health. What is it?

A dog is barking. Why?

Someone is working very hard on something. What is it?

Someone is wasting time. What's the person wasting time on?

Someone says, "I can't wait until that happens!" What is the person looking forward to?

Someone has a plan for his or her business, but something goes wrong. What goes wrong?

Someone says, "If only we did this, the world would be less violent." What could this be?

Someone's initials are S.T. What could the person's name be?

Someone gives someone else a present. What is it?

Someone admires someone else. Why?

Someone has something unwanted happen at school. What was it?

Someone feels more hopeful than before. Why?

Someone has a pet. What is it?

Someone is late. Why?

Someone goes somewhere on vacation. Where does the person go?

Someone has lost something. What was it?

Someone has set a goal for him or herself. What is the goal?

A person just had some really healthy food. What was it?

Someone put something on his or her "to do list" for the day. What was it?

Someone tells someone else a secret. What is the secret?

Someone invites someone else to do something with him/her. What do they do together?

Someone fixes something that was broken. What was it?

Someone earns some money. How does the person do it?

"Ah! Something smells good!" What is it?

Someone makes a big mistake. What is it?

Someone writes a nonfiction book that is meant to teach people something. What's the title of the book?

Someone got wet from a bunch of water falling on him/her. How did this happen?

Someone is very proud of him/herself. Why?

Someone does something silly. What is it?

A person got very rich. How did the person do it?

A person has a habit that he/she wants to change. What is it?

One person doesn't like a second one. Why not?

A person works very hard at something. What is it?

Someone wants to borrow a certain tool. What is it, and what does the person want to do with it?

Someone pays someone else a compliment. What exact words does the person say?

Someone has something named after him. What is it, and what's it named?

Someone did something really fun. What did the person do that was such fun?

Someone did something that wasn't much fun, but that the person was glad to have done. What was it?

Someone exercises the skill of conservation by saving or not spending some money. What choice does the person make?

Appendix 2: Choice Points

For any of these choice points, if the situation is too vague, not specific enough, feel free to make up any additional details so that you have a situation that is specific enough to work with in the way you'd like. Also, please cultivate the skill of changing the choice points a little so that they are suitable for whatever exercise you want to do.

Options for exercises:
Continue to list more choice points.
Brainstorm options.
Pros and cons.
Twelve thought exercise.
Four thought exercise.
List Important Variables.
Decisions Exercise.
UCAC fantasy rehearsal.
STEBC fantasy rehearsal.

Someone wants to save more money and spend less. What are things the person might avoid spending money on?

Someone has too many things cluttering up his or her house.

Someone is in a family where there are big financial problems. The person is working to make money, but other family members aren't working enough and are spending too much.

Someone has spent some money to get a recording studio to record some songs the person plays. But when the person hears the recording, the sound quality is low.

Someone is asked to join a club. The person doesn't really like the things the club does, but the person would like to have some more friends.

Someone gets an email saying that someone from another country would like to give him or her lots of money for doing very little.

You run a business, but you are not getting enough customers to make money in your business.

Someone in your family considers traveling by motorcycle. You are aware that motorcycle travel is very dangerous.

You have headaches. You go to someone whom someone else recommends. The person holds their hands over your body to transfer energy into your body and to help the energy in your body get aligned better.

You suspect that this won't really help.

You're the president of a college. The fraternities at your college seem to promote a lot of alcohol abuse dangerous hazing rituals.

Someone goes to a library to work and study. There are some people close by talking loudly, who are distracting.

Someone is under a lot of stress from having too much to do and not enough time to do it.

Someone has a boyfriend or girlfriend, that the person is pretty happy with, but meets someone else he or she likes more, at least for the time being.

Someone is principal of an elementary school. The school budget gets cut by a large amount. What does the person do?

You are choosing whether you want to try to get into an "elite" college, for which you'd have to work really hard and do very hard courses all during high school, or a less selective college, where you would have time to do more community service and fun things during high school.

Someone in your family drinks too much alcohol, too often. What do you do about this?

Someone is choosing a career.

You're the principal of a school. There's a problem that kids at your school are unkind and mean to each other a lot. What do you do about this?

When you try to do your academic work at home, family members keep interrupting you, plus there are temptations to watch TV, go on the Internet, and do other things. What do you do?

You run a business. You have a customer who uses your business a lot. But the person acts so unpleasant to you and to your staff that it is beginning to make everyone's job not enjoyable any more.

A friend of yours is getting so skinny that you think she is damaging her health. What do you do?

You can go to bed any time you want; what time do you choose?

You're at a rock concert, and somebody tells you that the star musician you went to see would like to meet with you privately after the concert. This person says he will drive you to where you will meet. What do you do?

Someone finds that he or she is spending so much time on the Internet that not much else gets done.

You have the choice of being homeschooled or going to school.

You are at the grocery store and can buy anything you want for your next few meals. What do you get?

You have some money that you have saved up. What do you do with it?

You pull a tick off yourself. You are in a place where Lyme disease is common. What do you do?

You have a choice about what subjects to study in school; what do you pick?

There's a bare patch in the back of your yard where a tree was cut down that doesn't have grass growing on it. You can plant something in that place, or leave it bare. What do you do?

Your English teacher tells your class that you should never ask questions in essays. You see lots of examples in essays of good writers where the writer posed a question and then answered it.

Someone downtown asks you for some money. Do you give some to them?

A friend you know is getting her navel pierced. Do you do the same thing?

A friend you know is getting a tattoo. Do you do the same thing?

There are several types of computer software that do something you want on the computer. Which do you pick?

You want to ask someone in your family not to use a clean glass each time, but to use the same glass over and over so there won't be so many dishes to wash. What words, and what tone of voice do you use?

You want to ask someone in your family to close the windows and turn the fan off before turning the air conditioner on. What words, and what tone of voice, do you use?

You have a sister with long hair, who tends to get her hair in her food when she eats. What do you do about this?

You want to lose some weight. What rules, if any, do you make for yourself about eating or exercise?

You have some things that you should study before long, but at the moment you'd rather play a game on the computer. Which do you do?

You want to take a course, and you have a choice as to whether to go to a class or just to study the subject on your own and go in and take a test on it.

You grow a little patch of kale for yourself in your yard, but a ground hog likes it and eats it up.

You have a summer where you don't have a lot planned; what goals do you want to make for yourself?

You have a choice about what goals are most important for you to accomplish during your lifetime.

Someone wants not to spend so much money on food. What does the person cut out?

You're a member of the Supreme Court. Some leaders of colleges admit people to their colleges more easily if the person is a member of a racial group that has been discriminated against. But a member of the other group sues and says that this policy is unfair to them. Do you let the colleges use "affirmative action," or not?

You're a child, and you get invited to go somewhere with a friend, with the

friend's parent driving you. You don't know whether the friend's parent is a safe driver or not. What do you do?

You're a child, and you've gone to a friend's house. The friend's parent is going to drive you and your friend somewhere. You're pretty sure that you've seen the friend's parent drink 5 or so bottles of beer shortly before you're to go.

You're the leader of a country. A man is in your country who's a citizen somewhere else. This person has found out how his own government spies on foreign people and its own citizens, and has leaked this to the press. Some people think he's a hero and some people think he's a criminal. Do you arrest him and turn him over to the other country, or let him stay in your country, or tell him he has to leave and go somewhere else?

You're a business owner, and you have the opportunity to put your picture and the name and address or your business where anyone can see it on the Internet. Do you do so?

You have the opportunity to put your picture and your home address on the Internet. Do you do it?

Someone invites you to take up sidewalk skateboarding. You don't have a helmet, but the person says that you won't need one.

You have a high powered blender that you use to prepare foods. But you have a child who likes to get into things and explore things, and you're afraid your child will try out the blender and get injured very badly.

You get a job that is about 3 miles from your home. You don't have a car. How do you get back and forth?

You are wanting to have study and work parties with a friend, so that you can get work done without being lonely. But the first friend that you invite to do this with you talks so much when you're together that you don't get work done.

You're married. Someone you had a romantic relationship with before you got married invites you to get together and have lunch.

Someone has been working on writing something for an hour. But then something happens to the person's computer, and all the work is lost.

Some friends from out of town invite themselves to come and stay at your house, fairly often. But each time they come, they stay for too long, and they

eat lots of your food without helping to pay for it.

You're a parent. Your teenage daughter stays out late at night with her friends and doesn't let you know where they are, and you are worried about her safety.

You're a parent. Your child is not working enough on schoolwork, and is not getting good grades.

You're a parent. Your child is getting into the habit of saying rude and disrespectful things to you.

You're a student. One of your teachers bullies the students in the class, being sarcastic and insulting to them, particularly some of them, nearly every day.

One person feels that the other should return phone calls and text messages right away, but the other doesn't feel at all obligated to do that.

One person gets really offended if the other doesn't remember birthdays and anniversaries; the other doesn't think it's such a big deal and wishes the other wouldn't.

You're a student. You have to get an operation and you miss a lot of school. When you go back to school, you're expected to make up all the work you missed, plus do the regular work. You still don't feel 100% well, and the expectations are too much.

Someone in elementary school is made fun of a lot because his ears are big. He thinks of the option of getting plastic surgery.

Someone is in fifth grade and still has the habit of sucking the thumb.

Someone has crooked teeth, and the family has the money for braces, but the person is afraid of dentists.

Someone has a phone that works just fine. But the person's friends all get phones that are the latest cool gadget.

Someone has a bad reputation for being reckless and impulsive and selfish. The person feels that this is not his or her true self. The person wants to change the image.

A child's parents are not married. The child lives with one parent, but wants to live with the other parent.

A child goes back and forth between two parents, and is fine with doing that. However, the parents fight with each other very often about the child and when the visitations are and how much time gets spent with each parent.

Someone in a family has a bad alcohol dependency problem. Someone else in the family drinks alcohol and doesn't have a problem with it. Should the person who doesn't have the problem continue to keep alcohol in the house?

Someone is on an athletic team in college. This is very demanding of the person's time, and it very much hurts the person's grades. But all the person's friends are also on the team.

You fix computers for a living. A person tells you a problem with their computer, and you tell the person how much it will cost. Then you fix the computer really quickly, but the person doesn't want to pay you as much, because it took such a short time. The person resents paying the agreed upon price. This same thing has happened several times with other people.

You make friends with someone at school. But someone else acts really resentful of you because that person thinks you are stealing the friend away from him or her.

Appendix 3: Options for the Pros and Cons Exercise

Someone considers ...

taking 5 very hard courses in school, which are a lot harder than the person has taken before.

adopting a pet cat from an animal shelter.

trying out for a football team.

buying another book on a school subject, to supplement what's in the textbook the school gives.

stopping playing video games altogether.

rewarding himself or herself with video games only when a certain amount of self-disciplined work has been done.

harvesting a weed from the yard that is supposed to be edible, and cooking up a big batch of it and eating it.

(The situation is that someone is being bullied in school.)

sending an email to the parents of the bully, telling them about what is going on.

writing down every day what is going on and sending what is written to the school principal.

ignoring the bullying.

going in to a school counselor and talking about the problem, several times if necessary.

asking one's parent or parents to talk with the leaders of the school.

(The situation is that someone has a family member who very often says mean and critical and hostile things.)

talking with the family member about this problem and asking the family member to try to change.

ignoring the hostile things the family member says and trying to respond enthusiastically to the nice things the family member says.

giving the family member daily feedback on how nice the family member was that day.

offering a prize to that family member when the person can

accumulate a certain number of points for being nice rather than being mean.

(The situation is that someone needs to have a computer program written for something she is working on.)

buying some books on computer programming and learning how to write the program herself.

hiring someone else to write the program for her.

(The situation is that someone wants to do some good for people who need help.)

contributing money to an organization that supplies cows or goats to poor families around the world.

starting an organization where volunteers take children hiking in the woods.

starting an organization where volunteers help children in math after school.

being in an organization that writes and speaks about the value of nonviolence and tries to persuade people of the importance of this.

(The situation is that someone wants to make sure that she doesn't get too fat.)

resolving not to eat anything between meals.

making a list of junk foods, and never eating them except in small amounts as rewards for self-disciplined work.

exercising for an hour each day.

giving up dairy foods and meat.

counting the calories of everything that is eaten each day and stopping when a certain total is reached.

(The situation is that someone has an employee who isn't doing the job correctly.)

firing the employee.

spending lots of time training the employee to do better, and checking up on how well the employee does.

(The situation is that someone's family doesn't have much money, and a youth in the family wants to help out.)

doing lots of babysitting to earn money.

working very hard on schoolwork to get a scholarship to college and to get a high-paying job afterwards.

(The situation is that you are governor of a state, and there are too many people getting killed by guns in your state.)

proposing a law that would only allow police to have guns.

proposing a law requiring anger-control and conflict-resolution training in all schools of the state.

proposing a law that would make all ammunition have a number on it that would identify the person who bought it.

offering lots of money each year to those counties of the state that have lowered their violence rate the most.

Appendix 4: Affirmations for Psychological Skills

Affirmations for Sixteen Skills and Principles

1. Productivity. I want to work hard and effectively to take care of myself and the people I'm loyal to. I want to work to make the world a better place. I want to better myself and prepare myself in the skills I need for working toward worthy goals.

2. Joyousness. I want to take pleasure and joy in the wonder of life and living. May I be grateful for being able to take part in the great adventure of life.

3. Kindness. I want to treat people as I would like to be treated. May I be unselfish and compassionate and work to make people happier.

4. Honesty. I want to keep my promises and tell the truth, without lying, cheating, or stealing.

5. Fortitude. I want to be strong and stay calm when things don't go my way. I want to be tough enough to put up with hardship when I need to. I want to focus on making the best choice, even when I feel bad.

6. Good decisions. I want to think carefully and systematically when important choice points arise.

In making joint decisions or resolving conflicts with other people, I want to think and speak calmly and thoughtfully to try to find a just and good option.

7. Nonviolence. I greatly value the right of people to live without being hurt or killed by others. I want to work for the day when this right is available to all.

8. Respectful talk (not being rude). I want to choose my words carefully, and be aware of the the effect my words have on others. I want to let my words support and nurture people. I want to avoid harsh and insulting words unless there is a very good reason.

9. Friendship-building. I want to build and maintain good friendships with others, including family members. I want to enjoy people despite their imperfections.

10. Self-discipline. I want to do what is best, even when it is not the most pleasant thing to do. I want to give up

pleasure and tolerate discomfort when necessary to achieve my higher goals.

11. Loyalty. I want to decide carefully which people to be loyal to. I want to stick up for those who have earned my continuing loyalty.

12. Conservation. I want to use scarce resources wisely, without wasting them. I want to avoid wasting my own money and time. I want to protect the earth for future generations.

13. Self-care. I want to be careful to protect my own health and safety and welfare, and that of all other people I affect.

14. Compliance. I want to comply with authority when it is right and good to do so.

15. Positive fantasy rehearsal. I want to rehearse in my imagination the thoughts, feelings, and behaviors I consider good and right. I want to avoid taking pleasure in images of other people's misfortune.

16. Courage. I want to be courageous enough to do what is best and right, even if I feel some fear of doing so.

* * * *

Affirmations for All 62 Skills

The following are affirmations for all sixty-two psychological skills.

Group 1: Productivity

1. Purposefulness. I want to work for the highest and best purposes. I want to cultivate reasons for living that I can feel proud of.

2. Persistence and concentration. I want to develop my power to concentrate for longer and longer times, so that I can accomplish more that brings happiness to others and myself.

3. Competence-development. I want to take joy in developing my own skills and abilities: schoolwork skills, skills in arts, recreations or sports, and especially the skills that will let me be productive.

4. Organization. I want to be organized in my decisions about how to use my time, how to use my money and where to place my papers and objects. I want to use organization skills to realize the greatest yield from the effort I expend.

Group 2. Joyousness

5. Enjoying aloneness. I want to find joy in the work and play that I do by myself, as well as from the things I do with other people. I want to have a good balance between doing things alone and doing things with others.

6. Pleasure from approval. I want to enjoy it when I receive compliments and approval, especially from the people I consider wisest about what is good and worthwhile.

7. Pleasure from accomplishments. I want to congratulate myself, thank myself, and celebrate in my mind when I do something smart, good, or worthwhile. I want to feel good about my good acts, even if nobody else notices.

8. Pleasure from my own kindness. I want to arrange my mind and my thoughts so that I feel very happy over making someone else happier.

9. Pleasure from discovery. I want to take joy in discovery, in finding out things about the world and how to live life.

10. Pleasure from others' kindness. I don't want to take for granted what other people have done for me, but to feel gratitude and happiness about whatever kindness comes to me from other people.

11. Pleasure from blessings. I want to be aware of the many blessings I have, the many ways in which I've had good luck and good fortune, and feel good about those things.

12. Pleasure from affection. I want to enjoy being affectionate with others in good ways.

13. Favorable attractions. I want to seek out and enjoy a person of the sort who is good for me.

14. Gleefulness. I want to be gleeful and to take joy in the childlike part of myself.

15. Humor. I want to enjoy laughter and humor; I want to help other people enjoy what is funny in our lives.

Group 3: Kindness

16. Kindness. I want very often to do kind acts, acts that make other people happier in the long run.

17. Empathy. I want to become aware of what other people are thinking and feeling. I want to see things from other people's points of view. I want to see how my actions affect other people.

18. Conscience. I am glad that I have a conscience and that I cannot harm

other people without getting signals from my conscience. When I have harmed another person, I want to listen to my conscience telling me that I should make amends if possible and should avoid inflicting further harm in the future.

Group 4: Honesty

19. Honesty. I want to tell the truth, and not deceive people.

20. Awareness of my abilities. I want to have a true idea of my own skills, abilities, and potentials. I want to be confident in how much I can learn to do if I really try. When I am not very skilled at something, I want to be honest with myself, as a first step in improving if I wish to.

Group 5: Fortitude

21. Frustration-tolerance. I want to handle it when things go badly, and not think things are worse than they really are. I don't want to feel overly bad about little things that go wrong.

22. Handling separation. Sometimes I may lose someone I've come to depend on or love. At those times, I want to find the strength inside me that lets me handle my loss and return to being happy.

23. Handling rejection. I want to handle it well when people reject me or don't want to be friends with me. If they don't like me because of a fault I can correct, I want to try to correct it. If they don't have a good reason for rejecting me, I want to go on being happy.

24. Handling criticism. When someone criticizes me, I want to learn all I can from what they are saying. If they have something good to teach me, I want to learn it respectfully. If they are criticizing me without a good reason, I want not to let it bother me too much.

25. Handling mistakes and failures. When I make mistakes or fail at things I try, I want to honestly admit to myself that I made a mistake. I want to think about what I can learn for next time and what I can do to make things better now, and not waste too much energy condemning myself or blaming someone else.

26. Magnanimity, non-jealousy. I want to be glad when other people have good things happen to them, even when I don't have those good things happen to me. I want not to be overly jealous when someone else experiences something good.

27. Painful emotion-tolerance. I want to be brave in handling the situations in which I feel bad. I want to try to learn as much as I can from those situations. I want to tolerate the pain that should be tolerated and avoid the pain that should be avoided. I want to do what is best even when I feel bad.

28. Fantasy-tolerance. I want to be aware of the difference between thinking and doing. Even though I think about many things, I will choose to do only some of the things I think about.

Group 6: Good decisions

6a: Individual decision-making

29. Positive aim. I want to keep myself focused on making things better, for others and myself. I don't want to make things worse by trying to get sympathy, consolation or revenge.

30. Planning before acting. I want to think and plan before acting, and avoid impulsivity. I want to devote more thought to important decisions and less thought to less important ones.

31. Fluency. I want to make full use of words as tools to express what is happening around me and within me. I want to use words to make life better for others and myself.

32. Awareness of my emotions. I want to be aware of what I am feeling, and why I am feeling what I am, and thus be better able to make decisions and live happily in the world.

33. Awareness of control. I want to be able to figure out how much power I have to change things. When I do that, I can know what to try to change and what to try to tolerate.

34. Decision-making. When I have an important decision to make, I want to take several steps: think about what the problem is; work to get the information I need; think of several options; think what will probably happen when the options are tried; assess the desirability of the things that might happen. I might also think about the advantages and disadvantages of each option. In this way I want to make as good a choice as I can.

6b: Joint decision-making, including conflict resolution

35. Toleration. I want to be able to enjoy a wide range of what people do and say, without needing to boss them around.

36. Rational approach to joint decisions. When I have a problem or joint decision to make with another person, I want to work to find a solution that makes us both happy, if such a solution exists. I want to think hard about how I want to act, rather than being ruled only by emotion.

37. Option-generating. When I have a problem to solve, I want to be creative in thinking of options for its solution.

38. Option-evaluating. When I have a problem to solve, I want to recognize the best and most reasonable options.

39. Assertion. I want to be able to take a strong stand, stick up for my own way, or continue to work against my opponents when it is wise to do that.

40. Submission: I want to be able to give in to another person's wishes, admit I was wrong, or allow myself to be led when it is wise to do that.

41. Differential reinforcement. I want to focus enthusiastically on the good that other people do, since that is a good way to bring it out and encourage it.

Group 7: Nonviolence

42. Forgiveness and anger control. While protecting myself, I want to be able to forgive people who have harmed me, not only for their sakes, but for my own. I want to avoid burdening myself with unnecessary anger.

43. Nonviolence. I want to commit myself to the principle of nonviolence and to work to foster this principle for the world.

Group 8: Not being rude (Respectful talk)

44. Not being rude, respectful talk. I want to be very sensitive and aware, and always notice when I get the urge to use words, vocal tones or facial expressions that are accusing, punishing or demeaning. I want to avoid these unless there is a very good reason.

Group 9: Friendship-Building

45. Discernment and Trusting. I want to get to know other people based on accurate information and not distort what I think about people with prejudice, overgeneralization or wish-fulfilling fantasies. I want to decide wisely what someone can be trusted for, and trust when it is appropriate.

46. Self-disclosure. I want to be able to talk about myself and share intimate

thoughts and feelings with another person, to the degree that it is appropriate and wise to do so.

47. Gratitude. I want to be able to communicate to others my gratitude, admiration and approval.

48. Social initiations. I want to start friendly talk with others frequently and comfortably.

49. Socializing. I want to give joy to other people and myself by talking with them and hearing what they have to say, and doing fun and useful things together.

50. Listening. I want to be a good listener. I want to take the time and effort to understand the other person's point of view, and to let the other person know I understand.

Group 10: Self-discipline

51. Self-discipline. I want to tolerate discomfort, pass up the temptation of certain pleasures, and expend tough effort when necessary to make good things happen.

Group 11: Loyalty

52. Loyalty. I want to stand by the people who have earned my loyalty, and keep my commitments to them.

Group 12: Conservation

53. Conservation and Thrift. I want to preserve Earth's resources for ourselves and future generations. I want to resist the temptation to waste my time and money on unnecessary luxuries. I want to be thrifty to the degree that is best.

Group 13: Self-care

54. Self-nurture. I want to think kind thoughts to myself, just as I wish to say kind things to other people.

55. Habits of self-care. I want to take the best care of my body and my mind that I possibly can. I want to avoid any drugs or toxins that I know will hurt my body or mind in the long run. I want to eat, sleep and exercise in ways that take care of my body.

56. Relaxation. I want to become expert in relaxing and calming myself when I wish to, and to enjoy my skills of relaxation and meditation.

57. Carefulness. I want to be aware of danger when it is present. I want to protect others and myself, and try to make us safe.

Group 14: Compliance

58. Compliance. I want to feel good about obeying reasonable and trustworthy authorities at times, especially when they tell me to do something I don't feel like doing but which I know is best to do.

Group 15: Positive fantasy rehearsal

59. Imagination and positive fantasy rehearsal. I rejoice in the use of my imagination as a tool in rehearsing or evaluating a plan, or adjusting to an event or situation. I want to practice in fantasy the patterns that are useful to me and avoid the ones that are harmful.

Group 16: Courage

60. Courage. I want to be confident and brave when I wish to be, especially when there is no danger present. If I feel unrealistic fear, I want to face what I fear, and thus take a step to conquer the fear.

61. Independent thinking. Sometimes people model wrong decisions or try to persuade me to enact wrong decisions. I want to think for myself and do what is right.

62. Depending. When I need help from someone, I want to be brave

enough to ask for that help and to feel comfortable in receiving it.

Appendix 5: Things To Say To Create a Positive Emotional Climate

Expressing gladness that the other person is here:

Good morning! Good afternoon! Good evening! I'm glad to see you! It's good to see you! Welcome home! Hi! I'm glad you're here!

Expressing gratitude and appreciation:

Thanks for doing that for me! I really appreciate what you did. I'm glad you told me that! Yes, please! That's nice of you to do that for me! This is a big help to me. Thanks for saying that!

Reinforcing a good performance of the other person:

You did a good job! That's interesting! Good going! Good point! Good job! Congratulations to you! You did well on that! That's pretty smart!

Positive feelings about the world and the things and events in it:

Wonderful! That's really great! Wow! Hooray! I'm so glad it happened like that! Sounds good! Look how beautiful that is!

Wishing well for the other person's future:

I hope you have a good day. Have a nice day! Good luck to you! I wish you the best on (the thing you're doing).

Offering help or accepting a request for help:

May I help you with that? I'd like to help you with that. I'll do that for you! I'm going to (do this job) so that you won't have to do it! Would you like me to show you how I do that? I'd be happy to do that for you! I'd love to help you in that way!

Accepting or declining an invitation to do something with the other person:

I'd love to! Yes, I'd love to do that with you!
I'd love to do that with you, but unfortunately I can't at that time. Let's do that together another time!

Positive feelings about oneself:

I feel good about something I did. Want to hear about it? Hooray, I'm glad I did this!

Being forgiving and tolerating frustration:

That's OK; don't worry about it. It's no problem. I can handle it. I can take it. It's not the end of the world.

Expressing interest in the other person:

How was your day today? How are you? How have you been doing? How have things been going? So let me see if I understand you right. You feel that _____. So, in other words you're saying _____. I'd like to hear more about that! I'm curious about that. Tell me more. Uh huh . . . Yes . . . Oh?

Consoling the other person:

I'm sorry you had to go through that. I'm sorry that happened to you.

Apologizing or giving in:

I'm sorry I said that. I apologize for doing that. I think you're right about that. Upon thinking about it more, I've decided I was wrong. I'll go along with what you want on that.

Being assertive in a nice way:

Here's another option. Here's the option I would favor. An advantage of this plan is . . . A disadvantage of that option is . . . Unfortunately I can't do it. I'd prefer not to. No, I'm sorry, I don't want to do that. It's very important that you do this.

Humor:

Saying or doing funny things, retelling funny things, or laughing when the other person is trying to entertain you by being funny - but avoiding sarcasm or making fun of the other person.

* * *

Appendix 6: Self-Ratings of Psychological Skills

The Psychological Skills Inventory

The following questions have to do with "psychological skills." How skillfully did you act over the last 24 hours? (This can be changed so that you rate the last week or the last month.) How good was the functioning in each of these areas? Use any number between 0 and 10, including odd numbers or decimals if you want.

0=Very poor
2=Poor
4=Not very good, so-so
6=OK
8=Good
10=Very good
n=Not applicable, not answerable, or not known

_____ 1. Productivity: concentrating, staying on task, getting things finished, working well, having high work capacity

_____ 2. Joyousness: feeling good about accomplishments; cheerfulness, pleasant mood, being happy, not being depressed

_____ 3. Kindness: trying to make others happy; sharing, consideration, courtesy, helpfulness

_____ 4. Honesty: Telling the truth, keeping promises, not cheating or stealing

_____ 5. Fortitude: handling not getting your way, putting up with hardship, not getting too upset when things don't go as desired

_____ 6a. Good individual decisions: Thinking before acting, using good judgment

_____ 6b. Good joint decisions or conflict-resolution: acting in ways that make it more likely that problems or conflicts with other people are solved peacefully and sensibly

_____ 7. Nonviolence: No physical hitting, kicking, etc., no threats to hurt

_____ 8. Respectful talk: Not being rude, not doing unkind talk, being tactful, expressing approval

_____ 9. Friendship-building: Having good chats, letting people get to know you, being a good listener, developing positive relationships

_____ 10. Self discipline: Being able to do what's best to accomplish goals rather than just doing what you feel like doing

_____ 11. Loyalty: Honoring commitments, preserving relationships, sticking up for friends

_____ 12. Conservation: Not being wasteful of money, time, or resources

_____ 13. Self-care: Taking care of your own health and safety, being careful

_____ 14. Compliance: Obeying parents, teachers, and the law, when they are reasonable authorities

_____ 15. Positive fantasy rehearsal: Not enjoying violent or cruel fantasies or entertainments; using imagination to rehearse ways of accomplishing good goals

_____ 16. Courage: Not being hindered by anxiety, unrealistic fear, worrying, or unnecessarily avoiding certain situations.

* * * *

One-Item Self-Rating of Psychological Skills

_____ Please rate your overall functioning. Good functioning is the thoughts, feelings, and behaviors that tend to: produce happiness and well-being in both oneself and others; produce good social relations and positive achievement; and accomplish worthwhile goals. Please rate how good, overall, your functioning was.

Index

activities
    and correspondence to goals, 233
activities, too many, 15
advantages and disadvantages
    exercise, 70
affirmations
    for 16 skills and principles, 300
    for all 62 skills, 301
affirmations exercise, 55
aloneness
    as technique in anger control, 152
alternate reading, 16
    mastery of, 24
    ways to enjoy, 18
anger out, 151
approval
    in tones of voice, 102
biofeedback, 197
    mastery for, 200
brainstorming options
    example of, 67
    mastery of, 69
    more examples of, 234
brainstorming options exercise, 65
breathe and relax, 174
breathe and relax exercise
    mastery for, 177
bullying
    discussed in an exercise, 99
celebrating others' choices exercise, 38
    example of, 38
celebration of others' choices exercise

mastery of, 41
celebrations diary, 37
celebrations exercise
    example of, 33
    how to do, 32
    mastery of, 37
    reason for, 35
choice points
    examples of, 291
choice points exercise, 165
    example of, 166
    mastery of, 168
clear speech, 23
cognitive therapy
    Big Idea of, 76
commands, criticisms, and
    contradictions, 155
competition
    conversation about, with reflections
        exercise, 47
    versus cooperation on guessing
        exercise, 169
compliance
    criteria for high ratings in, 225
concentrate, rate, and concentrate
    exercise, 202
    mastery for, 206
concentration
    techniques for, 206
concrete goals, 227
conflict resolution role play
    example of, 149

mastery of, 158
conflict-resolution
  criteria for high ratings in, 222
conflict-resolution role play, 146
consequences of options, 70
conservation
  criteria for high ratings in, 224
consonant sounds
  and clear speech, 23
convergent thinking, 26
conversation
  and divergent thinking, 27
cooperation
  on the guessing exercise, 169
coping fantasy rehearsals, 115
courage
  criteria for high ratings in, 225
criticism
  attitude toward, 208
criticism exercise, 208
decision exercise
  example of, 160
decision-making
  importance of options in, 65
decisions exercise, 159
  mastery of, 163
divergent thinking, 26
  example of, 28
  questions for, 288
Dr. L.W. Aap
  mnemonic for conflict resolution, 148
effort-payoff connection, 124
emotional climate
  list of things to say, 308
emotional climates, 120
emphasis on words or syllables, 20

ethics, 53
examples
  high and low quality reflections, 51
executive functions, 192
exercise, physical
  before relaxation, 175
expressive reading and speaking, 19
external rewards, 127
facilitations, 95
fantasy rehearsals, 112
fingertip temperature, 197
follow-up question, 96
food as reward, 133
fortitude
  criteria for high ratings in, 220
four responses
  for listening, 95
four thought exercise, 89
  example of, 90
  mastery of, 93
Franklin, Benjamin, 217
friendship-building
  criteria for high ratings in, 223
goal setting exercise
  example of, 230
goal-setting and goal-monitoring, 227
  mastery for, 233
good decisions
  criteria for high ratings in, 221
good will meditation, 185
guess the feelings exercise, 74
  example of, 75
  mastery of, 76
guessing exercise
  example of, 170
  mastery for, 172
happiness

and effort-payoff connection, 125
heart rate biofeedback, 199
homework
    used in concentration exercise, 203
honesty
    criteria for high ratings in, 220
imagining acts of kindness, 183
internal rewards, 127
jingle, for remembering skills, 13
joint decision role play, 146
    example of, 149
    mastery of, 158
joint decision skill
    importance of, 147
joint decisions
    criteria for high ratings in, 222
joyousness
    criteria for high ratings in, 219
kind acts, types of, 184
kindness
    criteria for high ratings in, 219
listening with four responses exercise,
    95
    example of, 97
    mastery of, 100
listing important variables
    example of, 138
    mastery of, 145
    more examples of, 244
listing important variables for a
    decision, 137
listing values and principles exercise
    mastery of, 56
listing values or principles, 53
loyalty
    critera for high ratings in, 224
mantra, 181

mastery fantasy rehearsals, 114
meditation
    with movement, 182
meditation techniques, 178, 181
    mastery for, 189
mental heallth, meaning of, 7
mental health skills, 9
menu for goals, 229
mind-watching, 178
    example of experience, 178
    mastery for, 179
motives
    for entertainment, power, and
        pleasure, 56
movement
    meditation with, 182
muscle relaxation, 174
musical notes
    task switching exercise using, 195
negative numbers
    rules for, 194
nonviolence
    criteria for high ratings in, 222
note-naming
    as task switching activity, 195
one-item rating scale
    for psychological health, 226
one-item self rating, 311
option-generating exercise, 65
options
    meaning of, 65
overgeneralizing
    in the twelve thought exercise, 83
physical exercise, 7
pitch of voice, 22
pleasant dreams technique, 185
positive emotional climate

things to say to promote, 308
positive emotional climate rehearsal
  exercise
  example of, 121
  mastery of, 123
positive emotional climate rehearsals,
  120
positive fantasy rehearsal
  criteria for high ratings in, 225
positive feedback, 96
positive reinforcement, 35
practice, importance of, 8
prefrontal cortex
  and task switching, 192
principles to live by, 53
productivity
  criteria for high ratings in, 218
pros and cons exercise, 70
  example of, 71
  more examples of, 240
  practice situations for, 297
pros and cons exercise,
  mastery of, 73
psychological skills, 9
psychological skills inventory, 310
psychological skills meditation, 187
quality of reflections, 49
rating scale
  for decisions, 140
rating yourself, 215
reading skill, 16
reflections exercise, 42
  benefits of, 42
  example of, 44
  mastery of, 52
relaxation
  benefits of, 174

relaxation techniques, 181
  mastery for, 189
respectful talk
  criteria for high ratings in, 223
responding to criticism exercise, 208
  examples of, 210
  mastery of, 214
rest, 188
retelling
  as test of learning, 23
role play
  of joint decision, 149
saving a reward for after self-
  discipline, 124
  examples of, 128
  mastery of, 133
self-care
  criteria for high ratings in, 224
self-discipline, 124
  criteria for high ratings in, 224
self-monitoring, 215
  mastery for, 226
self-reinforcement, 35
sixteen skills and principles, 12
skills and principles
  sixteen and sixty-two, 54
Skills Stories Exercise, 58
  example of, 59
skills, psychological, 9
skin conductance level biofeedback,
  199
social conversation role play, 107
  example of, 108
  mastery of, 111
  more examples of, 264
SOIL ADDLE

mnemonic for decision exercise, 159
song to remember psychological skills, 12
speaking skill, and reading aloud, 17
STEBC
    meaning of, 112
STEBC fantasy rehearsals, 112
    examples of, 113
    mastery of, 116
    more examples of, 252
survival
    and divergent thinking, 27
task switching, 191
    examples of, 191
    mastery of, 195
techniques to help you concentrate, 206
temperature biofeedback, 197
thoughts
    effects on emotions, 74
time on task
    for relaxation, 189
to do list, 134
    example of, 134
    mastery of, 136
tones of approval exercise, 102
    example of, 104
    mastery of, 106
TP Paarisec

mnemonic for criticism responses, 209
twelve thought exercise, 78
    example of, 81, 87
    mastery of, 88
    more examples of, 247
twelve thought recognition, 79
types of kind acts, 184
types of thoughts
    list of 12, 78
UCAC fantasy rehearsals, 117
    example of, 117
    mastery of, 119
    more examples of, 260
unearned rewards, 125
values, 53
variable
    meaning of, 137
virtues
    on Franklin's list, 217
visualizing relaxing scenes, 183
war
    and conflict-resolution, 147
weighting variables according to importance, 142
What are the Qualities (song), 12
word "one" as mantra, 181
work ethic, 14
worthy goals, 228
yelling
    in conflict resolution, 152

CPSIA information can be obtained
at www.ICGtesting.com
Printed in the USA
FFOW03n0828100117
31145FF